Dynamic local ministry

Dynamic local ministry

ANDREW BOWDEN and
MICHAEL WEST

CONTINUUM
LONDON AND NEW YORK

Continuum
The Tower Building, 11 York Road, London SE1 7NX
370 Lexington Avenue, New York, NY 10017-6503

First published 2000

ISBN 0-8264-4996-4

British Library Cataloguing-in-Publication Data
A catalogue record for this book is available from the British Library.

Typeset by SetSystems Ltd, Saffron Walden, Essex
Printed and bound in Great Britain by Biddles Ltd, Guildford and King's Lynn

Contents

ↄↄↄↄ

Acknowledgements

It is no light undertaking for dual-role ministers to write a book of this length. In our case it was made possible by the generous understanding of Bishop David Bentley and Archdeacon John Cox, who encouraged us to have a go; by our colleagues in the Diocesan Local Ministry Departments, who, despite the inconvenience to themselves, continued to believe that a book like this needed to be written; and by Bill Woodhouse, Stanley Emson and Richard Marlowe from the Watershed Parishes, who ensure that ministry carries on there, whatever the Rector may get up to!

The visit to New Zealand was generously supported by the Swire and the Sylvanus Lysons Trusts and was facilitated by the wholehearted support of Garth Cant, Bill Bennett and Bishop Murray Mills.

Our profoundest thanks are due to the members of Local Ministry Teams in this country, in Australasia and in America, who, because they have accepted the challenge and followed their vocation, have lived the stories which form the core of this book.

Last, but not least, thanks are due to our families, who continue to put up with us despite our literary ambitions.

கூஉகூஉ

Foreword

Whether it's a field of wheat, a flock of sheep or the Church's ministry, country people judge by results. This is an important book because it records changes that are actually taking place in the Church's ministry and, in particular, the development of a new style of ministry now widely called 'local ministry'.

The changes that have transformed society and the Church in recent years have made it imperative that the Church's ministry should evolve and adapt. Whilst older styles of ministry, particularly those in rural areas based on George Herbert's *The Country Parson*, are deeply valued, it is acknowledged that such patterns of ministry cannot be replicated in the modern Church.

A new style of ministry has evolved which, in this country, has its roots in the work of Roland Allen, in the desire of urban priests to indigenize the Church's ministry and in the need in rural areas to provide ministry over increasingly large clusters of parishes. Variously called *all member, collaborative, mutual, total* or *local* ministry, this new pattern has emerged not just from the demands of the contemporary situation but also from a close study of the development of ministry in the early days of the Church.

Much of the book is concerned with examples and illustrations which the authors, wisely, allow to speak for themselves. This is neither exhortation nor theory but a report of a widespread development within the Church which has until now been largely unacknowledged. Part of the richness of this book comes from the fact that these initiatives have been taking place in different parts of the Anglican Communion within different traditions of church life and within very different social contexts.

A former archbishop has written that writing a book is a hazardous undertaking for a parochial clergyman. Many will be thankful that two parochial clergy who have been pioneers of this new style of ministry have made their experience and wide knowledge of local ministry available through this book. It is hoped that many will find it challenging and stimulating. It is widely recognized that the Church will have to continue to change its patterns and styles of ministry in the future, and much has been written of a speculative nature. Here we are privileged to read the reports of what is actually happening to meet these challenges; it is an account that deserves to be widely read and acted upon.

Dr Anthony Russell
Bishop of Ely
September 2000

එංඑංඑං

Introduction

Bill is a small farmer and a member of a ministry team in an English rural benefice. Jane is an administrator in the Health Service and an ordained local minister working as part of a team that is planting a church on the large housing estate where she lives. Brian is the bishop of a diocese in Australia that is working to promote local ministry in a large diocese with a small number of scattered Anglican churches and Joyce is the principal of a local ministry scheme in a rural diocese in England. She has worked hard to establish a training scheme of high quality designed to prepare lay people for new roles in the local church.

All share a vision in common. All are part of a development that has swept through the church over the last twenty years and is now becoming established in the Anglican Communion in England, Australia, New Zealand, America and Canada. All are involved in local ministry.

What Is Local Ministry?

Local ministry is hard to define because it is not a programme or a movement. Rather it is a collection or family of beliefs about the nature and work of the Church and the way that ministry is understood and expressed in the local church. At the heart of local ministry is a vision of the Church as a priestly and prophetic community which values and honours the ministry of each of its members. Using the pithy and energizing phrase, 'the ministry of all baptized Christians', it affirms that members of the Church are called, through baptism, to a life of prayer and service which may find expression, at certain periods in their life, in a ministry that is authorized and supported by the church community.

Under the banner of local ministry, bishops, clergy and lay people have worked across the mainstream Christian traditions to re-energize the life, work and witness of local churches. They have found ways to support church members as they have explored what God is calling them to be and do, and they have set up schemes, where appropriate, to train local church members for an exciting variety of new roles undertaken in the service of Christ.

Taking the Local Church Seriously

Local ministry has not emerged to preserve the structures of an ailing church, but rather to free the local church to explore new ways to engage with the community in which it is set. Local ministry is, by definition, local and therefore it needs to take seriously the community that the church is called to serve, and the places in which individual Christians are called to work. In New Zealand, Australia, Canada and America this can mean working with an indigenous culture, e.g. among Indian peoples. In England it can mean embedding the church in the culture of the inner city or of small villages through the active and acknowledged ministry of those who live and work there.

What Kinds of Ministry?

Within the Anglican Church, lay people have been encouraged for many years to take responsibility for areas of local church life and many have been churchwardens, treasurers or PCC secretaries or have taught in Sunday school or helped with the youth group. However, local ministry has helped the church to recognize that work formerly considered the preserve of the stipendiary priest can be done equally well, and in some cases better, by members of the local church. Local ministry teams have freed the gifts of lay people to work alongside the parish priests as pastors or teachers or worship leaders. In many parishes, those called to reader ministry have embraced the need to work with other members of the congregation in ministry teams and some members of local church congregations have felt called to be priests and to exercise a sacramental ministry among the people in their community. In England the ordained local minister, emerging from within the community to serve that community, is ordained into the catholic ministry of the priesthood and licensed as an assistant to the stipendiary priest.

Because of the different contexts in which dioceses operate in England and abroad, and because of the different preferences expressed by their bishops and senior staff, dioceses that have embraced the vision of local ministry have developed it in many different ways. This is its strength, and the inevitable consequence of taking the local seriously. Some dioceses have embraced ordained local ministry but some have developed local ministry schemes to predominantly support lay ministry. Some have concentrated their resources on the development and maintenance of local ministry teams while others have stimulated local ministry in a variety of other ways.

Catholic and Local

Local ministry is inevitably a partnership between the local church and the diocese. The Church of England is an episcopal church and the bishop has a key role to play in the way that the diocese develops its life and ministry. He also has a particular role in the discernment, training and practice of those called to be readers or ordained local ministers. Those that emerge from the local church for these accredited ministries need to recognize the part played by both the local and the broader church in confirming and supporting their vocation.

What's in a Name?

The world is full of acronyms and this book is unfortunately no exception. They are mostly explained as they occur but there is a need to identify two sets of acronyms that are at the heart of local ministry and can lead to confusion. The first set refers to those who emerge from the local church to work as priests within that community. Since the publication of the report *Stranger in the Wings* in 1998, they are normally referred to as ordained local ministers (OLMs). However, many referred to this ministry in its early stages by the term local ordained ministry (LOM) which in turn gave way to the title adopted for a time in the nineties, local non-stipendiary ministry (LNSM). The term ordained local ministry and the acronym OLM will be used in this book although the other titles do appear in official documents that are referred to from time to time.

The second set of acronyms refers to the group in the Church of England that advise the House of Bishops on ministry and are particularly responsible for advising the bishops on the selection of individual candidates for ordination and for accrediting the colleges, courses and schemes that train them. This group was known as the Advisory Council for the Church's Ministry (ACCM), changed its name in the nineties to the Advisory Board for Ministry (ABM) and is now known as the Ministry Division of the Archbishop's Council (Ministry Division). The various reports that this body has produced over the years that are relevant to ordained local ministry will have each of these names in their titles and the reader should expect this body to appear under its various names in the pages that follow.

The Story of This Book

The story of this book will be the story of those individuals and dioceses that have embraced local ministry in its various forms in various places. It will outline the practical pressures and theological imperatives that have contributed to the development of local ministry and will tell the story of those called to be members of local ministry teams, those called to be ordained local ministers, those officers who have been called to provide training and support for them, and those bishops who have promoted local ministry in their own dioceses. It will concentrate on the Church of England but will embrace the vision and the practice of some of the Anglican dioceses abroad and of our ecumenical partners in this country.

Because each diocese, scheme, minister and locality is different, this book weaves together the experience of many people around common and recurring themes. The names of individuals have been changed for the sake of confidentiality but their experiences are a matter of record. This is not a book of fiction but a weaving together of a large number of true stories. Together they comprise a record of what it has meant to work with a particular vision of God, Church and world, and they chart the way in which the ministry of many people, from many lands and cultures, contributes to, and further develops, that vision.

This is a time when the Church is asked again to travel along a road of exploration. Old definitions of Church and ministry are breaking down but there is as yet no new consensus, no clear way forward. It is an exciting time to be the Church, but not for the faint-hearted. Local ministry has pushed back the boundaries of ministerial experience and has sought new insights about God, the Church and the world.

To the members of local ministry teams in this country, in Australasia and in America who, because they have accepted the challenge and followed their vocation, have lived the stories which form the core of this book.

1

cocococo

Local Ministry:
the Practical Pressures

'A boat is safest when it is at anchor in a sheltered harbour. But that is not what a boat is for'. Local ministry is about taking risks and trusting the Spirit.

Local ministry is happening everywhere these days. Wherever congregations respond to God's call to work together for the coming in of the Kingdom, there is local ministry. It is like a breath of fresh air and has begun to transform the churches. It is also beginning to be recognized formally. Churches are beginning to 'authorize' local ministry, to 'commission' local ministry parishes, to 'mandate' local ministry teams and to ordain ministers with local licence.

This book tells the stories of some of the people involved in authorized local ministry.

But how did it all start? What is driving it? Is it a way of stopping the gaps or has it a respectable theological rationale? This first chapter looks at the practical pressures which have forced the churches to look at alternative models for ministry. It then goes on to record some of the practical responses and alternative models that have been tried.

Practical Pressures

No one likes change, and no one can see why they ought to change unless they are uncomfortable where they are. But as he always does, Jesus speaks from the edge to the self-satisfied centre, and over the last half-century has succeeded in making us feel distinctly uncomfortable.

SOCIETY IS CHANGING

We are uncomfortable because we can no longer effortlessly believe. It is interesting to compare the novel *Jane and Prudence* written by Barbara Pym in the 1960s with *A Question of Integrity* written by Susan Howatch in the 1990s. Both are about the Church, both describe a genuine form of Christian belief and practice, but what a difference of atmosphere. Jane is a dutiful and secure Christian who is rather puzzled and surprised that her friend Prudence does not believe. Her sense of guilt about being a hopeless vicar's wife is funny and endearing. In contrast, Howatch's Anna and Helen are desperately serious characters, tormented souls wallowing in a 600-page-long course of psychotherapy. Gone are the certainties of inherited belief. Certainty is now virtually impossible unless you have made belief in Christ 'your own'.

Within the latter part of the twentieth century, and within a culture often labelled 'high' or 'post' modern, the notion of the Church has undergone significant change. Formerly the Church of England's role in society was clearly recognized. It was the nation's church and membership was extended to every citizen. As a Christian institution which embraced the whole of life in its theology, its ritual and its moral thinking, the Church of England represented organized English religion. However this notion has been steadily eroded.

In the atmosphere created by the 'post' or 'high' modern culture in the latter part of the twentieth century, we have witnessed the breakdown of all major belief systems, whether religious or secular. The great hierarchical institutions of government, industry and commerce have largely disappeared and have been replaced in many cases by small self-managing units in which the roles and functions of employees are constantly shifting in dynamic networks tied together by computer technology and worldwide telecommunication.

We are living in a global economy in which the old allegiances to Queen and country are breaking down to be replaced by new regional identities within a united Europe. The Internet and television are changing the landscapes of our lives. Society is becoming increasingly complex, and change increasingly rapid.

Although the Church of England is still the established church, there is a tendency in society to view religion as a matter for the individual conscience – a personal lifestyle choice that has no place in the public domain. In a multiracial, pluralistic society, the Church of England increasingly struggles to provide any kind of moral or spiritual leadership and is in danger of being relegated to the margins of public life. Even in the village, the church's traditional stronghold, it can no longer rely on general support and approval.

Living and witnessing in the rapidly changing world of 'post' or 'high' modern British culture has proved difficult for the Church of England and it has struggled to define its role as a national institution. However, the atmosphere of post or high modernity has also stimulated the church to change and adapt.

Living at a time of rapid change, the church has learned to value the stability provided by its history, tradition and fellowship. Being pushed to the margins of society, it has been forced to reaffirm its commitment to mission and outreach. Living in a world in which hierarchical institutions of state, commerce and government are giving way to decentralized decision-making structures with dynamic, collaborative networks of workers, it has been stimulated to explore new ways to minister. At a time when the historic resources that have supported the church for generations are running out, local churches are being encouraged to take responsibility for the church's present life and future work. And no one is likely to shoulder that sort of responsibility unless they are truly committed and have made the church's ministry 'their own'.

It is clear why there is so much difference between Barbara Pym's 'Jane', and Susan Howatch's 'Anna', and why many Christian congregations feel beleaguered. But taken together, the pressures of 'post' or 'high' modern society in Britain have provided an atmosphere in which the church has been challenged to rediscover a vision of Church and ministry that is New Testament in origin but is able to respond to the needs of the modern world.

FINANCIAL PROBLEMS

We are also uncomfortable because there is not enough money available to maintain church buildings and to pay for someone else to do the ministry for us. In most places it is still possible to raise money to maintain church buildings (which are perceived as 'heritage' rather than as 'places for worship'), but, partly as a result of the decline in inherited belief, raising money for 'ministry' is much more difficult. Further, the cost of ministry has escalated dramatically over the last twenty years.

In the little village of Coates in Gloucestershire the quota has risen from £550 in 1978 to £8,500 in 1998 (or by 72 per cent per annum), and for that they get one sixth of the stipendiary ministry they used to have. The reasons for this are complex. First, the Morley Report *Partners in Ministry* of 1967 recommended a new deal on clergy pay and conditions which has proved expensive. The stipend, while still low in comparison with other professions such as teachers or social workers, is at least adequate, which it often was not before 1967. To this has been added a good occupational pension. Before 1967, there was no clergy pension and many could not afford to retire at all, which was bad for them and often very bad for parishes. But in 1998 the cost of pension provision absorbed 68 per cent of the Church Commissioner's income, and more was added by the dioceses. In retrospect, the worst mistake of the Commissioners during the 1980s was not that they lost money on property investments, but that they failed to make separate provision for pension funding.

The extent of the change is well illustrated by a passage from *Ministry in the Countryside*:

> Many parishes do not understand where the quota money goes, and the reason for this is not just obtuseness on their part. In Gloucester in 1959 only 7.3% of parochial income was on average needed to meet the quota, compared with 50.3% in 1989. In 1960 the parson was paid by someone else and there was vociferous complaint because for the first time the parish had to find money to pay some of the bills on the parsonage. Expense claims were almost unheard of. In the 1970s everything changed. 'They' at the diocesan office confiscated 'our' glebe, sold 'our' parsonage, and removed 'our' parson. In the 1980s, having stripped us of 'our' assets 'they' increased the quota tenfold, and now expect us to pay the new parson (who lives six miles away) for the petrol he uses to visit us. In one generation not only do the goal posts seem to have been moved, the game itself has been transferred to another pitch. As it was so aptly put to the Acora Commissioners:

Within the lifetime of some of the people in this place, the vicar has changed from being the person who distributed money to those who were the chief charge on the community, to now being the chief charge on the community himself.

Looking at the view through the villagers' windows, it is hardly surprising that there is a problem.

So it is not just that church members are less generous than in the old days; it is that the paid ministry costs far more in real terms than it ever did 'in good King George's glorious days'. And the situation is very uncomfortable, both for lay people and for the paid clergy.

NOT ENOUGH MINISTERS

We are uncomfortable because there are fewer stipendiary ministers. Despite a recent upturn in the number of those ordained, it is still estimated that by 2003 there will be 250 fewer paid clergy in the Church of England than there are today.

Nor, if we have any sense of justice, is it 'comfortable' that paid ministers should be replaced by non-paid ministers, and that we should carry on as though nothing had happened. Ministers are often accused of stopping lay people from sharing their ministry. But lay people are equally to blame, in that, either through laziness or lack of commitment, they often collude in leaving it to the vicar 'because that's what they are paid for'. Clearly if the minister is not paid there is absolutely no justification for such evasion of responsibility. And that is a truth we would much rather not face up to, and which makes us feel very uncomfortable.

THE MULTI-PARISH BENEFICE

The fall in numbers of paid ministers has made life very uncomfortable indeed for those living in small villages. A parson in every parish, the priest in his 'living', makes some sort of pastoral and theological sense in the context of English social history and of the enduring reality of parish boundaries (at least in the countryside). But as soon as the clergy no longer live with those who they represent at the altar, and as soon as they no longer share the day-to-day social context of those they are pastoring, the theological and pastoral rationale of the model breaks down. The multi-parish benefice, run as if nothing had happened, is unsatisfactory for parishioners who cannot have the undivided attention of their minister, and deeply unsatisfactory for the clergy spread ever more thinly over a larger area, whose guilt at what they have left undone knows no bounds. When two yoked settlements escalate to five or even ten, an absurd situation becomes a disgrace, and the sooner we declare that this particular emperor has no clothes the better. To live in a rural parish these days can be very uncomfortable indeed.

THE NEED FOR INDIGENOUS MINISTRY

Nor is it very comfortable in the inner cities, though for rather different reasons. The Sheffield formula has seen to it that inner-city parishes still have their fair share of full-time paid ministers, and the reallocation of historic resources has seen to it that, despite local poverty, there is usually enough money to pay them. What is uncomfortable is the recognition that the strategy for ministry which seems to work in the suburbs (and even in some rural areas) does not seem to pay off in the inner cities, largely because of an incompatibility of cultures. Back in 1965, Nick Stacey, the Rector of Woolwich, gave an interview which was given front-page coverage in the Sunday Times in which he declared, with his usual forthrightness, that the clerically led church had failed. He and five curates, the cream (sic!) of the Church's officer corps, had worked for five years in an inner city area doing all the right things, making the fullest use of their considerable talents – with absolutely no tangible results. Of course we all said at the time that it was a monstrous travesty of the situation (and a lot more besides!), but he was right to make the point and was fully vindicated by the findings and recommendations of the *Faith in the City* report. Stacey had recognized what Roland Allen had recognized in China at the turn of the century, that, if they are to thrive, churches need to 'localize' the good news and to make the gospel 'their own', and that every church needs its own indigenous ministry. Outsiders, like Columba the Irishman who played such an important part in the evangelization of Scotland or Boniface the Devonian who laid the foundations for the establishment of the German church, can often stimulate vision, train, organize, galvanize, but the maintenance of ministry has to be the responsibility of local congregations. They must be given the confidence and the training to minister to each other.

Ted Roberts writing in *Partners and Ministers* in 1972 put it this way:

> Overseas it has long been accepted that if a genuinely indigenous church is to grow it must have an indigenous ministry. After much painful change in thinking and attitudes, Western missionaries are accepting their servant role overseas. But we have failed to see that local people are likewise best equipped to lead the church in the inner-city areas of Britain.

Now that was a very uncomfortable thought in 1972, for it called into question the whole accepted strategy for ministerial training in the Church of England.

Practical Responses: Finding More Clergy

IMPROVING THE PAY AND CONDITIONS OF CLERGY

The discomfort felt was initially perceived as being due to a shortage of clergy. The immediate reaction was to harangue the congregations and to trawl the (private) schools in search of more candidates for the ministry. This exercise brought it home to those involved that the career opportunities offered to a young man by the church were, to say the least, poor. The system of payment (and appointment) was Byzantine, there was no pension, and all but the chosen few ended up in an impossible rectory in an impossibly depressing rural parish wondering why no one came to Prayer Book services – 'the glory of the Church of England' – any longer. The Paul report, the Morley report and new experimental forms of service began to remedy all this, but still the numbers at theological colleges dwindled.

CLERGY TEAMS

The loneliness of the sole cure also came to be recognized, and it was noted that Jesus sent out his disciples two by two rather than singly. Clergy Teams and groups were formed both in large urban areas and in deep rural dioceses, and they certainly brought new life and hope to a number of parishes. The Hempnell Group in Norfolk have published *The Group* a celebratory book to mark the 21st anniversary of their foundation which bears witness to a generation of quiet effective Christian growth. (Incidentally, this group has now developed into a collaborative local ministry team which includes lay people as well as clergy, and one of their number has now become their ordained local minister.)

Minster ministry was a variation on the theme of the clergy team, the idea being to locate the clergy in a central settlement where they could live a semi-monastic life 'like the canons of old' and go out to the surrounding villages to minister as need arose. The 'Minster' vision is beautifully expressed by Christopher Donaldson in his book *The New Springtime of the Church*. But it must be said that the vision has only twice found lasting practical expression, at Beaminster in Dorset and Leominster in Herefordshire, and it appears to be significantly more attractive to clergy than it does to lay people.

The tight structure of clergy teams did not suit everyone, and the report *Team and Group Ministers* includes many a sorry tale of clergy who cannot or will not get on with each other! Nevertheless, informal groups of clergy, meeting over coffee once a fortnight, soon became a normal part of the clerical scene with excellent results; while the upgrading of clergy chapters, the introduction of serious CME (Continuing Ministerial Education) and the launching of regular clergy appraisal in many dioceses, together led to a significant revival in clergy morale.

But still the numbers of paid clergy continued to decline.

THE USE OF READERS

The discomfort of not having a resident minister is felt most obviously went it comes to Sunday services. In the 1960s even small village churches ran two or three services on Sunday, not to mention the Sunday school which every child had to attend regularly – as ex-Sunday school pupils, now in their fifties, will always tell you! But now they have to make do with one service on Sunday. Even this would not any longer be possible if it were not for a growing army of readers (there are now more than ever before) who help to plug the gaps. Readers are very highly trained and are increasingly being called on to take baptisms and funerals as well as non-liturgical Sunday services. Some dioceses (e.g. Gloucester and Lichfield) are specifically training readers for children's ministry and for the taking of family services, and this is proving especially helpful in rural benefices. Of course some parishes have far too many readers and some, often the more remote ones, have no one on whom they can call. But thanks to the (voluntary) work of readers the vast majority of parishes who want it can still have a weekly service at a time which is reasonably convenient.

The use of readers mirrors the use of non-ordained authorized ministers in other churches. The Free Churches have for many years relied on the services of 'local preachers'. The Methodist Church in particular has, over the last fifteen years, revolutionized its local preacher training and brought it up to a very high standard indeed. The Roman Catholics, whose clergy numbers have fallen dramatically, now make full use of (married) deacons and eucharistic ministers (men and women) to ensure that regular services are provided.

USE OF RETIRED CLERGY

Until the introduction of the clergy pension the numbers of retired clergy who could help with services was relatively few. Today, however, there are over 7000 of them as compared to 9600 active stipendiaries, and though they are not always 'where they are most needed', there are few rural benefices which do not make use of them every month, if not every week. In some cases they are prepared to take a 'house for duty post' which gives them a free house in return for two or more (usually far more!) days a week working in the parish.

There are few other professional people who show such devotion to duty that they are willing to sacrifice their retirement in this way, but it has to be said that there are sometimes problems. Retired clergy are very likely to carry on ministering in the same way and with the same assumptions they have always had. They keep the show on the road but they often don't move it forward. It could be argued that for a parish to make use of retired clergy to plug the gaps simply puts off the day when congregations will have to face the hard realities which God wants them to face.

NON-STIPENDIARY MINISTERS

Despite the measures described, the numbers of stipendiary clergy continued to dwindle, and during the 1970s and 1980s the need for priestly hands was felt to be acute. At the same time, there was a real shortage of money to pay them.

At this distance it seems extraordinary that there should have been such a furore about the ordination of 'non-stipendiary' priests. Perhaps it was that the idea was first mooted by industrial chaplains who were regarded by the parish clergy with considerable suspicion. Industrial chaplains had come to believe that there was a desperate need for priestly ministry 'to the structures' of society and industry, but who would do it? Parishes were less and less inclined to fund full-time chaplains and so the obvious solution was to ordain some of the lay people who had caught the vision and who would not need to be paid since they had a full-time job. It was envisaged that they would not act as parochial clergy but as 'chaplains to industry'. Most industrial chaplains believed that the Church was becoming obsessively congregational and needed to recognize anew that God was interested in the whole of life, not just what happened on Sunday. (Hence the book *God on Monday* by Simon Phipps.) They believed that, as the established church, the Church of England had a duty to provide chaplaincy to the 'structures' as well as ministry to the 'hearth', and the hope was that NSMs would begin a process of radical reappraisal of priorities.

But, once the idea of NSM became accepted, another group of candidates began to offer for ordination. These were people who had taken early retirement, or who, approaching middle-age, had paid off their mortgage, educated their children, and now wanted to do what they had really always wanted to do – that is, be parish priests. They were not, at least initially, interested in being paid for their services. There are now more than 2000 NSMs ministering in the Church of England, and in many parishes they provide the backbone of the priestly ministry.

LOCAL THEOLOGICAL COURSES

The chief fear about NSMs was that they were, or would be seen as, second-class priests who were not properly trained. In order to counter this, initially candidates for NSM were separated from their families and packed off to semi-monastic institutions to ensure that they would become 'proper' priests. The folly of putting such unreasonable burdens on such obviously suitable volunteers – not to mention its expense – soon became apparent and led to the setting up of local theological courses which allowed people to live a 'normal' life while training for the priesthood (both NSM and stipendiary). On most courses the candidates meet each other weekly, but in some areas, such as East Anglia, the distances are so great that tutoring has to be done locally and the ordinands only meet together for occasional weekends and during the summer school. It is a system which recognizes and affirms the validity of the vocation to non-stipendiary ministry, which gives proper recognition to the claims of home and family, and which makes full use of the rich life-experience of the individual candidates. It is good to report that, in this way, older candidates have helped to break that 'clerical mould' which was an inevitable consequence of using only one particular form of theological education. It has not, however, done anything to question the assumption that high academic standards are a prerequisite for 'proper' priesthood. Indeed, colleges and courses vie with each other in the pursuit of bigger and better – some would say more pointless and pompous – qualifications.

INDIGENOUS MINISTRY

It soon became apparent that among NSMs there were a variety of vocations. A small number felt called to be worker priests, some to be parish priests wherever, within reason, the bishop might send them, but some were clear that their calling was to minister in the place where they lived. Theirs was a calling to *stabilitas*, to the steady lifelong love of the neighbour in a frenetic world. These people were labelled NSMs, but were in reality the prototype of indigenous priests or what we now call ordained local ministers (OLMs).

In fact, a debate had been taking place within the Church of England for most of this century about the acceptability or otherwise of ordained local ministry. However, it was not until the publication of the report *A Supporting Ministry* by ACCM in 1968, which set out a case for auxiliary pastoral ministry, that various experiments with local ministry were initiated. One such scheme operated in Bethnal Green and has been documented in the book *Partners and Ministers* by Ted Roberts.

Ted recognized that the experiment began with the question, 'Can a docker be a clergyman in the Church of England, and even if it were possible is it desirable or necessary?' Would it help to overcome the alienation of the working class from the church? These initial questions gave the experiment its central context; the establishment of a ministry that was indigenous to the East End of London. Trevor Huddleston had recently returned from Africa to be Bishop of Stepney and the African church had long cherished the principle of indigenous ministry. Ted Roberts writes, 'Two societies which at first sight could not be more different – Masasi and East London – in principle have the same need in common. If God is to be given His due glory, both communities must have a church that grows out of and belongs in the local community.'

Ted argued that the East End church had been blessed over the years by the sacrificial ministry of many full-time professional priests. However, in spite of this the church appeared to him to be weak. It therefore seemed possible that, if a way could be found to share the leadership of the church with people who really belonged to the East End, a step could be taken towards the establishment of a church that genuinely belonged to the area and was not run by people who came from a different social and educational milieu.

The experiment in 'supplementary ministry' that followed had six essential characteristics. Firstly, the ministry was to be conceived as a team enterprise. Two reasons supported this, one essentially practical and the other theological. On the one hand the demands of ministry made sharing within a fellowship desirable and, on the other, God's gifts were perceived as being varied so that no individual could be in possession of them all. Secondly, the call to local priesthood would come initially from the local church rather than being an outside appointment, although it would be confirmed by the centrally administered Advisory Council for the Church's Ministry. Local priests would therefore start with the enthusiastic support of the local congregation. Thirdly, the ministry would be settled rather than itinerant, have local roots and allow local strengths to emerge. Congregational authority would therefore be encouraged and local initiative be released. Fourthly, supplementary ministry would enable experimentation with training methods different from those used to train full-time ministers. A five-year training programme was therefore devised which took the experience of the individuals very seriously and established a pattern of training that was essentially practical rather than academic and which operated in the local parish rather than in a residential college setting. Fifthly, supplementary ministry was to be for a specific term of service, initially a seven-year period, to encourage a flow of leadership and to challenge the tradition of lifelong ministry. Sixthly, it was to establish the principle of volunteer service and to break the division of the church into givers and receivers, professional ministers and lay receivers of ministry.

It is a vision of remarkable clarity which has been in every aspect vindicated by experience, and it established most of the essential characteristics of OLM in this country.

ORDAINED LOCAL MINISTERS

The initiative of Ted Roberts was the direct inspiration for other inner-city ordination schemes in Manchester, Southwark and Liverpool. They are all schemes which aim to train 'indigenous' clergy to minister in a particularly intractable local situation. They have always claimed that their candidates are every bit as well trained academically as those at theological colleges and one of their particular contributions to local ministry is that they have achieved these standards by a remarkable revolution in teaching method. In Appendix 5 to *Stranger in the Wings*, David Leslie of Liverpool sets out the educational rationale for this development. The teaching is essentially interactive and it is grounded in reflection on experience rather than the recitation of dogma. In this way theology is brought out of the academy and once again put within the grasp of lay people, and the results are truly amazing.

Although candidates are not trained in the parish, it is a guiding principle of these schemes that the congregation has to become fully involved in the process. Before they can field a candidate a parish has to have conducted a parish audit, to have taken part in schemes of lay training, and to give evidence that they not only believe in 'all member ministry' but that they are trying to put it into practice.

At the same time, though driven by a different sort of discomfort, the Diocese of Lincoln developed its own form of local ministry. In their case – predominately deep rural and tiny parishes – they felt the need to build up authorized teams of lay people who would share with the stipendiary minister the responsibility for overseeing the ministry in their parish. Team members are nominated by the congregation, and the diocese delivers a three-year training course in the parish. In the second or third year, one or more members of the team may be recommended for ordination. The driving idea in this version of OLM is that the ordinands should not be raised on to a lonely clerical pedestal but should remain 'just one of the team'. To this end, most of their clerical training takes place locally with other members of the team and, not surprisingly, the academic hierarchy in London has accused them of not being up to scratch academically.

Nevertheless, the principle of lay team first, OLM candidate second, has been taken up by a number of other dioceses, notably Gloucester, Hereford and Lichfield.

THE BISHOPS RESPOND

In 1979 the Diocese of Lincoln decided to embark on a strategy for ministry which was committed to the development of OLM. These proposals gained the approval of the House of Bishops in 1984 and it soon became clear that a number of other bishops were going to ordain local priests 'as they saw fit'. For instance, the Diocese of St. Edmundsbury and Ipswich launched a pilot scheme in 1988 without accreditation and, by 1996, there were already twenty OLMs operating in Suffolk. In order to maintain some semblance of order, the House of Bishops produced *Guidelines for Local NSM* in 1989 and ABM Policy Paper No.1 with *Regulations and Guidelines* in 1991. A further report followed in 1994 and another, *Stranger in the Wings*, in 1998. There was general agreement that any diocese which wanted to be accredited should submit a 'scheme' to show how OLMs would be chosen, trained and supported. This was to be vetted by ABM (the Advisory Board for Ministry) and approved by the House of Bishops. The Manchester scheme was approved in 1989, followed by Southwark in 1991 and Truro in 1992. Fourteen others have followed, with a further one in the pipeline.

LOCAL MINISTRY BECOMES A MOVEMENT

Clearly a head of steam was building up and, in 1993, a conference on OLM was organized for all interested parties. This has become an annual event and, in 1998, twenty-five dioceses were represented. Meanwhile, the Edward King Institute at Lincoln has run a number of conferences on local ministry, and a new journal called *Ministry* has been produced to service an increasingly large interest group.

Practical Responses: Encouraging the Laity

The practical reactions to the felt 'discomfort' outlined above have all contributed something to the refashioning of the model for ministry inherited from the Victorians. But they are all clerical solutions to what is still often perceived as a clerical problem. (Even the use of readers is, in this sense, a 'clerical' solution since they are in this context being regarded as service-takers.) But, alongside these initiatives, are a host of others which start from a quite different premise: that the Church is the whole people of God. We not only, therefore, need to ordain more clergy; we also need to identify, encourage, develop and use the God-given gifts of lay people. Or, to put it bluntly, God doesn't just want more priests; he wants more motivated lay people.

COURSES AND CONFERENCES

Time would forbid me to tell of the lay-training initiatives undertaken by the churches over the last generation: Lent Groups, Parish lectures, house groups, the running of courses in Christian belief, parish audit days, Spring Harvest, Lee Abbey weekends, retreats, the development of spirituality and spiritual direction, the blossoming of the ministry of healing, music groups, Taizé chant, Iona liturgy, to name but a few. Since the 1960s the laity of the English churches have been put through an 'A' level, if not a degree course, in 'religious development' and, as a result, many congregations have developed a confidence and spiritual maturity which is simply miraculous.

THE BEGINNINGS OF DIY IN THE PARISHES

These initiatives have helped some individuals to sort out their faith intellectually and helped others to have a personal experience of God which has changed their lives for the better. But it has not just been of benefit to individuals. It has spilled over into helping congregations to have confidence in their own abilities.

The stewardship movement of the 1960s and 70s developed in Christians an awareness that they had talents – gifts – which should be put at the disposal of the Church. The Tiller report affirmed that all the baptized were called to ministry and that this, far from being the prerogative of priests, was the privilege and duty of every member of the congregation. Study groups up and down the country began to take on board the implications of this new way of 'being the Church', and 'gifting exercises' became a normal part of a parish audit.

LAY PEOPLE BEGIN TO DO THEOLOGY

In a quiet way, one of the most significant developments of all this Bible study and waiting on the Lord has been to bring theology once again within the grasp of lay people. Anyone who has been a member of a study group can instance moments of insight when, because of what someone has said, they were able to view life in a new way, and though the participants would not often see this as 'theology', that it most certainly is. The development of 'cells' and 'liberation theology' in Latin America is just another and more highly developed example of the same phenomenon: the rescuing of theology from the academy and putting it back where it belongs – in the Christian community.

CHURCHWARDENS AND PCCS

Buoyed up with a new confidence, many lay people have taken the first steps towards making theirs a DIY local church. Churchwardens are no longer saddled with the job for life. Increasingly, they make a conscious decision to do a five-year stint with some sense of vocation. Members of PCC's and church meetings are beginning to recognize that they too can be 'instruments of his peace'. Most ministers now have a regular informal 'staff' meeting with a group which includes not only authorized ministers (such as readers) but often lay people who play a key role in the running of the church. Many larger parishes sport a network of lay-chaired subcommittees which would make even Shire Hall blink.

PASTORAL ASSISTANTS

Apart from the provision of church services, the major 'discomfort' of having fewer clergy is that there just isn't the time for visiting and pastoral care that there used to be. But who else can do it? The right to talk personally to someone who is not a member of your own family, an invitation to come into peoples homes, is a great privilege and an awesome responsibility. Perhaps for this reason lay people have been shy of allowing anyone to visit and 'counsel' them except the minister and, consequently, those who have natural gifts with people have been reluctant to use them formally for the Church. They are surely right to tread delicately on ground which is so sacred.

Nevertheless, all of us do plenty of visiting and listening and caring which is nothing more than simple neighbourliness, for which we need, not so much technical training, as a prayerful compassionate heart and a good sense of humour. Building on these simple foundations, a number of parishes have developed teams of visitors, some trained and authorized like the pastoral assistants of Salisbury and Winchester Dioceses, others trained but not officially authorized. Many readers have become involved in pastoral as well as liturgical ministry. And though some people feel there is still nothing quite like a visit from the minister, a visit from a member of the congregation is a great deal better than nothing. In Dymock, in Gloucestershire, back in the late 1980s, a lay member of the local ministry team faithfully visited an old housebound gentleman who lived in her hamlet. When he died the family asked that his funeral should be taken, not by the vicar, but by the lady who had visited him and been for him the compassionate Church. Perhaps St James had got a point!

Those lay people who feel called to undertake ministry soon feel a need for training. Indeed, they may not be prepared to take on some aspects of ministry unless they have been properly prepared. Most dioceses now provide training in bereavement visiting, marriage preparation, baptism visiting, care for the elderly and support of those with learning difficulties. Particularly helpful is training for adults in how to initiate work with children and young people, and it is a remarkable tribute to diocesan officers that there is hardly a parish in the country which is not in some way reaching out to the under-20s through the ministry of lay people.

Part of the contract when a parish nominates a candidate for OLM is that lay people will join with them in the learning process. The 'education teams' thus formed are another growth point for lay people. 'I hope,' said a member of one such team in Cornwall, 'that our visitor will sense how exciting we find this process and how wonderful it has been for us to take part in it.'

Similarly, those who become members of local ministry teams in Lincoln and Gloucester dioceses contract to spend eighteen or more evenings a year in the study of set modules, two Saturdays a year on day conferences, and to attend one residential weekend a year on top of that. When they start they invariably feel daunted; when they finish they are usually crying for more!

Practical Responses: Collaborative Ministry

We have suggested that a series of practical pressures has called forth a series of practical responses and, for the sake of clarity, we have suggested that for a generation the Church has either tried to provide more clergy or tried to encourage more lay people to accept their responsibilities for ministry and mission. In practice, it has usually been both/and rather than either/or. Most dioceses are persuaded that God is calling his Church to a 'collaborative' model of ministry where clergy and laity work together to bring about that transfiguration of the world which we believe to be his will.

NON–AUTHORIZED COLLABORATIVE MINISTRY

As we have seen, local ministry is not so much a model as a movement. It is happening virtually everywhere in one form or another. Wherever congregations or members of congregations are hearing God's call to collaborative service and responding to it, there is local ministry. Sometimes it is recognized in the church magazine, sometimes it goes humbly unnoticed; sometimes it is called 'ministry', sometimes it is called 'church work' or, simply, 'being a good neighbour'. It is undoubtedly 'core' work for God but it is often fuzzy at the edges. Those involved are frequently not formally elected; they have neither contract nor status and obligations are largely self-imposed.

AUTHORIZED LOCAL MINISTRY

It is useful to draw a distinction between local ministry in general and 'authorized' local ministry. Authorized local ministry involves recognition, formal approval and training on the one hand, and contracts and obligations on the other. In one sense such a definition covers members of PCCs, church wardens, lay pastoral assistants, and informal ministry teams. But in the context of this book there is another distinction we need to draw between these forms of authorized local ministry and local ministry teams as they have evolved within the Church of England over the last decade.

COLLABORATIVE LEADERSHIP

Authorized local ministry teams specifically recognize that leadership should be collaborative. As the Gloucester Local Ministry handbook puts it: 'the team is a sign that God calls lay and ordained in partnership to ministry and mission in the world and to leadership in the church'.

From lay involvement in collaborative ministry it is a logical step to begin moving towards collaborative leadership. A local ministry team is a group of lay and ordained people who work in partnership, to lead, co-ordinate and develop the ministry and mission of all – to build up the worshipping, witnessing Body of Christ locally. The team is nominated by the congregation and authorized by the bishop but the members are not there to do everything themselves – they are there to encourage everyone to recognize God's call as real and to respond to it. The clergy person is a member of the team and inevitably has a special stake in what happens but it is no longer 'my' parish, or 'my' church, or even 'my' team – the burden of leadership has become a shared responsibility.

Inevitably collaborative ministry throws up issues about 'authority' and 'leadership' and the relationship between clergy and laity. These issues have not yet been resolved, or if they have been 'resolved' it is only a local and temporary accommodation while we gain experience of what it is like to work collaboratively. The theory is straightforward enough but, as we shall see from the stories which follow, local practice can vary and the shock of cultural change can be painful.

LOCAL MINISTRY TEAMS AND OLMS

Local ministry teams in this latter sense are authorized and trained teams of lay people and clergy who together share responsibility for seeing that ministry happens.

In most but not in all dioceses, one (or more) of the team may be recommended as a candidate for the ordained local ministry (OLM), and if this happens a significant part of their training will take place along with the other members of the team. But there is another ordination track which OLM candidates can follow. They may also, as it were, precede the formation of the lay team. In this case, a candidate is commended locally, their vocation is tested by the Ministry Division (the national body set up by the House of Bishops to oversee the training of authorized ministers), and the congregation, or a team within the congregation, undertakes either to share in their training or to train to work with them once ordained, or to do both.

As we saw, the felt discomfort of not having enough ministers drove the church to take action. One response was to ordain more priests, while the other was to mobilize lay people to share in ministry. In this formalization of local ministry teams the two strands meet.

REGULATIONS FOR AUTHORIZED LOCAL MINISTRY

The Church of England suffers from the structural problem that at General Synod level there is a Ministry Division which covers all ordained ministers and readers, while responsibility for the training of lay people is divided between the Board for Education and the Board for Ministry. Clearly authorized local ministry teams are hybrids that do not fit into this structure. However, the Ministry Division has gone a long way towards adopting the whole movement, and its Policy Papers, ABM 1 and ABM 4, together with the recently published *Stranger in the Wings*, are the best guide we have to what is happening – and to what, in the light of fifteen years' experience, the House of Bishops feel should be happening – as authorized local ministry develops.

ABM Policy Paper No. 1 includes the following passages:

Necessary Marks of OLM

2.11 The following three marks of this form of ministry appear to be necessary for its effective functioning.

I   Catholic order in the service of the local church and community

2.12 Perhaps the mark which most distinguishes OLM from other ordained ministries is its concentration on a particular locality and church. It recognises that each local church's ministry can include ordained men and women locally chosen, trained and deployed.

II   The collaborative ministry of the whole local church

2.18 Experience suggests the OLM cannot be planted in isolation in a traditional local church community and expected to flourish. Nor is it sufficient to say that an OLM must be 'part of a team of people, ordained and lay'. It is recognised increasingly by a variety of dioceses with OLM schemes that this ministry must be the fruit of a commitment by the local church to the ministry of the whole congregation.

III   A commitment to working in teams

2.20   Diocesan experience again suggests that OLM should be exercised in close relationship with other ordained and lay leaders in the local church.

[The paper goes on to stress that an OLM scheme must have a full place in the life of the Diocese.]

2.24   One implication of an OLM scheme being 'local and catholic' is that it needs to be properly owned by the diocese and to have its place within the mainstream of diocesan life.

THREE MODELS FOR LOCAL MINISTRY

ABM Policy Paper No. 4 recognizes that there are at least three different models for local ministry being used by dioceses. It recognizes that this is not surprising since each 'local' context will be different. In its desire to listen to local needs, the House of Bishops 'wishes there to be scope for a plurality of approaches'.

The working party set up by the House of Bishops identified three models, all of which were commended by their dioceses as being especially suitable to the local context.

• The Lincoln Diocesan Scheme (Model A) is founded primarily on an understanding of baptism as a basis for the ministry of every member of the Church. This priority is carried through into training, where groups are selected from parishes and enter a three-year training period together by means of a locally-based study group with a tutor. This model was judged to be especially suitable for the scattered rural communities of the diocese, since there was a desperate need there to foster local self-confidence and self-reliance.

• The Truro Diocesan Scheme (Model B) envisages local study groups as an element in the training, and these include an ordinand as well as lay members from the congregation. The aim of the group is to prepare the ordinand to foster the Christian life of the laity. While the ordinand will share in his or her training with lay people from the local community, the distinctiveness of both their vocations needs to be recognized from the start.

In commending this model, which is avowedly clerical, the diocese argued that:

> We wish to affirm the primary task of lay ministry to be the people of God in the world, served and resourced in that discipleship by the worship, pastoral and sacramental life of the Church. In addition, we would argue that due to the particular circumstances of Cornwall the formation of lay ministry teams would be more likely to serve the aspirations of newcomers to the countryside and the County, but might suppress a genuinely local ministry. Lay ministry teams are only one expression of the practice of a genuinely shared and corporate ministry.

- The Manchester and Southwark Schemes (Model C) were developed in dioceses with large urban areas, within which a significant proportion of parishes were either explicitly designated Urban Priority Areas or came near to this category. They provide explicit training for the ordination candidates only and the candidates are selected before entry to training. The ordination candidates meet together by year-group at a common teaching centre on week nights, and the collaborative emphasis is found in the way that ordinands train together as a group. The group does not include lay members from the parishes. The dioceses believe that this model is particularly suitable since it provides an opportunity for serious interactive education which has proved very effective in developing the confidence of ordinands from UPAs. Nevertheless, they insist that parishes in the scheme must have a good track record of collaborative ministry.

In the event, the wish of the House of Bishops that 'there should be scope for a plurality of approaches' has been fully realized and, of the existing schemes, there are no two which are precisely alike. Each diocese has taken the local context very seriously indeed. The one common denominator is that they all believe God is calling his Church to embrace a collaborative model which encourages the ministry of all the baptized.

HOW THE FREE CHURCHES HAVE RESPONDED

Not surprisingly, other mainstream churches in the UK are facing much the same pressures as Anglicans. Obviously it is valuable to listen to how they are responding.

Within the United Reformed Church (a union of the Congregational Church in England and Wales and the Presbyterian Church in England) response to the pressures we have identified has taken two forms. The first is that the office of 'elder' or 'deacon' has been upgraded. It is now policy to identify individuals in each congregation who will not only run the local show but will take services if no ordained minister is available. These people are recognized by the local congregation as 'holy people' and their appointment is confirmed by the District Council. There are 'elders' training days' run by the District and these elders meet on a monthly basis with ordained ministers of the area. The second response has been to upgrade the monthly or quarterly 'church meeting' and to try to give it an agenda which will ensure that all members of the congregation feel that it is worthwhile coming to.

The Methodist Church is not, of course, one of the churches of the Reformation but is a later offshoot of Anglicanism, which, in its centralized order, is much more like Presbyterianism. Although the priesthood of all believers is a core doctrine, the focus of 'the church' is seen as the circuit, or the Connexion, rather than the local congregation. For Methodists the practical experience of 'church' is much more like a typical Anglican multi-parish benefice than a typical Anglican parish. Stipends, assessments and deployment of ministers are all the responsibility of the circuit rather than the congregation.

The other big difference is that Methodist ministers have, from the first, been peripatetic – short-term 'visitors from outside'. And even though they have, for obvious family reasons, become residents, it is still very unusual for a Methodist minister to be in the same station for more than seven years. (It was, after all, Wesley's battle with the clergy of the Church of England about peripatetic ministry which was the catalyst for schism in the first place.) Nevertheless, Methodist ministers still exercise an authority in the circuit quite disproportionate to their numbers.

The responses within Methodism to the pressures we have

identified have been as follows. The training of local lay preachers has been revolutionized. Local preachers continue to be local people with local knowledge and local insights, but they are now highly trained on a nationally accredited course. It is worth noting that local preachers are local to their circuit rather than to their congregation. They are unlikely to take the service in 'their own church' more than once a quarter, though all the services they take will be within the circuit. They are, therefore, 'networkers' at a local level.

Methodists have recognized the need to reform their forms of worship. 'Worship leaders' are now being trained to take part of the service alongside the minister or local preacher. Monthly 'all age worship' has become usual, even in small rural churches.

At an organizational level, the importance of circuit allegiance and circuit meetings are being stressed. Without inter-congregational collaboration the smallest congregations are bound to go to the wall. Also within Methodism there is still a will to ecumenical co-operation, and there are numerous examples of LEPs where the worship of God in small settlements is kept alive by means of sharing worship and/or buildings with a congregation of another denomination. Given the significant difference between the congregationalism of the Reformation churches and the centralism of the Methodists, it is not surprising that the Methodists have often managed to stay open when others have closed. Methodism has survived in many villages, while the others have in most cases retreated to the market towns.

THE RESPONSE OF THE ROMAN CATHOLIC CHURCH

A shortage of priests

If anything the pressure of 'discomfort' on Roman Catholics is even greater than that on Church of England congregations. Canons 150 and 121 state that the office of pastor requires the order of priesthood: 'An office which carries with it the full care of souls, for which the exercise of the order of priesthood is required, cannot validly be conferred upon a person who is not a priest' (Code, 1983, Canon 150). But 'the numbers of (celibate) priests is declining and their average age is increasing. This decline is not steep at present, but it will accelerate'. (*The Sign*

We Give, p. 15). In the Americas the shortage is so great that many parishes are now run by 'non-priest pastors' of whom a majority are women.

Gilfeather reported as long ago as 1977 that over 80 nuns in Chile were acting as administrators of priestless parishes. In 1991, Wallace recorded that there were 214 parishes in the United States that were being administered by non-priests of whom 74 per cent were women. She went on to point out that this can cause real problems for the faithful.

> The idea of a woman pastor is so incongruous for many Catholics that they can hardly imagine it. A woman in charge of a parish does not look like a pastor, does not sound like a pastor and does not behave like most previous pastors. . . . Their modus operandi, their leadership style has to be different: it is collaborative, based on equality rather than hierarchy. (p. 36)

Though there are no 'non-priest pastors' in England, there are already a significant number of parishes which are run in all but name either by married priests or by deacons who are often married. To the traditional Roman Catholic this in itself can be very perplexing. John was an Anglican priest who became a Roman Catholic and has just been made priest-in-charge of his local parish. Trying to explain this to her old mother who has always been Catholic, his wife met a blank wall of complete incomprehension: 'But, my dear, he's married.' Some of the other responses of the church to the fall in clergy numbers have certainly proved difficult for the faithful to swallow, as we shall see. We are not, however, concerned here with why the numbers of priests have dwindled or with the question of clergy celibacy. What is important to note is the enormous pressure that this has put on the Roman Catholic Church to rediscover a theology of the laity and to embark on collaborative ministry.

An inherited folk Catholicism

As with all churches, the Roman Catholics have to live with a strong inherited 'folk' religion. In their case it is focused in the Mass. Catholics 'must attend Mass' and will still go to great pains to do so. But attendance at Mass is rarely perceived as implying an obligation to become involved in the congregational life of the parish: 'it is my obligation to attend Mass, it is the priest's job to run the church'.

Since the priest is the one who alone can say Mass he is vested with special dignity and authority. (The idea that it is the congregation who, with the priest, offer the valid eucharist would be foreign to Catholic folk religion.) The authority of the priest has been overlaid and enhanced by centuries of somewhat simplistic teaching and cultural practice, and, as in the Church of England, it continues to be reinforced by what clergy do in church together with the way they behave and the language they use in their dealings with lay people.

Naturally, like the Church of England, the Roman Catholic Church wants to escape from the clutches of folk religionists, but even when they restate their theological case in more sophisticated terms Roman Catholics still believe that the Mass is the focus of all the Church's activity, and that the episcopacy and the presbyterate are given by Christ to his Church and are essential to its existence. So the hierarchy find themselves in a no-win situation. The laity, for good or not so good reasons, expect priestly eucharistic-centred ministry – which the hierarchy also believe to be what God wants for his people – but this cannot be provided because there are not enough (celibate) priests. Further as Reinhold Stecher has argued in 'A challenge to the Church' – (*The Tablet*, 20/27 December 1997, pp. 1688, 1689), if the Church is indeed a eucharistic community, it is surely more important that local people be ordained to celebrate the eucharist than that all those ordained should be celibate seminarians. There is no shortage of local people who could be ordained, there is only a shortage of traditional priests. Is not the church putting the cart before the horse?

Vatican 2 and The Sign We Give

The beautifully written and presented report *The Sign We Give*, the Report of the Working Party on Collaborative Ministry, illustrates how far the Roman Catholic Church in England and Wales have moved in adapting to the pressures of the situation. 'Since Vatican II much has been done to renew the Church according to the Council's vision'. Non-Roman Catholics, brought up on the folk religion image of that church, would be amazed to realize how much ministry is already being done by lay people. Many lay people and religious are employed in full-time pastoral work alongside priests, and the 'Network for Lay Ministry', started in 1991, now has 200 members.

Permanent deacons

The office of permanent deacon has been revived since Vatican II, and Liverpool Diocese alone has more than 200 of them. A deacon is a member of the clergy and may perform all priestly functions except saying the Mass and the Sacrament of Reconciliation. He may also be married. Ron was one of the first deacons to be ordained. His secular job was as a pastoral counsellor in prisons. His parish priest and other members of the congregation encouraged him in his vocation which was tested by the bishop. After three years training he was ordained and appointed by the bishop as administrator of a hostel for seamen. He was then also asked to become 'non-priest pastor' of a small parish. He found the work stimulating but trying to do both jobs at once was too much for him. He now continues to run the hostel, helps out in the local prison (which has its own priest) and does various representative jobs on behalf of the diocese, largely connected with the world of (secular) work.

Ron is very happy indeed in his job and professes not to want to 'move on' to be a priest. Indeed, he is saddened by the attitude of so many of his fellow deacons who he believes would seek to leap into priest's orders if the church decided that it wanted a married priesthood. He believes that there is a specific role for the permanent deacon which is not just liturgical and certainly not just to plug clerical holes. The deacon is called to teach, to expound the Bible, to live a Christian life of service and involvement with the world, and to be a bridge between the laity and the clergy – a foot in both camps! He also believes that deacons are called to serve on their own home patch – they are not called to be peripatetic or deployable – and in this sense his vocation is similar to that of ordained local ministers in the Anglican Church.

Special ministers of the eucharist

Special ministers of the eucharist, who may be male or female, may distribute the communion in both kinds and may conduct a

'Liturgy of the Word and Communion'. They may not preach but they may make some comment on the Bible readings for the day. They do not dress as clergy but they do sometimes wear a scapula. Most parishes have them; one parish, with an average congregation of 200, has ten such ministers.

People are recommended for this ministry by the parish priest, who may act on the advice of members of the congregation, and they will be expected to have a strong spiritual life of their own – for instance, there is an obligatory annual quiet day. Training is carried out by the priest or the diocese or both, and varies widely from diocese to diocese. They are publicly commissioned for a year at a time. They are rarely called on to conduct a 'Liturgy of the Word and Communion' on Sunday except in very dispersed areas, but they frequently do so on weekdays. The service includes distribution of communion from the reserved sacrament, and though it does not include the Prayer of Thanksgiving it is for many indistinguishable from the Mass, except that it is taken by a lay person who is not vested and who is often female. It also takes less time! Hardly surprisingly, a number of lay people find this muddling. John, who is a deacon, reports that the faithful are happier when he is taking the (exactly the same) service 'because he is properly dressed and looks like a priest', though ironically a service taken by a deacon does not 'count' as a Mass. It is all rather confusing and at a subconscious level it must contribute to what one Roman Catholic writer has tellingly described as the 'greying of the priesthood'.

Catechists and other ministries

Cathechists do a remarkable job. They help with baptism preparation, (adults and children), marriage preparation, preparation for confirmation and reception into the church, and in the taking of parish house groups. (They are, of course, firmly under the direction of the priest and it varies enormously from parish to parish as to what exactly they are allowed to do.) They are trained by the diocese and by the parish priest. Most parishes now have them, and there can be as many as eight in one parish.

Besides this, many lay people are involved in the 'music ministry', in looking after the fabric, in running the finances and in helping to run parish events. So far, there are not many 'pastoral care groups' in Roman Catholic parishes, but this may be because pastoring is perceived not so much in terms of ordinary neighbourliness as 'the cure of souls', and that really is still seen as the job of priests or trained lay pastors.

But is it collaborative?

So there is plenty of lay ministry going on, but is it collaborative? Over the last generation the Roman Catholic Church has begun to introduce its own form of synodical government, though it is not yet part of canon law and is therefore more a means of consultation between clergy and laity than an instrument of government. There is a Parish Pastoral Council which elects to the Deanery Pastoral Council which elects to the Diocesan Pastoral Council. Membership of these councils is partly through nomination by the parish priest, partly through election by local congregations and partly press-ganged volunteers! How they work, how they are run and how far they are collaborative will depend on the parish priest, though the report *The Sign We Give* provides plenty of practical guidance on good practice. The enthusiasm with which pastoral councils are run does also depend on the personal inclinations of the bishop of the diocese!

In all of these ways Roman Catholic parishes are involving lay people in ministry more effectively than many of their Anglican or Free Church counterparts. Nevertheless, they are trying to effect a huge cultural change in a very short time and, hardly surprisingly, the good news is not happening everywhere. Mary was employed as a lay pastor in a large rural parish and was so well thought of that she was nominated to represent the Roman Catholic Church on a national body. The old priest retired, a new priest arrived, and within weeks Mary no longer had a job. 'He felt that he should do all the pastoring in the parish'. Andrew converted from nominal Anglicanism to Roman Catholicism and was soon trained and commissioned as a special eucharistic minister. Week after week prayers were said and appeals were made for vocations to the priesthood. Sensing a real need, he felt called to offer for the permanent diaconate and was given a supporting letter to the bishop. All he was told raised his hopes and confirmed his sense of vocation, until after two interviews he suddenly received a curt letter from the bishop telling him that he wasn't right for the job. No offer of seeing the bishop, not a word from his parish priest, not a word from other members of the congregation, let alone the possibility of an appeal. The bishop had spoken and that was that.

Finally, a reminder that the Roman Catholic Church is controlled, not from Westminster but from Rome.

A Vatican instruction entitled, 'Instruction on Certain Questions Regarding the Collaboration of the Non-ordained Faithful in the Sacred Ministry of the Priest', released on 13th November 1997, warns against abuses of lay ministry and emphasises the unique position of the ordained ministry based on apostolic succession – which it says is an essential part of Catholic ecclesiological doctrine. Though supporting the involvement of the laity in the pastoral ministry of clerics in parishes, the document insists that this should be allowed only where there is a shortage of priests, not for reasons of convenience or 'ambiguous advancement of the laity'. The document gives the impression, difficult to avoid, . . . that lay participation is accepted without enthusiasm, a non-optimum solution constrained only because of the shortage of priests. (*The Tablet*, 22 November 1997, p. 1524)

TOTAL MINISTRY

Local ministry is not only happening here in the UK. Churches in other parts of the English-speaking world are also under pressure and have begun to go in for what they call 'Total Ministry'. For them the pressures are even greater than for us. Indigenous ministry was developed in Alaska in villages which were only accessible by ski or by plane, and where a visit from a stipendiary priest was a twice-yearly event. In small rural settlements in the Americas and in Australasia there was a stark choice between closure and DIY, and with the help and encouragement of visionary bishops a number of parishes have had the courage to go for Total Ministry.

In these Total Ministry parishes, a 'gifting' Sunday (when the gifts of all the members of the congregation are recognized) is followed by a 'choosing' Sunday (when the congregation nominate potential priests). These parishes were on the point of closing their doors for good. Today, local people lead the worship, local people pastor the congregation, local people spearhead evangelism and social outreach, and local people are priest-presidents at the eucharist. In these parishes we can see 'all-member ministry', not in theory but in action. And to support them there is the apostolic, peripatetic, enabling, vision-keeping, trouble-shooting, ministry of the bishop and his stipendiary clergy-facilitators.

The experience of these Total Ministry parishes will be examined in greater detail in a later chapter but it is perhaps appropriate to end this chapter with a quotation from one of the pioneers of total ministry, Wesley Frensdorff (in Borgeson and Wilson, 1990, pp. 2–6) formerly Bishop of Nevada, who was killed in a plane crash in 1988.

Let us dream of a church

> in which the sacraments, free from captivity by a professional elite, are available in every congregation regardless of size, culture, location or budget.

> In which every church is free to call forth from its midst priests and deacons, sure in the knowledge that training and support services are available to back them up.

> In which members, not dependent on professionals, know what's what and who's who in the Bible, and all sheep share in the shepherding.

> In which discipline is a means, not to self-justification, but to discipleship.

> A church in which worship is lively and fun as well as reverent and holy; and we might be moved to dance and laugh; to be solemn, cry or beat the breast.

Let us dream of a church

> so salty and so yeasty that it really would be missed if no longer around; where there is wild sowing of seeds and much rejoicing when they take root, but little concern for success, comparative statistics, growth or even survival.

> A church so evangelical that its worship, its quality of caring, its eagerness to reach out to those in need cannot be contained.

2

〇〇〇〇〇

Local Ministry:
the Theological Pressures

In this chapter we see how 'having a conversation with our past' has freed us up to think radically about models of ministry and the role of the priest. We then look at the way recent ecumenical documents have begun to give a new clarity to our thinking about ministry and we examine the way in which the English Free Churches and the Roman Catholic Church are responding theologically to the pressures outlined in chapter one. We conclude that there is a growing consensus about a new way forward: the development of local collaborative authorized ministry.

Theological Pressures and Reactions

INTRODUCTION

No one likes change. All change is difficult and cultural change usually takes at least a generation to become accepted. Some believe passionately that local ministry is not about rearranging the furniture but about redefining the meaning of 'ministry' and the meaning of 'Church'. It is about moving from all-clerical ministry towards all-member ministry. It is about recognizing baptism, not ordination, as the supreme commissioning sacrament. It is about reaffirming 'local' and redefining authority. It is highly revolutionary and very dangerous, and we can only dare to walk this road if we truly believe that God is saying to us 'this is my path – walk in it'.

Many would not see it this way. They see local ministry as a way of plugging the clerical gaps on the cheap. The last chapter shows why they think that, and it would be silly to pretend that God does not often use 'discomfort' to prod us into doing the right things for the wrong reasons. This chapter, however, attempts to set out what the 'revolutionaries' dimly perceive to be God's vision for his future. Like most revolutionary thought, it begins as we commune with our past.

THE JEWS IN EXILE HAVE A CONVERSATION WITH THEIR HISTORY

The way in which religion can develop as people ponder on their history is well illustrated by an article of Walter Brueggemann reprinted in *A Social Reading of the Old Testament*, pp. 263 ff. He suggests that the exiled Israelites managed to refocus their understanding of what God wanted them to do when they set about re-editing their sacred texts and thus inaugurated a 'communing with their past'. There is no space here to develop his fascinating thesis, but he suggests that, by a careful reading of the texts, we can identify a Mosaic understanding of 'Church' with its central themes of covenant and holiness and its emphasis on the moral demands of God. This was the tradition which formed Israel in the early days when there were no stable institutions. It was a community that had to improvise. 'In the most radical way possible Israel was a new-start church.' However, when the Israelites settled in Canaan this 'pink elastic' church was replaced by a highly structured 'red tape' state religion. 'Cultus' and the state were intertwined and religion was there to undergird the status quo. With the centralization of worship at Jerusalem, religion and state had become intimately connected, the temple and priesthood being not unlike the Chapel Royal of medieval England. (Though even within the Jerusalem framework the great prophets kept alive the vision of the Kingship of God over and above human beings, and repeatedly challenged Israel to be a holy people.)

But then the whole sophisticated structure collapsed like a pack of cards. For the exiles, says Brueggemann, the landmarks had been destroyed and they inevitably asked 'How can we sing the Lord's song in a strange land?' Were they to go along the path of syncretism, either with the great religions of Mesopotamia or with the local religions of Canaan? Were they to turn in on themselves

and root out from their midst the Canaanite women, thus secur-
ing their future by a total exclusivity close to tribalism? Or were
they to wait on the Lord, less certain than before, less conceited
than before, less voluble than before, so that the Lord could make
of them a truly holy people who he could use for his purposes?

It was, says Brueggemann, in communing with their past that
they began to perceive their destiny. Most scholars would now
agree that the final editing and much of the writing of the Old
Testament took place during the exile. The work of editing and
rewriting allowed them to have a sort of conversation with their
history, and in the process they began to perceive where they had
come from, why they were there and where they should be going.

Chapter one has suggested that for us, too, the old structures
have collapsed or are in an advanced state of decay; the landscape
has changed. As we pick ourselves up, dust ourselves down, and
look to the future we too need to ask ourselves some hard
questions. Are we to lose our identity in a 'world religion'? Are
we to retreat into a 'fortress church' and bicker amongst ourselves? Or do we also need to have a conversation with our past?

A CONVERSATION WITH THE EARLY CHURCH

The young Billy Graham ran an evangelistic crusade in Los
Angeles. Thousands were converted but a number of local ministers accused him of setting the churches back a hundred years.
'I'm sorry,' he said, 'What I hoped I was doing was setting them
back 2000 years.' What has inspired local ministry in all its forms
has been reading again about how the Church operated when, in
Aposolic times, it first left the hands of its maker. Not so much
the frankly triumphalist accounts of the Pentecost church but the
tantalizingly incomplete snapshots of small, compassionate,
whingeing, spirit-filled, cantankerous, hospitable, factional, above
all believably human congregations we find in the Epistles.

Granted that we cannot be dogmatic because the evidence is
so slight, and granted also that the congregations are inventing
structures as they go along and are therefore different from each
other, what we see are congregations which are essentially local.
For instance, Paul writes separate letters to the Colossians and to
the Laodiceans, and tells them to swap their mail when they have
read it (Col 4:16). The congregations are small enough for Paul

to know many of them by name; the letter to Philemon, for example, gives an enchanting insight into the human scale of the early church. It is a Christ-centred Spirit-filled do-it-yourself church. For instance, although Paul tries to drop in as frequently as possible at Corinth to make sure things there are going along all right, there is no suggestion that in between his visits everyone hangs fire until he returns. They run their own show. He is the (rather heavy-handed!) facilitator.

Although the congregations were small, they were extraordinarily committed. It must have been exhilarating to be a member of that sort of church. Everyone was there because they wanted to be there. Everyone had been touched by the Spirit and had something to offer either as a contribution to worship – tongues, singing, healing, prophecy, wisdom – or in building community life and helping to bind up its wounds. 'Behold how these Christians love one another', said Pliny. Love, compassion as God has compassion, is reckoned to be the supreme gift of the Spirit (1 Cor 13).

They were also brimful of expectation – expectation of the coming in of the Kingdom of God. Perhaps they were deluded about that, perhaps they didn't quite understand what Jesus meant by 'time', perhaps their eyes were not wide open enough to spot the kingdom coming and the crop growing under their noses, but at least it kept them on their toes, and at least it meant that for them everything was, as C.K. Barrett (1985, p. 13) put it, 'provisional, temporary, penultimate'.

THE EARLY CHURCH AND BUILDINGS

The early Christians had no buildings to look after. Though the book of Acts suggests that they continued to worship in the temple and that, wherever he went, Paul first joined the local synagogue, the whole concept of 'the holy place' had been given a new twist. Jesus was remembered as having disparaged the magnificence of the temple (Matt 24:1–2, Mk 13:1–2, Jn 2:13–20), and was accused of plotting to destroy it (Matt 26:61). Stephen was arraigned for speaking against the Temple and, in concluding his defence, is said to have referred to the futility of building a house of God (Acts 7:48–50). Clearly buildings, and particularly the temple, were an issue for early Christians. But what Paul and Peter did was to help them see beyond the physical and to understand themselves as 'a holy temple' (1 Cor 3:16–17 and 1 Peter 2:4–5), which is not rock solid and set in English Heritage aspic but is still being built, living brick by living brick, (sometimes, sadly, straw bale by straw bale: 1 Cor 3:12–13), until ultimately we become the true temple of God (Eph 2:19–21). Not that any of this is incompatible with the use of an earthly shrine, but it does put it in its place!

LEADERSHIP IN THE EARLY CHURCH

In one of his earliest letters to the church in Thessalonica, Paul refers to workers who lead and guide the church (1 Thess 5:12). In Phil 1:1 he refers to overseers (bishops) and servers (deacons). In Acts 20:17–28 the leaders of the local congregations are invited to meet Paul at Ephesus, and they are described first as presbyters (elders:v.17) and then later, as overseers (v.28). Ephesians 4:7–16 recognizes that there are specific gifts of leadership which are bestowed by Christ for the building up of the congregation (though no mention is made of particular offices). In the later letters (1 and 2 Timothy and the epistles of John) the importance of 'authority' in the face of 'false' teaching is stressed, but authority in this sense is only one aspect of leadership. The impression is that we are looking at a developing situation where leadership is exercised in different ways in different congregations depending on the local situation.

What is quite clear is that, wherever we glimpse it, leadership in the early church is corporate. Nowhere do we discern anyone who might be described in modern parlance as 'the minister' of a local church. For example, the leadership at Antioch in Acts 13:1 consisted of a group of 'prophets and teachers'. From among these, two – Saul and Barnabas – are commissioned to go on a missionary tour. Paul never operated alone, always with the support of a team. What is also clear (1 Cor 12 etc.) is that everyone in the congregation was recognized as having God-given gifts, that everyone was expected to put these gifts at the disposal of God and the Church, and that the 'highest' gift was not oversight or the presbyterate or leadership in any form, but love.

THE IMPORTANCE OF BAPTISM

Another thing that emerges from the documents of the early church is that, for them, the sacrament of baptism with the laying on of hands was of supreme importance. It was regarded as an astonishing privilege and carried with it the awesome responsibility of being a member of the body of Christ. What is at issue is not when in a person's life baptism should take place, but what the sacrament implies. Some of the most striking passages in Paul's letters remind his readers of the significance of their baptism (Rom 6:3–11, 1 Cor 12:13, Gal 3:27–9). The theme is constant: because of your baptism you have become a new creation and this has implications for how you live and what you do. By baptism you are commissioned for ministry within the congregation and for mission in the world. The methodist Covenant Service (see *Oxford Book of Prayers*) exactly captures the essence of this new relationship:

> I am no longer my own, but yours. Put me to what you will, rank me with whom you will; put me to doing, put me to suffering: let me be employed for you or laid aside for you, exalted for you or brought low for you; let me be full, let me be empty; let me have all things, let me have nothing; I freely and wholeheartedly yield all things to your pleasure and disposal.
>
> And now, glorious and blessed God, Father, Son and Holy Spirit, you are mine and I am yours. So be it. And the covenant which I have made on earth, let it be ratified in heaven.

THE HOLY TRINITY AS A PATTERN FOR MINISTRY

We also need to hear what the doctrine of the holy Trinity, as it developed in the early church, has to say to us about 'ministry'. The doctrine in its final form did not emerge until the Great Councils, but in John's Gospel we can already glimpse something of its importance for our consideration of collaborative ministry. In chapter 17, John allows us to, as it were, listen in as Jesus talks with the Father. The whole passage conveys the sense of a team working together, of intimate conversation between friends. As the conversation proceeds, first the apostles, and then the rest of us, are caught up into the ministry of the 'Holy Team'. Reading the passage in an English translation we are bombarded with plurals – 'they', 'them', 'those'. The model for ministry we find here has nothing to do with the solo yachtsman, it has everything to do with the ship's crew or, to change the metaphor, with the many members and organs of the body of Christ. The Russian icon painter, Andrei Rublev, exactly caught the mysterious atmosphere of absolute unity and absolute diversity in his icon of the three angels who visited Abraham. This extraordinary work of art also expresses another truth of the developed doctrine – that within the Trinity there is no hierarchy, only a harmonious unity of purpose.

Robin Greenwood, in his seminal book *Transforming Priesthood*, describes the doctrine of the Trinity as 'a relational theology'. The report of the (Roman Catholic) working party on collaborative ministry *The Sign We Give*, puts it this way:

> The central mystery of faith is the Trinity; the belief that God's very being is relationship. God is Father, Son and Spirit, a communion of persons. . . . As human persons we are made in the image of a God who is Trinity. . . . It is in relationships, in our communion with each other, rather than in isolation from others that we find fulfilment. . . . This is the basis of the mission we share through baptism and confirmation.

THE EUCHARIST AS AN ACTIVITY OF THE WHOLE CONGREGATION

After half a millennium of bloodshed over the meaning of the sacrament of holy communion, it is refreshing to return to the New Testament and to find that – no doubt in their naiveté – they just did it. They met together, they gave thanks, they broke the bread, they shared the wine, they remembered the death of Christ, and they looked forward to his coming again. Paul had to exhort the congregation at Corinth to recognize the profundity of what they were about; but then he would probably be saying the same to us today in our post 'Parish Communion Movement' church.

It is not clear who presided at the eucharist, though we can probably assume that it was one or all of the local elders. It may even have been the host, the owner of the house where they were gathered. What does emerge from the Epistles is an assumption that the eucharist is different from the sacrifices at the Jerusalem temple in that it is an action of the whole local congregation. This is well expressed in the recent report *Eucharistic Presidency* (General Synod, 1997), 4:16.

> It would seem that the event of worship for the early Christian communities was typically an experience of the immediacy of God's presence to the whole Christian community through the power of the eschatological Spirit in their midst. Active participation in worship by every member of the congregation appears to have been understood as the norm (1 Corinthians 12 and 14). In the Epistle to the Ephesians, temple imagery is used to demonstrate that the liturgical divisions of the past have been overcome in Christ. The old temple placed different categories of people in different degrees of relation to God's presence, but the new temple is formed in the new humanity of Christ and through him we all have access to the Father by the Spirit (Ephesians 2:18). In the Epistle to the Hebrews we are told that whereas before only the high priest was allowed to enter the inner court of the temple, and then only once a year bearing the blood of sacrifice in his hands, now Christ has opened the way into the sanctuary of God's presence because by the offering of his body 'he has achieved the eternal perfection of all who are sanctified'. (Hebrews 10:14)

The report quotes with approval the conclusion of the International Anglican Liturgical Consultation: 'In, through and with Christ, the Assembly is the celebrant of the Eucharist' (4:17).

A further implication of our glimpses of practice in the New Testament is that the president(s) at the eucharist were people who were either local people themselves or who knew local people intimately. Presidency at the eucharist carries with it a presumption of pastoral oversight. The Anglican Liturgical Consultation document continues: 'The liturgical functions of the ordained arise out of pastoral responsibility. Separating liturgical function and pastoral oversight tends to reduce liturgical presidency to an isolated ritual function.'

It would seem, then, that in the early church each congregation expected to have among their own number those who could celebrate the mysteries, and that these people were in a close pastoral relationship with those who they represented at the altar. Further, since the church is a eucharistic church, every Christian community has a right to the celebration of the eucharist; a right that, in the earliest days, took precedence over any insistence that the eucharist should only be celebrated by highly trained, let alone celibate, ministers.

FREE TO ACT

Many writers and practitioners this century have had this sort of 'conversation with the past' and have found the experience liberating. The exploration has suggested that our whole understanding of the Church (and of priesthood too) is very different from that of our New Testament ancestors. It is not that, because *they* are in the Bible and *we* are not, *they* are right and *we* are wrong. After all the New Testament evidence suggests that what we are looking at is a church which is developing under the guidance of the Holy Spirit and which has not yet reached anything like a definitive form. The point is that such a conversation shows beyond doubt that our inherited model for ministry is only one of many, and if it isn't any longer effective it is no sin to move to another that will do the job better. The burden of our inheritance is removed from our shoulders. 'Provisionality' is a gift of the Holy Spirit to us, just as it was in the early church. All too often today, church members feel like a young aristocrat who has inherited the family mansion – and the family debts. They feel obliged by loyalty to the past to sacrifice their lives to maintaining the edifice, complete with threadbare carpets and impossibly uncomfortable sofas. What our conversation with the New Testament does is give us the courage to as it were sell the mansion and move into the dower house or even the flat in town!

LOCAL PRIESTHOOD AS PART OF OUR HISTORY

As we continue our conversation with our history, moving beyond New Testament times, a number of other assumptions are called into question. An important issue for our subject is whether 'local' priesthood is a new invention or the recovery of a truth we had all but lost.

In this respect it is useful to look sideways at how priesthood has developed in the Orthodox Churches. For them as for us, the understanding of priesthood is grounded in ecclesiology and in their belief in the centrality of eucharistic worship.

In their understanding, the celebration of the liturgy is the supreme function of the priest and his other functions are, in comparison, insignificant. Indeed, they are not so much 'functions' as 'charisms' which individual priests may have, but only if they are perceived to have them will they be licensed to use them. Teaching and preaching are regarded as 'charisms' and by no means all priests are licensed to teach or preach.

All priests are seen as 'local' priests (the representative of one particular congregation) and they can neither celebrate the liturgy nor preach for any congregation other than their own without the express permission of the bishop. While this is a matter of 'order', the theological reason for the regulation is that the liturgy is held to be true (valid) because of the worship of the congregation (assembly) expressed through their particular representative. Move either the priest or the congregation and the equation no longer balances.

Vocation to the priesthood may come initially through the call of God to an individual, or the call of a congregation to an individual. The fact that many priests are effectively 'pressed into service' is reflected in many Orthodox ordination rites. First, the part played by the congregation in signifying that they believe the ordinand to be worthy is an essential part of the sacrament. Second, the ordinand approaches the bishop supported on either side by a priest – in case he may be tempted to try to run away!

Although during the Middle Ages in Western Europe bishops and priests became distanced from the rest of the congregation, in practice priests were often local people who had been sent to the bishop for ordination and who then ministered in their local place for the rest of their lives. (Although monks often did officiate in parishes belonging to their monastery – see the Ellis Peters 'Brother Cadfael' stories – this practice was frowned on by the authorities.)

After the Reformation, the early Anglican ordinals put considerable stress on the inseparability of ministerial office and the church community. This was brought out partly by the requirement (in the Preface to the 1550 Ordinal) that candidates for ordination be duly tried and tested, partly by their public interrogation by the bishop and partly by the requirement that ordinations should be 'upon a Sunday or holy day, in the face of the church'.

Anglican priests have never been 'local' in the orthodox sense but, in practice, many clergy returned to minister in the parish in which they had been born. For instance, the Leir family were rectors of Ditcheat in Somerset, father followed son for 256 years. As Anglicans we have always valued the local place and the local congregation, and the fact that this is a central feature of our tradition is still very much evident today. The authors of *Believing and Belonging*, much the most extensive survey of rural Christianity in this country ever carried out, reflecting on the evidence write as follows:

> It is easy to debate the nature of Anglicanism in terms of a three-fold order of ministry set amidst Prayer Book, the place of Reason in interpreting scripture, and Church Tradition. A better way of characterising the Church, however, might be in its parish organisation and ethos. The Parochial System constitutes the Church of England. It is the parish not the diocese which forms the centre of gravity of Anglicanism. (Winter and Short, 1990, p. 20)

Of course things are changing but, in *The Clerical Profession*, Anthony Russell shows that the clergy only came to regard themselves as a professional class in the early Victorian period. The 'invention' of theological education, the adoption of a distinctive dress, the reordering of churches and changes in the way services were performed all led to the raising of the clergyman and his family to a pedestal separating them from the rest of the local society. Initially (particularly in rural areas) many of these 'new' clergy served for most of their lives in the same parish and thus carved out for themselves a 'local' position (though a subtly different one from that of their predecessors), but this too has changed so that now it is unusual for a priest to remain in the same benefice for more than ten years.

Ronald Blythe (1986), a perceptive commentator on the rural scene, writes in *Divine Landscapes*:

> The parish as a unit of landscape is the most associative, contentious and distinctive personal region. It is venerated as the landscape of nativity and cursed as the landscape of limitation. Parish scenery pulls us this way and that, it is in control of us. Even the twists and turns

of a city parish's streets have their special private direction for the born parishioner. In the country, where one can often see an entire parish from boundary to boundary, one can also see one's entire life. It is comforting – and painful. For those who have remained in the same place a parish is not an address, it is somewhere you don't need one. But if one moves away after only a few formative years there is no severing the umbilical link that feeds one with its particular parochialism. One of the great difficulties experienced by a priest today, is that his flock never really understands that their parish can never be his – not in anything like the sense in which they possess it. Unless, as frequently happened at either end of Christian parish history, he happened to be a son of the village. Medieval farmer's son, Victorian squire's son, there is a BROKEN tradition of the local holy man taking charge of the local holy ground.

And of course the multi-parish benefice only exacerbates the break in the tradition.

What Blythe draws attention to here is the fact that for most of Christian history, and for much of English history too, there has been a close link between the local settlement, the local congregation and the local priest. 'Local' priesthood is not, therefore, a new invention but can be seen as a recovery of healthy rootedness.

THE DEVELOPMENT OF CLERGY 'OVERSIGHT'

Another all-important issue is the development of 'oversight' or 'episcope'. By the end of the second century AD the need to cope with the problem of 'false teachers', and who was to decide what was or was not false teaching, seems to have led to the emergence of the bishop as the chief focus of leadership, and the presbyters ordained by the bishop gradually came to exercise oversight within local congregations. This is not the place for a full theological statement of the development of the priesthood; that has been done in the ARCIC final report, the Lima (WCC) document *Baptism, Eucharist and Ministry*, and has been most recently rehearsed in the report *Eucharistic Presidency* (General Synod, 1997). What we do need to recognize is that all of these documents suggest that the practice of ministerial priesthood which was developed in the Western churches needs to be reconsidered in the light of New Testament studies.

One of the reasons why these reports have re-examined 'order' in the Church is because scholars have come to question a number of developments surrounding the offices of bishop and priest which have taken place since New Testament times. Among the most influential books on this subject has been that of Edward Schillebeeckx, *Ministry – A Study of Ministry in the Life of the Church*. He identifies a number of trends during the first two centuries which tended to increase the authority of the clergy. He draws attention to the move from charismatic to official leadership and suggests that what had originally been the exercise by individuals of gifts bestowed by the Spirit became institutional offices.

He also suggests that there gradually crept back into the Church the concept of 'the sanctuary' which only the priest can enter and of the eucharist as a holy mystery, a sacerdotal ceremony: and that this had the effect of elevating the priest above other Christians. By the end of the first century, we find images of 'sanctuary' being used in Christian writings along with references to the sacredness and the special holiness of the office of the bishop. This is in marked contrast to the teaching of the writer of Hebrews rehearsed above who says that Jesus has broken down the barrier into the sanctuary so that not only the priestly caste but all the baptized may enter.

Ultimately, it is suggested, these changes led to the situation we find in the high Middle Ages in Western Europe when leadership rooted in community finally gave way to leadership by private individuals. What was originally: Jesus → the people of God → clergy and leaders, became: Jesus → clergy and leaders → the people of God.

Even the Reformation did not fully reverse this process, because within the reformed churches leadership remained focused on an elite group of 'learned' ministers. These came to be regarded as 'first class' Christians, a church of the 'chosen' in a far larger church of the 'unchosen' who had become a sort of baptized proletariat.

The effects of this are elaborated by Bishop Wesley Frensdorff in his essay 'Ministry and Orders: a Tangled Skein' (Borgeson and Wilson, 1990, p. 20). Analysing the inherited situation in the United States churches, he writes:

> Our ministry delivery system, the delivery of service in the name of Christ, is basically the English village model, but in overload. The

model is centred and heavily dependent on the 'cleric', who at one time was the most educated person in the village and thus also the primary teacher. The church buildings, as a result, are set up as classrooms. This model tends to create vicarious religion, centred on the priest as the holy person, in whom is focused the religious power and knowledge. It also tends to create dependence, rather than interdependence. If the priest is 'father', church members are children, who never reach sufficient adulthood in Christ to exercise much of their ministries.

The 'need' for professional training for the office has locked us into a dependence on money and vocation to full-time ministry. But when the money or the vocations run out who is to administer the sacraments? As a result there is a high degree of sacramental deprivation where the conditions of the model cannot be met. As Roland Allen pointed out more than fifty years ago, we have a situation in which we claim that the eucharist must be central to the life of the church wherever it gathers, but we have locked up its presidency in a professional, highly educated order.

Responding to these problems the ARCIC and Lima documents make a number of points:

- The ordained minister has responsibility for 'oversight'

ARCIC (para 9) states that 'An essential element in the ordained ministry is its responsibility for "oversight" (*episcope*). This responsibility involves fidelity to the apostolic faith, its embodiment in the life of the Church today and its transmission to the Church of tomorrow.' (ARCIC 1 (1982); Lima Text (1982))

Seen in this light, 'oversight' has a much wider significance than it is sometimes given. It is clearly leadership, and yet it has nothing to do with authoritarianism. On the contrary, like all Christian leadership, it is a form of service.

- The ordained minister has responsibility for the ministry of the Word

ARCIC (para 10) states that 'A ministerial vocation implies a responsibility for the Word of God supported by constant prayer.' But traditional preaching is only one form of the ministry of the Word. Anglican law and practice have always envisaged that some priests might not be able to preach, though they were provided with homilies to read. Moreover, preaching itself is not confined to ordained ministers, and the essential point is that regardless of who preaches on a particular occasion the ordained minister has the essential oversight of that ministry.

• The ordained minister should preside at the eucharist

Lima (para 14) states that 'it is especially in the eucharistic celebration that the ordained ministry is the visible focus of the deep and all-embracing communion between Christ and the members of his body'.

What is also perceived is that, as Schillebeeckx has urged, every Christian community has an apostolic right to the celebration of the eucharist. This means that it is vitally important that in every locality there should be a body of ordained ministers.

Further, the liturgical functions of the ordained arise out of pastoral responsibility. Separating liturgical function and pastoral oversight tends to reduce liturgical presidency to an isolated ritual function.

• The ordained minister as 'icon'

The ordained minister will often have to represent the Christian community to those outside. In an established church like ours this can still be a very demanding aspect of the priestly ministry, and ministers deserve to be properly trained for it.

• The collegiate nature of all ministry

Finally, what is particularly stressed in these documents is the belief that the church is *community* and that this applies just as much to the priestly offices as it does to the congregation. Bishops, priests and deacons all ought to exercise their ministry within 'a college of ordained ministers sharing in the common task'. (Lima Text, para. 26)

THE ENGLISH FREE CHURCHES

In some ways local ministry is the birthright of nonconformists. While it is dangerous to generalize, two of the doctrines which are enshrined in the Congregationalist and Baptist traditions are (a) that the fullness of the church is present in every Christian congregation and (b) that by baptism all are ordained to a priestly ministry.

These doctrines are still worked out in practice in most areas of their church life. Lay people are responsible for the governance of the local church, and the church meeting of all members elects elders and deacons and is the ultimate decision-making body. Lay people run the finances, look after the fabric and undertake basic pastoral functions. They contribute to worship if they are gifted as speakers, interceders, musicians or encouragers. The ministry of lay people in daily life has always been recognized and the compassionate caring tradition in English social life owes much to the way in which Free Church people have heard and practised 'the social gospel'.

Nevertheless, like the Anglicans, the Free Churches are re-examining the New Testament. If there is one basic reason for this it is because, like Anglican vicars, Free Church ministers have, largely unintentionally, captured authority for themselves and this has tended to let the baptized off the hook. Partly this is a result of Free Church history. A renewed study of the Bible in the original Hebrew and Greek played a key part in bringing about the Reformation, and book learning was therefore highly revered by Protestants. What seems to have 'converted' people to the reformed churches in that generation was the reading of pamphlets and the hearing of sermons. Again, it was by and large 'the learned' who were writers and preachers. It is hardly surprising, therefore, that congregations should come to believe that the minister might properly be brought in from outside and that they should invest that luminary with special respect, inadvertently failing in the process to recognize the Spirit-given gifts which were all the time within themselves. Nathaniel Hawthorne's novel, *The Scarlet Letter* gives an accurate and vivid account of the exalted position of the minister in seventeenth-century New England.

The nineteenth century was another period when preaching and the charismatic appeal of individual preachers became the focus of Free Church activity. Free Church worship revolved around the sermon and, with the removal of restrictions on the building of chapels, preaching houses went up all over the land.

In *The Myth of the Empty Pew*, Robin Gill shows how the efforts of congregations to outbuild each other were self-defeating and in many cases led to financial ruin and a decline in numbers. But the memory of the 'great preacher' continues to dominate the Free Church psyche even today.

As we saw in the first chapter the Free Churches are doing all they can to 'recover their birthright'. But an important question remains. These are essentially lay-run churches and yet they seem on a numerical count to have 'failed'. Does this mean that the whole concept of local ministry is flawed? This issue is fully discussed in *Ministry in the Countryside* (Bowden, 1994, pp. 195–201), to which the reader is referred. The problems identified are as follows.

- That the theology of the Free Churches is at heart 'associational', and that the challenge given sits uneasily with the sociological pressures of the small settlement.
- That the pattern of worship in the Free Churches somehow got stuck in the 1950s, and this meant that they were unable to adapt to the felt needs of new (largely urban) people moving into the villages.
- That in a small congregation dominated by family allegiances it requires the dedicated ministry of a gifted outsider if hard decisions for change are to be made and carried through.
- That changes in demographic and employment patterns have undermined the raison d'être of many chapels.

> Rural Anglicanism has always been accused of being the Conservative Party at prayer. By contrast, Nonconformity has strong links with Liberalism, and Methodism played an important part in the rise of the Labour movement. It would seem that in many cases chapels flourished in the hierarchical society of pre-1939 village life as either the church of the tradesman or the working man's church, and became just as culturally 'fixed' as rural Anglicanism. That society has gone or is fast going, and in particular farming no longer dominates either villages or the rural labour market. As a result, the rural chapel now often finds itself 'a rebel without a cause'.

> What the evidence seems to suggest is that the closure of the village chapel is at least in part a historical and cultural

phenomenon. The moral to be learned is not that lay ministry is a blind alley, but that even locally rooted lay ministry must respond to change if the doors are to stay open.

THE ROMAN CATHOLICS

Vatican 2 and The Sign We Give

The Sign We Give, the Report of the Working Party on Collaborative Ministry, illustrates how far the Roman Catholic Church in England and Wales have moved in adapting to the pressures of the situation. It begins by stressing the importance of the second Vatican Council:

> The decree on lay people affirmed that they have an active part of their own in the life and action of the church. Their action within the church communities is so necessary that without it the apostolate of the pastors will frequently be unable to obtain its full effect (AA10).

The 1985 Extraordinary Synod speaks explicitly of collaboration.

> Since Vatican II a new type of collaboration between lay people and clergy has happily come about within the Church . . . In this there is a new experience of the fact that we are all Church.

The theology of collaborative ministry

The report goes on to define what it means by 'collaborative' ministry:

> Collaborative ministry is an ecclesial activity; it brings together into partnership people who, through baptism and confirmation, as well as ordination and marriage, have different vocations, gifts and offices within the Church . . .

> Involvement in collaborative ministry demands conscious commitment to certain values and convictions. These include a recognition that Christian initiation gives us a shared but differentiated responsibility for the life and mission of the Church, and calls us to work together on *equal* terms . . . an agreement that we are accountable to each other for how we work and what we do (italics added).

Powerful stuff!

The ecclesiology which underpins collaborative ministry is

then explored. 'Communion' ecclesiology is based on the belief that God's very being as Holy Trinity is relationship, and that

> it is in relationship, in our communion with each other, rather than in isolation from others that we will find fulfilment. This is the basis for our equality in dignity as members of the Church and for our awareness of the Spirit's activity within and between us.

Hierarchy and authority

There follow sections on 'hierarchy', 'authority', 'leadership', 'the role of the priest' and 'the role of the bishop' which, while clearly addressed to the particular Roman Catholic context, have a lot to say to all ministers who are seeking to re-understand their role in this new collaborative world. In particular, the Roman Catholic understanding of the role of the bishop – based on the belief expounded in the writings of Ignatius of Antioch that the 'local' church is the diocese and that where the bishop is, there is the church – while at first sight anathema to most Protestants, would seem to offer a way of coming to terms with the issues of authority which local ministry will increasingly throw up. It is not insignificant that in Anglican Total Ministry parishes in New Zealand the bishop is an ex officio member of every local ministry team.

So Where Do We Go from Here?

A GROWING CONSENSUS ABOUT THE WAY FORWARD

In chapter one we saw that a number of practical pressures were making the Church feel decidedly 'uncomfortable' and we looked at some of the practical responses of the Church to try to relieve those pressures. In this chapter we have suggested that the theological imperatives, quite apart from the practical pressures, are actually so great that it is no longer a matter of patching the old tyre; we are going to have to get out our cheque book and go and buy a new one.

The good news is that, as a result of our experiences over the last generation, all over the English-speaking world Christians are coming to a consensus about which way we should be going, at least until we come to the next crossroads! This consensus is based on:

• A theology of all the people of God as ordained to ministry and mission by baptism.

• A model for ministry based on a new understanding of the 'relational' working of the Holy Trinity.

• An understanding of ministry and priesthood which finds its focus in the eucharist.

• A model for ministry which is rooted in the local congregation.

• A model for ministry which is based on ministry teams rather than on individual ministers.

Or, put another way, there is general agreement that we need to move from an 'all-clerical' towards an 'all-member' model for ministry, and that we should encourage each congregation, whether they are in a geographical area or within some other base community such as a school or hospital, to develop a model that is:

LOCAL: Recognizing the gifts of local people. Directed towards supporting local people. Seeking to meet local needs. Trusting that in the power of the Spirit we can 'Do it Ourselves'.

COLLABORATIVE: Lay people and clergy working together, each using their God-given gifts for the building up of the body of Christ.

AUTHORIZED: Recognized by the wider Church. Guided and supported by the wider Church. Recognizing obligations to the wider Church.

MINISTRY: Called to do a 'priestly' task which in some way 'transfigures' people and places. A ministry grounded in listening to God and to others, and committed, not to structures, but to swimming with 'the flow of God's story'.

The Human Face of Local Ministry

What this book will try to do is to give authorized local ministry a human face – to tell stories rather than to argue about theories. The stories do, of course, illustrate many of the issues which are thrown up in practice but, first and foremost, we hear from practitioners what it is like to be an OLM, an incumbent, a team member, a bishop, a local ministry officer – one of those involved in this exciting enterprise which we believe to be of the Spirit.

3

ഗ്രഗ്രഗ്ര

The Parishes' Tale

In this chapter we look at local ministry from the perspective of the parish. Who becomes a member of a local ministry team and what are their worries? How do they work with each other and how do they relate to the rest of the congregation? Most significantly, how do they relate to the incumbent and to those of their own number who 'break ranks' to be ordained as OLM? Finally we ask the bottom-line question: is it a success?

A Variety of Parishes

One of the remarkable facts about the practice of local ministry in our churches is that it is truly local. It is a truism that every place is different and yet the model for ministry which the Church of England has traditionally offered is monolithic. The 'parish system' has to do duty in the hills of Northumbria and the fens of Lincolnshire, in the UPAs of Bristol and the suburbs of Torquay. Local ministry seems at last to have broken the log-jam. It appears in a multiplicity of guises and is moulded to a multiplicity of needs.

Lincoln Diocese has been training local ministry teams for longer than anyone else and its introductory booklet *Exploring Local Ministry* gives the following examples:

1. Nine people are crammed into the vicarage study. Including the Vicar and the Reader they form the Local Ministry Team for a large urban parish in the north of the Diocese. They meet in this way once a month to pray and plan their activities. The seven who have done the Local Ministry training are an interesting group: two teachers, a

nurse, someone who runs his own business, a shift worker and two who are retired. Their ages range from mid-thirties to – well we had better not say!

The team members main job is pastoral work, visiting young families, the sick and the bereaved: though they do help to lead worship from time to time.

They enjoyed their training together and are glad of the chance to continue it. One of the teachers is now much more aware that her teaching is her own very special Christian ministry – and the businessman has found to his surprise that he has got just what it takes to lead the church youth group!

2. Come now to a more rural area where three small parishes share an incumbent – the sort of place where everyone seems to commute for everything – work, shopping, schools and leisure.

Three years ago at a joint meeting of the PCCs ten people were chosen for training within the Local Ministry Scheme. Two had to drop out after a few months, but two others have now been selected to train for ordination as priests.

The new priests will still be part of the team, but there is some excitement at what they may be able to contribute to the life of the local congregation. The incumbent speaks of a new sense in all the villages that the church is alive; folk in the locality are already getting the message that the church is the people rather than the building.

3. In a country town parish further south in the Diocese they chose their team in a completely different way. Each one of the seven local people represents at least one different area of the church's life and work. There's a Sunday school teacher, an MU member, one of the choirmen, a young mum who has children at the play group and three others. They meet each month with their Vicar and Churchwardens and they have an important job co-ordinating what goes on in the life of the church.

All the members of the group now feel a lot more confident about calling themselves Christians and some have discovered skills they never knew they had. In fact two of them have dropped out of the work they used to do for the church so that they have more time for these new ventures.

One of the women in the group discovered early on that she was being called to ordination, and she is now the focus for some exciting work on a housing estate some distance from the parish church.

The benefice of Caldwell was to be linked with the next-door benefice making six parishes in all. Many in the congregations could remember the days when each of the villages had their own clergyman and folk used to sit back and criticize the vicar and his wife. Of course lots of people still complained that 'we don't see much of the vicar these days', but for some time those who really didn't want their church to shut up shop – as the post office and the garage had done – had realized that things would have to change. The trouble was knowing quite what to do. They kept the church clean and tidy, and the fabric was in tiptop order. By making judicious use of retired clergy they ensured that there was a weekly service in their churches at a time people could manage. But it proved more difficult to maintain regular visiting, welcome newcomers and provide effective ministry for children and young families. Then the diocese ran three very successful conferences for clergy and lay people and expectations of a new deal were raised. The parishes were asked to nominate a ministry team, and team members committed themselves to two years of training plus a three year stint. In return the diocese offered professional training, ongoing support and episcopal authorization. It seemed to be just what was needed to turn good intentions into a model for ministry which local people could understand and accept.

Wenfold is a large suburban parish with a dynamic vicar and 700 worshippers on a Sunday. It is a terribly exciting place to worship where you really get a sense that the church is alive and kicking and well. It is the sort of congregation where there is a great need for pastoring and for priestly ministry – for counselling, confession, laying on of hands. Nor is it just the Sunday services which have to be covered; it's also the weddings, funerals and baptisms which such a parish attracts. If the stipendiary clergy are to be released to have vision and spiritual relaxation there is a clear need for more priestly hands to be available. But there are no more stipendiary clergy available and as soon as an NSM from the congregation is trained he or she disappears over the horizon to minister somewhere else. The news that a local person (provided they really are committed to staying local) could be locally trained and ordained for the exclusive use of the parish seemed like an answer to prayer. There were a number of people in the congregation who seemed to fit this particular bill and there were others who were only too ready to form an education team to join in the training. It was like being a member of a really high-quality discussion group and doing something useful at the same time.

Clearly local ministry has something to offer all sorts and conditions of parish.

A Variety of People – the Unexpected Ones

Not only does local ministry seem to suit a variety of parishes; it also appeals to a wide variety of people. One team includes a farmer, a housewife, someone who runs a very successful bed-and-breakfast business, and an opera singer! Another team includes, among others, a young couple who have a flair for producing youth musicals, a retired headteacher, a farmer's wife and an industrial executive. Most team members are 'the obvious choice' but always there are one or two who never expected to be asked.

Sarah is very shy indeed and was amazed to be asked to join the team. 'But I thought – well, if they really want me, it would be rude of me to say no'. She found the first residential training event excruciating in anticipation, though when it came she thoroughly enjoyed it. She was trained as a secretary and other members of the team soon came to recognize her organizational gifts. 'She's the one who keeps us together and fixes dates and reminds us about meetings'. She had certainly never seen herself as having pastoral gifts but the team has given her the confidence to take up a visiting role (with other team members) in a number of local residential homes. 'They asked me to go along with them, and I didn't find it nearly as difficult as I expected. In fact I rather enjoyed it'.

Sylvia has had a very difficult life and has a pretty low sense of self-esteem. But she is committed to prayer and is the sort of person anyone can talk to. She too was amazed to be asked, and every now and then 'can't think what she's doing in this team – everyone's doing so much more than I am'. But the truth of the matter is that prayer – for their town and for each other – is the core of the team's work, and deep intercessory prayer is second nature to Sylvia. She even found herself hosting a group for a very successful Alpha Course.

Bill is a small farmer, the only one of his family who takes church seriously, each of whom still live in the parish where they were born. A marked man! No one was surprised that Bill should be asked to join the team – except Bill. He left school at 14, and has always been acutely embarrassed by his lack of educational background. When the archdeacon came to the parish to take a day on 'collaborative ministry' it wasn't until after lunch that Bill twigged that 'collaborative' didn't mean 'working with the Germans'. But what Bill does have in full measure is 'Wisdom' and, three years down the line, the team has given him the confidence to recognize what a great gift God has given him. In fact, ever humble, Bill's chief worry is that the team always seems to defer, not to the opinions of the bright young incumbent, but to him!

Reservations People Have

TIME

When the vicar calls and asks someone to 'join the team' even the most assured have reservations. Worries concerning time for instance. Being the member of a team involves a major commitment of time: probably twenty or more evenings a year when in training and a number of Saturdays or weekends too. That may be why the majority of team members are fifty-plus. And yet those who stay the course are often devastated when it finishes.

The Lower Vale benefice had a wonderful parish day to clear the decks for the formation of a team and over forty people were nominated. But when the incumbent went round asking individuals to join, she soon felt like the householder in the parable who bid many to his wedding feast. One would shortly be moving, a second could only say yes if he reneged on another commitment, a third couldn't because it would cause a family row, and so on. A number said they would love to have a go next time round but, as of now, only three of the 'obvious' candidates could or would say yes.

In Ashmere everyone agreed that John would be just right as an OLM candidate and that finding a local education team would be easy. After all, half the people in the congregation had first-class university degrees. And then they tried to fix a date for the first team meeting. One member runs the Bank of England, so his first free evening was in three months time; another always spends the winter months in Florida, a third spends the summer months in Greece, and so it went on. The luckless John was fortunate if his 'education team' met three times a year.

And yet even busy young executives do find the time and, having done so, find the time well spent.

> *I rarely get home before 6.30, so it's a real wrench to come out again for the team meeting at 7.30 and of course I feel extremely guilty about leaving my wife to look after the children yet again. But I have to say that the way the meetings and the worship are conducted, and the support I get from the team, makes it worth the effort – far more so than the PCC, I may add!*

At a gathering of five teams which marked the end of their three-year training, far from there being a general sigh of relief everyone wanted training to continue. And three of the teams have found the transition from twenty study meetings a year to no more than a monthly team meeting extremely difficult. At the other end of the 'training tunnel' the problem of finding 'time' now seems to have moved to the bottom of the agenda.

I'M NOT CLEVER ENOUGH

'I'm not clever enough' and 'what have I to offer?' also feature high on the reservations list. Of course a module on Christian belief can come across as intellectually impossible if it's taught in a university lecture style, but a number of dioceses use 'experience-led' teaching methods which overcome this problem. The rural evangelism video, *Hidden Treasure*, is often used as a discussion starter for this module, and the reaction is usually 'Well, I think *I* could do that' or even 'Well, that's not *real* evangelism, is it?'

The village of Paston has a large and enthusiastic education team who are helping to train their OLM. Only one of them has a degree, none of them has previously studied theology, and the ordinand herself has had no formal education since she left school at the age of sixteen. The OLM is trained at a central location along with NSMs and stipendiaries. She then has to pass on what she has learned to the team and initiate a discussion. A tutor helps her to prepare her presentation and monitors the meeting.

The topics range from 'understanding the doctrine of the Trinity' to 'what do we make of Genesis 1–11?' to 'the future of the family' to 'the ethics of intensive agriculture'. 'I do hope,' said one member 'that our visitor experiences the vigour, fun and comradeship that our mutual chemistry manages to generate. We have really enjoyed these sessions, and they have got us fired up about being members of the church as never before.'

Where some do feel the intellectual pinch is that any course inevitably questions 'party dogma'. James is a free churchman born and bred, and has always believed the Bible to be literally 'true'. He found the module on the Old Testament extremely difficult and was particularly upset when the tutor described the creation stories as 'parables'. It hurt him at a very deep level and his reaction was inevitably 'irrational'.

Don and Sheila are a lovely couple with young children, and for them to get away on a residential involves a real sacrifice. Their spirituality is Bible-based and they are accustomed to using extemporary prayer. The residential on 'spirituality' was billed as a time which would help team members to grow spiritually and to experience new ways of praying. In the event, the weekend was devoted almost exclusively to reflective silence: traditional Bible-reading and discussion didn't get a look-in. There were massive silences which left Don and Sheila cold, and an encouragement to inner questioning which they found deeply threatening. Their unhappiness was exacerbated by the fact that nearly everyone else seemed to think that it was all absolutely wonderful!

It was the same difference for Mark, a devout Anglo-Catholic who was, with much trepidation, attending his first residential. For the first time he was exposed to extemporary prayer in all its fullness and he found it very uncomfortable indeed. Not a structured service in sight – even the ASB would have done!

Obviously, team members have to learn to develop a theological framework for considering ethical issues. As authorized church ministers they are bound to have to respond coherently as society flounders deeper and deeper in a moral quagmire. At some stage in the course they will have to talk through issues such as abortion, divorce, homosexuality, agricultural methods and so on, which is fine provided you have not had a termination yourself, have not been divorced, don't have a son who has just been 'outed' and are not a farmer. Claire spent much of one residential in tears and if it hadn't been for the wonderful support of other members of her team she would certainly have jacked it all in. Eric, a farmer, came straight to the residential from dispatching day-old calves for slaughter and incineration – (part of the fallout from the BSE crisis) – to join a group of suburban-minded zealots who wanted to discuss the ethics of animal welfare. Fortunately, one of the local ministry officers had once been a farmer himself so there was someone who could clear up the debris after Vesuvius had erupted!

FAMILY LIFE

As with any vocation to any ministry, people are apprehensive about what it will do for their prior vocation to family life.

It would be silly to gloss over the problems but it has to be said that most of the stories are encouraging. Diana is an exuberant young mother, with three children and a high-flying husband, who succeeds in juggling her time with admirable skill. Her husband always was supportive but his own faith has grown as the team has trained. It was lovely to watch the children, eyes all agog and remarkably quiet, at the cathedral service when their mother was mandated with her team.

When the team thrives, the family seems to recognize the value of the project and their own faith grows. But contrariwise, when the team falters, or worse still fails, it can be disastrous. Phillipa was an enthusiastic member of a team which developed rapidly and began to show the first-fruits of success. Her agnostic husband was impressed and for the first time began to think of the C of E as something other than Trollopian. He even began to offer his very considerable skills in the service of the team. After a year or so it was suggested she offer for local ordination and, after considerable discussion, she agreed to test her vocation. She was accepted, ordained deacon, and everything looked set for a happy ending. But then the incumbent changed and almost immediately decided that he could not accept women priests. When he tried to stop Philippa being priested her husband was understandably very angry indeed, partly on her behalf, partly as a businessman faced by what he saw as crass mismanagement. It won't shake their marriage but it has certainly shaken his embryonic faith.

THE READER

Many readers feel threatened by local ministry. John had gone through a long and demanding course to become a reader, and it had meant real sacrifices for him and his family. He had to admit that he had been disappointed by how little this hard-won experience had been used in the parish. Because most of the services were communion-based, all he ever seemed to do was to take the residual matins or evensong which only a few people came to. The one way he did feel he was contributing was at the staff meeting when he and the incumbent planned the services and discussed parish policy over a cup of coffee (or something stronger!). Now the local ministry team was to invade that cosy huddle and he strongly suspected that, before long, team members – who hadn't been really properly trained – were going to be allowed to take services.

Peter had other reservations. He knew his limitations. The call to readership had been a genuine one; he had a real flair for doing the liturgy and for preaching. But he was not good pastorally and he was not a natural team player. Further, he had a very demanding job and well knew that there are only twenty-four hours in the day. What he could offer he did offer, but he couldn't also be a member of the team. He knew this was the right decision but it still made him feel guilty.

Anne was originally equally as suspicious but, after a sticky start, the team began to study a module on 'telling our faith story'. To her surprise, the other members all looked to her as the 'expert' and she felt more appreciated and valued as a reader than she had ever felt before.

Nancy was a local person who was used to doing what the incumbent said. He told her that, as a reader, she had to join the team and so she did. She was secretly amused to see that the team were not prepared to let the incumbent get his own way in everything and she began to see how healthy a lay team could be. Like Anne, she was truly amazed and humbled when the team suggested that she should consider offering for OLM. 'I would never have thought of putting myself forward, and if I didn't know that I was part of a team I wouldn't dream of doing so now'.

Relations with the Rest of the Congregation

WHEN LOCAL MINISTRY BECOMES TOO LOCAL

The avowed aim of local ministry is to enable the whole congregation 'to be church', as the latest jargon has it. It's all about 'whole body ministry', or 'total ministry' as they call it in the Diocese of Nevada, USA.

But it can have quite the opposite effect. Ordaining an individual to minister locally can result in the perpetuation of a 'very-reactionary-indeed' clericalism because it is so locally rooted. A lay team, even if called out by the congregation, can become an elite group which effectively discourages initiative in the rest of the congregation.

Eddie was the obvious candidate for OLM. Born and brought up in the village, he was a good kind person who everyone respected. But Eddie was a timorous mortal who could always be relied on to see a hundred good reasons for not taking risks. If he had been just one member of a ministry team his gifts would have been invaluable; set above the congregation on the pedestal of ordination, he kept 'his' church anchored in the past.

The parishes of Elansby benefice had only ever been able to raise a team of five, all of whom were well over fifty. Over the years, the reader was ordained, two members moved over the border of the parish (though they continued to attend 'their' churches), the incumbent left, and the benefice was enlarged. Inexorably the team became an overwhelmed group of 'vicar's helpers' with no vision apart from keeping 'their' churches open – just about. The congregation came to blame the team for the spirit of defeatism and disillusion which set in and, not surprisingly, they have failed to recruit new team members. In the words of the Free Church aphorism 'it's them that keep the church open that keep the church empty' and, sadly, their situation now closely mirrors the experience of many village chapel congregations.

MISUNDERSTANDINGS ABOUT WHAT THE TEAM IS FOR

However, it isn't often that the team are at loggerheads with the congregation because they are felt to be getting too big for their boots. Much more often it is that there is mutual misunderstanding about what local ministry is for. Local ministry should perhaps be seen as a way of moving the church along a continuum line from all-clerical ministry towards all-member ministry. This shift in emphasis constitutes nothing less then a cultural revolution and, as change consultants tell us, such a change does not happen either easily or overnight. There are many stops on the continuum line: the clerical team, a group of vicar's helpers, a stipendiary supported by a team, a team supported by a stipendiary, and so on.

Misunderstandings about ultimate aims abound and the most common is for a parish to think they have 'arrived' when the team thinks they have only just started. After all, things have moved very fast. Hardly a generation ago, the rural parish priest with a sole cure was 'expected to do everything'. The multi-parish benefice and the single minister circuit have finally persuaded most congregations that today the vicar can't any longer do it all. The solution which everyone can understand is for each parish to come up with a band of 'vicar's helpers' who will do corporately what the minister used to do in the old days but can no longer do 'because (s)he has five parishes instead of one'. But for all major decisions, for the choice and authorization of helpers, and for the preparation and conduct of services, the vicar remains the boss. For many of those in the pews this seems an admirable solution and certainly it is a great deal better than the old model. But, as the team proceed with their training, they soon come to realize that local ministry proper is about empowering the whole congregation to share in decision making and in ministry, and that is a long way further along the continuum line than 'vicar's helpers'.

The mismatch of visions shows most vividly in the expectations congregations often have of teams. However much hard work is put into trying to explain to them that the team is not there to do it all themselves but to 'enable the whole people of God to recognise their own special gifts and to exercise their various ministries' (*sic!*), they invariably want to know 'what the team is going to *do*'. And if, after a year, the team hasn't undertaken a high profile project, the congregation tends to be perplexed and become dismissive of the experiment. This can be very hard on the team whose identity is always fragile in the early stages of team formation.

The Duntisbury team was soon involved in an interregnum and, very sensibly, decided to devote the time to training rather than rush into doing lots of things which a new incumbent might well wish to undo. The churchwardens (who in this case were not team members) were invited to team meetings and the link proved extremely positive. The team came to understand the churchwardens' predicament at first-hand and were able to give significant moral and practical support, while the churchwardens got to know and value the quiet professionalism of the team. The congregation, on the other hand, could not understand 'why the team weren't doing anything' and, at every team meeting, one or other of the team remarked on the hurt this caused, which, of course, they could do nothing about.

Highbury is an old mill town where, historically, the coming of the established church post-dates the founding of the chapel. As a result, the two flourish on a more or less equal basis, meaning that an ecumenical team could be formed from mutual strength. Team members have found the shared experience exhilarating and there seems little doubt that the seeds are being sown for the formation of a 'proper' LEP in the town. But, inevitably, an ecumenical team cannot have as its focus practical decisions about the running of any one of the churches involved. They are in much the same position as a Council of Churches which has to concentrate on a limited number of 'community' activities. In the circumstances, what the Highbury team opted for was to concentrate on mutual support and prayer. Because they have chosen a low profile road they are constantly having to field misunderstanding and even jibes: 'the team is an expensive luxury for those who are members'. The fact that every one of them thoroughly enjoys being a member and gets tremendous support from it only adds to their sense of guilt! Periodically the local ministry officer has to have a 'justification session' with them, revisiting step by step the core aims of the group and reassuring them of the authenticity of their vocation. On one such occasion they identified two very successful Alpha courses, an excellent course on intercessory prayer, and the preparation of an ecumenical church information leaflet for newcomers, none of which would have happened without the support of the team. It helped them to feel much better!

Teams which can combine prayer and mutual support with

the running of the odd project seem to have less trouble about justifying themselves to their congregations. Barnscombe is the one large village in what has become a six-church benefice. The team is local to Barnscombe and dates from the balmy days of one parish, one vicar. The members have a wide variety of talents and are fully representative of both PCC and congregation. After eighteen months together they concluded that 'we all do just the same as we used to do, but we do it a lot better because we give each other so much mutual support. We are a really working team'. Barnscombe people recognized and accepted this development, and when the incumbent took over another four parishes, more and more 'local' ministry was devolved to the team. After a pretty rocky start to the shotgun marriage, the incumbent moved and the new benefice was plunged into an interregnum. Interestingly the churchwardens of the 'new' parishes have recognized the authority and professionalism of the team at a number of joint meetings and have asked team members to help with services and projects across the benefice.

Formal local ministry has a short history but the parish of St Saviours, Bunton has had a fully operational team for over ten years. The incumbent is not a fit person and yet, in that period, the congregation has doubled, the church has been re-ordered and a number of valuable social projects have been inaugurated in this inner-city area. There is an assurance and poise about the twelve-member team which is impressive. They are split half-and-half between original members and new additions. Their business meetings always have a double agenda, part studying a topic and part devoted to practical business matters. 'I think most of the good things that have happened in the parish started life in this group but we certainly haven't done everything ourselves.' And are they seen as an elite? 'If you asked many members of the congregation I don't think they would know who was in the team and who wasn't.'

SOME USEFUL METAPHORS

The question 'what is the team meant to *do*?' is so clearly at the heart of the local ministry enterprise that it may be valuable to list some of the metaphors or images which have been used to describe it.

- The roots of a tree: Underground, unseen, an integral part of the tree. The roots are as extensive as the branches; without the roots the tree would not stand up and there would be no leaves or branches.
- The foundations of a building: a similar image to that above.
- The pillars of a crypt chapel: massive rather than beautiful, a place where (usually) meditative prayer takes place, rarely visited or seen but supporting the whole structure.
- An oratorio: The performance of an oratorio requires tenor, bass, contralto and soprano singers. Assuming that all can sing in tune (!) they will sing that much better if they cluster around someone who has a firm hold on the part line. (A number of Renaissance illuminated manuscripts illustrate the principle.) The choir needs a conductor but the conductor also needs the choir. Both need to 'listen' to the inspiration of the composer.
- A French restaurant: In the old days the 'patron' would do everything: take the orders, cook the food, wait at table and wash up. This way (s)he could serve perhaps four tables an evening. To serve more customers the patron takes on a chef, a head waiter, a wine waiter, and a washer-up. As the reputation of the establishment grows the team must recruit a number of assistants and, by that time, the 'hierarchy' is probably invisible except to those who know the restaurant well.

Working as a Team

As the old adage has it: 'If you want something doing properly you'd as well do it yourself.' Collaborative ministry is not an easy option. In fact perhaps it's only because Jesus showed us so forcefully that it is the only way from 'here' to 'there' that we continue to struggle with such an impossible challenge. As we have seen, relations between the team and the rest of the congregation can be difficult, as can relations between team members.

The benefice of Grimthorpe combines two overgrown suburban villages on the edge of a thriving industrial area and within easy range of the motorway. As so often, such a location – relatively affluent but not plush – attracts people from all over the country who move there to further their career. Such people are independent and used to speaking their mind – not at all the qualities naturally associated with local people whose families have lived in the area for generations and who remember the Grimthorpes when they were separate villages. It can be an explosive mix and, initially, the members of the Grimthorpe team did not understand why hurtful conflict surfaced so often in their group. Only when members had been introduced to the insights of the Myers Briggs Type Indicator, and the Belben Test, did they begin to appreciate each other's gifts and learn to accept each other's approach to teamworking.

Historically, Errington is an Anglo-catholic parish, and the incumbent is a sincere and forward-looking exponent of catholic spirituality. When the team was chosen, a number of people who shared the spirituality of the incumbent declined the invitation to join, while two convinced evangelicals accepted. In a group of eight or so, the evangelicals would probably have made a positive contribution to the life of the team but, with only five people accepting the invitation to join, the group was too small to accommodate the different backgrounds. Things were not helped by the fact that the incumbent (quite rightly) didn't want to dominate the team but didn't want the team to 'get out of control' either!

There are no shortcuts in the process of team formation but professional consultants can help. The Ederton benefice comprises four small villages and has a quietly successful team. Two members left the area and a new enthusiastic young incumbent arrived. At this stage the team went on a team-building residential together. It's not always easy for an incumbent to get away with the team, but in this case clerical enthusiasm prevailed and the experience was formative. 'I hadn't really understood what local ministry was about in this diocese until I started "playing games" with the team, nor had I truly valued their remarkable range of skills'. The team members were equally enthusiastic. 'Our new incumbent obviously values us and doesn't seem to want to call all the shots. As we tackled our projects as a team, we really began to appreciate what "consensus" and "collaborative" can mean in practice'.

Adding to the Team

When someone leaves a team, or a new member joins, the old team dies and a new team is born. We recognize this in family life and provide rites of passage to help us to cope with the trauma of change. We need to be just as assiduous in the care of teams.

In Heartly their major concern was to find new team members to join a depleted and (as they saw it) very overworked and over-aged group. So the first meeting after their mandating was given over to planning a strategy for attracting new recruits and for training them for mandating in three years time. Targets were set and there was a detailed discussion about how the new members might be integrated and trained. Forward planning like this is necessary if we are to bring new blood into old teams.

In Forthly and Weston what happened was that one or two new people popped up in the congregation who 'obviously would be good to have in the team'. At that stage there were no clear guidelines about how they should be 'joined' or trained, and the lack of clarity has proved something of a problem. The diocese insists that the new members need to be trained but has found it hard to work out ways of making this possible, while the new members 'don't see why they need to go through all this training'. It has not helped that the only training on offer has been in a nearby parish alongside a new team which is being set up there. Their team-bonding experience is not therefore with their own team but with another group altogether.

There had been a team in Garton for three years before they were absorbed into the benefice of Tow Valley. The incumbent was impressed by the team and wanted to foster local ministry in the other parishes. The selection procedure was put into operation and so successful was the process that the team now consists of not two but seventeen members. However, the very success of the experiment is a problem. Such a large group is in danger of becoming unwieldy and makes team bonding more difficult. It has been a traumatic time for the 'old' team, who have not just 'died' but been taken over in a big way. There is also an issue about whether the 'old members' should (or would wish) to do the training course again, yet how else can they hope to bond? So far things are going very well and, despite the obvious difficulties, this approach seems more healthy than that employed at Forthly and Weston.

Relations with the Incumbent

Local ministry does seek to move a parish along a continuum between all-clerical and all-member ministry but it does not seek to remove the cleric from the equation. It is not a matter of making the minister redundant but rather of changing the ministerial job-specification. The Methodist Church in Singapore includes in its ordination service the following charge, which seems particularly apt as a description of the theological role of the stipendiary who is to lead a local ministry group.

Called to something smaller

We are not ordaining you to ministry; that happened at your baptism.

We are not ordaining you to be a caring person; you are already called to that.

We are not ordaining you to become involved in social issues, ecology, race, politics, revolution, for that is laid upon every Christian.

We are ordaining you to something smaller and less spectacular: to read and interpret those sacred stories of our community, so that they speak a word to people today; to remember and practice those rituals and rites of meaning that in their poetry address man at the level where change operates; to foster in community through word and sacrament that encounter with truth which will set men and women free to minister as the body of Christ.

We are ordaining you to the ministry of the word and sacraments and pastoral care.

God grant you grace not to betray but to uphold it, not to deny but to affirm it, through Jesus Christ our Lord.

The minister in a local ministry parish will be called on to 'minister' as perhaps never before in their ministry but (s)he will also have to abandon inherited roles, and that will inevitably be painful. There are plenty of stories to illustrate how painful it can be.

The benefice of Inchcombe formed a team under the inspiration of a visionary incumbent who was soon to retire. He was determined to include in the team all the most important 'church workers', even though two of them did not share the vision. Despite initial uncertainties the team began to settle down and thrive – until the incumbent retired. His departure allowed the uncertainties to surface and, during the interregnum, the two 'dissidents' came to the conclusion that what they really wanted was an old-style vicar who told them what to do. The new incumbent was a senior churchman who had clearly not recognized the implications of local ministry for his style of leadership when he accepted the living. He had hitherto worked in large town parishes and was used to planning strategy at the clergy staff meeting, with churchwardens in occasional attendance. From the start he looked askance at the team and decided that if he was going to have a team at all he certainly wouldn't have picked that particular group of people. To do him justice he was also genuinely surprised that the team didn't seem to know what it was supposed to be doing. He was a little shocked that the parish rather than the incumbent had nominated the team and certainly did not consider it his role to be an equal member of a team which did not consist of authorized ministers. The fact that two members of the team shared his mystification only confirmed him in his conviction that local ministry was anticlerical and wrong for the Church of England. Within a year the team had to be dissolved, with deep hurt to a number of individuals.

Darfield is a market town with a long-established team and a genuinely home-grown OLM. The new incumbent came with excellent credentials and the best intentions, and the bishop and everyone else was extremely happy with the appointment. When the honeymoon was over, the incumbent became increasingly frustrated with the process of teamworking, which he found slow and inefficient, and he came to believe that the team members were opinionated, self-satisfied and unrepresentative of the congregation. He ceased attending team meetings and began to use a small staff of readers and NSMs as the decision-making body for the parish. Not surprisingly the OLM felt torn apart by this development. If he was to continue to function as a priest he had to work with the incumbent, yet he felt himself to be inextricably a member of the team who had affirmed his vocation in the first place. He became a very unhappy person.

Other tales have a happier conclusion but they do illustrate some of the problems. Topton is a largish village which is geographically 'on the edge'. Over the last few years it has been in and out of three deaneries and benefices. It would be unkind to say that it shouldn't be there, but certainly the pastoral committee has little clear idea where it should be. An inspired incumbent persuaded them that the best thing they could do in this impossible position was to form a local ministry team and run their own show. No sooner had they done this than the benefices were reorganized yet again and Topton found themselves linked to a large wealthy village further down the valley. Their new incumbent didn't want them and probably they didn't want him, and for six months vicar and team tiptoed gingerly around each other. Eventually the incumbent came to realize that he simply could not fulfil a traditional pastoral role in a village which, on a bad day, was twenty minutes drive from the vicarage, and he concluded that he needed the team. The team, for their part, longed to keep alive the worship of God in their beloved church every Sunday but they needed someone to teach them what to do. The incumbent, who has real liturgical flair, showed them how, and Topton's two services a month have become a service every Sunday, with said evensong once a week thrown in for good measure. They have come to respect his expertise and he has come to respect their commitment.

Barnscombe, mentioned earlier, is a large working village which is close enough to a motorway interchange to attract both developers and incomers. It is lively rather than pretty. The incumbent took to the *idea* of local ministry like a duck to water. Unfortunately the idea never percolated from mind to heart, and what actually happened was that the team became a separate unit with its own agenda, aims and objectives. He was perfectly happy to give them a free hand, but his own relationship to the team was to be strictly semi-detached. For their part, the team found this puzzling and expected lots of clerical TLC. It took them a good two years to recognize what the incumbent expected of them. Fortunately they were an extremely gifted and varied group of people, and were nurtured by an experienced and understanding local ministry officer. But they still have to badger the incumbent to come to meetings and to give them the theological and professional support they need if they are to minister effectively. Local ministry does not work if the clergy abdicate their responsibility; collaborative ministry requires clergy and laity to work *together*.

The story of Deepwell is an interesting one because it illustrates admirably why teams need a stipendiary – 'the person from outside' – and the real pain this can involve. Deepwell is a small village with a very traditional BCP (*Book of Common Prayer*) congregation who look after their church extremely well. The other half of the population who don't usually come to church are relatively young, considerably less affluent, and their local paper is definitely not the *Daily Telegraph*. When the benefice team was formed, the only two people who would accept the call in Deepwell did not represent the BCP congregation. In fact they ran a regular family service and were all for out-and-out revolution to bring the church into the twenty-first century. The incumbent had great sympathy with their aims and ambitions and, as a true-blue collaborative ministry incumbent, he also believed in consensus government and shared decision making. On the other hand, he was an experienced parish priest who knew quite enough about villages to know that in a settlement of less then 200 people the church cannot possibly afford to go in for confrontational politics unless there is a very good theological reason indeed to spur you on. When push came to shove he just could not allow the enthusiastic young revolutionaries to have their way. This was very upsetting for him, very frustrating for them, and very perplexing for the team who had naively supposed that with collaborative ministry the incumbent is 'just' one among equals.

It needs to be recognized that not everyone has an equal stake in the ministry enterprise. Local people who will never move away have a different stake from those who will move on elsewhere in a few years; those who work in a place are involved there in a way that those who commute are not; the young have a stake which is quite different from that of their elders. And the stake of the incumbent, who is in one sense an outsider, but in another – as the representative of the bishop – is the oldest inhabitant, needs to be talked through by the team and respected.

The Interregnum

The departure of an incumbent is always a time for apprehension, never more so than in a local ministry parish. Rural deans do not always understand the rationale for teams and tend to ignore them. If the churchwardens are neither members of the team nor invited to team meetings, they can become surprisingly possessive about their brief hour of glory. But, above all, the team is apprehensive about 'who will we get?' and 'will (s)he approve of us?'.

Billington is a small town on the edge of a conurbation that could expect to have an incumbent of its own, and someone of high calibre. It had a relatively new team who were very aware that they needed to wait and see what the incoming incumbent wanted to do before taking too many initiatives of their own. They worked with the congregation, supported the churchwardens and, in fact, did all the right things in the circumstances, but they remained apprehensive. In the event, an excellent incumbent was appointed, a mature ordinand who had a great deal of experience of the world and of people management. He appreciated the team, recognizing their abilities and valuing their support, and immediately became a hands-on member.

His particular uncertainty was that he had come from another diocese where 'local ministry' meant something quite different. Inevitably he was inundated with bits of paper about the diocesan scheme, but practice in action and practice on paper do not always overlap. An induction course where he met other new incumbents in a similar situation helped to clarify the terminology but it could not give him a grasp of his role as incumbent within the team. For that he needed to visit another team and see how they operated. He contacted the local ministry officer to explain his concerns, and a visit was arranged to another benefice where a team had been in place for three years. The experience of seeing another team at work and sitting in on their team meeting answered his questions and allowed him to shape a clear vision of what his role should be in his own team.

The interregnum is a time when a good team is valued, and when good OLMs are worked off their feet. Edward is a local person and a natural team player. When the incumbent who had set up the team left, his first job was to put the rural dean right about the nature of OLM. The rural dean wanted to treat Edward as an autonomous cleric, while Edward was clear that his locus within a parish leadership team should be recognized. As a result of his quiet wisdom, the parish settled down to a creative ten months during which churchwardens and team co-operated in the running of the parish. Then the new incumbent arrived. He was very nice, very clever and very well meaning, but utterly disorganized. He was not against the team, but seemed quite unable to make use of them. Edward, as a priest, was asked to do services but usually at the very last minute, and the level of frustration in the now unused, unconsulted, and apparently unwanted team rose to boiling-point. Fortunately the diocese have supported Edward and the team, and a 'strategy for survival' has been put in place but it underlines how important it is from the team perspective for a diocese to do everything possible to get the right incumbent for a local ministry parish.

The OLM and the Team

THE LOCAL PERSON

OLMs come in all shapes and sizes, and the teams they have to relate to are equally varied. The Ministry Division guidelines stipulate that OLMs must operate 'within the context of collaborative ministry'. That may mean that the OLM works within a lay leadership team (as in Lincoln and Gloucester dioceses) or within a clerical leadership team (as is frequently the case in Guildford diocese) or the OLM is part of an educational team who work with the candidates while they train for ordination (as in Truro and Oxford dioceses).

In the first case, the OLM usually emerges from among the lay team, with the support and encouragement of other members. Not surprisingly, relations with other members of the team usually remain good and ordination does not greatly alter the group dynamics of the team.

Diana was a reader of some experience when the team was formed and initially she found the experience unsettling. She felt she had done it all before, and having worked with a fairly autocratic vicar was unused to shared decision making. However, when the team started to study a module on worship it all suddenly slotted into place. Instead of being treated as a second-class parson, she was suddenly looked up to as the resident authority on worship. As the team prepared to take a service themselves (part of the module), 'I found my vocation as a reader being truly affirmed for the first time.'

Diana is a very local person indeed and would not dream of offering for NSM, but when the team heard about the OLM option they immediately recognized her as the obvious person to preside at the eucharist in their church. They encouraged her and much to her amazement, she sailed through her selection conferences and has now been made a deacon. At her ordination she was adamant that she wanted the other team members to be involved in the ceremony 'because I couldn't possibly do it without them and, in a sort of a way, I am representing them – they are being ordained with me'. During a recent interregnum it was interesting to observe the dynamics of the group. Diana did not chair the meeting but the group deferred to her when it came to organizing the Easter services. She did not take responsibility for planning the services by herself – this was very much a collaborative affair with lots of people throwing in ideas and undertaking various tasks – but the team did recognize her co-ordinating role in getting the show on the road. She is a very humble person and there was no hint of jealously or 'who does she think she is?' from other team members.

THE OLM AND LEADERSHIP

Brian is an OLM in a team of eight which is responsible for a group of villages in the East of England. He is still in full-time secular employment while a number of other team members are retired. Most of the villages have one member in the team and that person tends to take overall responsibility for ministry in 'their' settlement. The team has just been joined by a new incumbent who, without being dominant, has natural leadership gifts. Brian, therefore, is not under pressure to take on a tra-ditional priestly role. He is quiet, slightly shy, and a good listener rather than a compulsive talker, and he apparently required a great deal of encouragement from the team before he would even offer for ordination. He only wears a dog-collar when on 'clerical' duty and a visitor to the group would not immediately pick him out as the OLM. The group defer to his opinion about the settlement in which he lives and listen attentively to him when he speaks but they do not seem to expect him to take a major part in the discussion.

Geoffrey, by contrast, is an obvious leader with a rather conventional army background. The team has served a number of very small villages for ten years. Their numbers have dwindled to four, and three of those, including Geoffrey, now live outside the benefice. There have been long interregnums and Geoffrey has had all the burden of traditional priestly expectation thrust upon him. Both Geoffrey and the team have colluded in this but it is not a happy situation. Everybody feels put upon and rather tired, and resent the fact that the congregation and the diocese are quite happy to leave it all to them. Unsurprisingly, they cannot get new members to join them and the other members of the team almost unconsciously seem to blame Geoffrey, in much the same way as a generation ago congregations tended to 'blame the vicar' if things went wrong.

THE OLM AS AN EXTRA PAIR OF PRIESTLY HANDS

Some dioceses need more clerical hands and have ordained OLMs to fill the gaps left by departing stipendiaries. These OLMs are either local people or those who are retired and have 'become' local, and the context of their collaborative ministry is a clergy and reader group.

Gervase, a former housemaster in a private school, lives in a multi-parish benefice 'and the parish wanted a vicar'. He is part of a benefice team but he exercises a largely pastoral ministry leaving policy decisions to his colleagues.

James, a retired banker, has lived for fifty years in a 'village' of 12,000 where the vicar needed help. James tried for stipendiary ministry but now feels that OLM is exactly the right slot for him. He is the classic 'perpetual curate' and the team both appreciates and supports him. Frank, also retired but with an army background, also works in a multi-parish benefice but his experiences have not been so happy. As with the others, what pushed him to ordination was a combination of his own congregation wanting its own priest and the vicar wanting help. All went well until the vicar moved and his successor 'ran totally amok'. Frank's story illustrates the potential problems for an OLM who is locked into a small clerical team.

Malcolm works in a huge suburban parish with a staff which, at the moment, comprises eight readers and five clergy. He is regarded as 'permanent curate-in-charge' and seems very happy with the situation. Francis is in a similar parish but, in his case, OLMs will replace three stipendiary clergy. Integrating a new incumbent into the team has not been easy and he expects that the next five years will be a pretty bumpy ride. Jane is a young mother who is OLM in a city-centre parish. They have a parish centre open seven days a week and her ministry is with the young people who come there. She finds her work exhilarating but exhausting and she has excellent relations with the other members of the team, who are no doubt delighted to have her. Bill was the only one of the group who was still in full-time employment and he found it extremely difficult to find the time to play a full part in team life. He is born and bred in the area and so has considerably more 'local wisdom' than the others but feels that the other members of the team get irritated with him because he can't make daytime meetings.

This group of OLMs have all been trained with readers and this has greatly enriched their vocation. It means that, on the one hand, readers know why they are readers and are not hankering to become priests, and, on the other, OLMs remain both lay oriented and perfectly happy to play a 'curacy' role within the team. The model does not, however, necessarily help to move the parishes along the road towards all-member ministry. One of the projects that an OLM has to do is to get the training team to consider 'what is different about priesthood?'. Christopher's report makes interesting reading. The reader believed that 'an ordained minister is clearly in charge and is the leader, part of the clergy establishment, i.e. one of "them". The OLM should be seen primarily as one of "us"'. Two lay members of the education team clearly saw the priest as the leader 'and everyone else has to work with him'. A churchwarden writes, 'The fact that the ministry team do not act as a team reinforces the idea that the priest is ultimately the leader and bears responsibility.' Not much that St Paul would recognize here!

The attitude of education teams to the OLMs they are helping to train is generally one of profound relief that someone has agreed to take on the job – and that *someone* isn't me! Jealousy, or even 'who does (s)he think (s)he is?' is hardly an appropriate reaction in this situation. The teams tend to fall into two categories: those who really enjoy the experience and those for whom it is very low on their list of priorities.

Mary's team is a splendid example of the former group. Eight to twelve people meet regularly in their remote village and she works through with them the module which she has been studying with other OLMs at the diocesan centre. A tutor monitors the meetings and everyone learns from the experience. It helps that study groups are something quite new for this particular congregation. The team members all think that Mary is wonderful and they will be heartbroken when she is ordained and the modules finish.

Garry and Henry are on the same course but for various reasons they find it much more difficult to get the team together. The team who are training with Garry tend to patronize him and one senses that they feel they are doing him a major favour by turning up at all. Henry is a 'doer' rather than a 'thinker' leading one to suspect that his ministry will be essentially pastoral rather than a teaching one. If it were not for the prodding of the course tutor, he would probably not worry too much if the team never met.

Brian, who is on another course, has to find a training team for himself and act as convener as well. Last year the team managed to meet only three times and the members clearly felt that PCC's and PCC subcommittee meetings had a higher priority than team meetings. Brian has to write most of the project reports himself.

Mercifully, many education teams take their responsibilities rather more seriously. In another diocese Melanie, who left school at fifteen and is a local person born and bred, joins NSMs and stipendiaries for university-style lectures and then comes home to her support group and tells them all about it. The lectures are interspersed with experience-based modules which Melanie facilitates with the help and advice of a tutor. The support group greatly admires her tenacity and much enjoy the discussions. In fact two of them testify that their whole lives have been changed by the process.

Does It Work? Is It a Success?

'It's exciting, it's frightening, but it's a privilege,' said Bill from New Zealand and his words would be echoed by many in ministry teams in England.

TOWARDS ALL-MEMBER MINISTRY

If the future of the Christian Church depends on reviving the 'all-member ministry' that we find in the Epistles, then local ministry teams have a lot to offer. They move congregations along the continuum line between 'all-clerical ministry' towards 'all-member ministry'. There is, of course, a danger that they may become a ministerial elite but, in fact, this rarely happens.

Three years down the line, the multi-benefice team of Fulford write, 'Catching a vision and confidence are what local ministry is all about – a vision of building up our confidence together so that the gifts we all have can be released and used in ministry within the Church and in mission in the world around us. It's about growing up and standing on our own feet as churches . . . It's about ordained and lay Christians sharing responsibility together for building the faith and confidence which will enable us to be a truly dynamic presence in our community.'

'People were worried,' writes a correspondent from Tiptree, 'that we would cut others out of ministry. In fact, since we've been involved in local ministry, we've come to realize just how much there is that is needed – we couldn't do it all even if we wanted to.'

Mary, from Alston, writes, 'We've been accepted by the parish for what we're doing and not for what we might have done (i.e. interfering). The parish was suspicious at first but not any longer.'

GROWING IN CONFIDENCE

A year ago the rector at Fulford became ill and had to take early retirement. During the long interregnum that followed, the benefice has – against all the odds – flourished. 'The sudden illness of our rector, whilst being a personal blow for the whole team, has had the effect of demonstrating to us all just how much we have, as a benefice, drawn closer together and grown in confidence as we have taken our first steps together in local ministry. In the past, the removal of a full-time vicar often proved disastrous but, where a local ministry team is in place, the ministry and mission of the local church can continue and develop.'

A MINISTRY THAT IS ACCEPTED

Ten years ago the benefice around the market town of Dunfold established an unofficial ministry team under the leadership of their dynamic – and at times somewhat abrasive! – vicar. All the pundits believed that it would fail, above all 'because village folk want to see the vicar and nothing else will do'. The pundits have been comprehensively confounded, as is illustrated by the following story. One of the members of the team was a former school-mistress who lived in one of the smaller hamlets a mile or so from Dunfold. Armed with her (unofficial) badge and a new-found confidence, Alison began to visit on behalf of the church an old gentleman who lived locally and who had once been a bell-ringer. After a year or so he died, his links with the church and God having been renewed. When it came to arranging the funeral, his family, instead of expecting the service to be taken by the vicar, specifically requested that it should be taken by Alison – a woman, an off-comer, an unauthorized lay person, yet the one who had shown Christian love to their father. As a Herefordshire farmer said in *The People the Land and the Church*, 'Country folk always assess by results; be it seed corn, breeding ewe, their neighbours – or their rector.'

LOCAL AND CATHOLIC

Local ministry takes the local congregation seriously. In a church which all too often seems to encourage and reward the central-izers, local ministry underlines the truth that the centre is there to support the local rather than vice versa. So it is a completely unexpected outcome of the local ministry initiative that it seems to break down the 'them' and 'us' barrier between the parish and the diocese. A district nurse writes, 'The local ministry course has given me a greater awareness of the needs of the wider Church and a deeper understanding of Anglicanism.'

In 1994, six benefices covering eighteen parishes enrolled on the diocesan scheme – in all there were forty trainee local lay team members. For eighteen evenings a year the diocese went to them for module training. On two Saturdays and one weekend a year the same very timorous, very local people were enticed from their stockades and herded together into a central place. 'A prickle of porcupines' would perhaps be an apt way to describe them as they reluctantly occupied their chosen positions in the assembly room. Three years later the same group of lay people embraced at parting, swore eternal friendship, determined on the founding of an Old Students' association, and generally behaved just like any other group of degree students at the end of their course. Furthermore, some of them have offered for OLM or for reader training, while others have become tutors or facilitators for diocesan local ministry events or now serve on diocesan synods and committees. With few exceptions they have come to recognize what the Catholic Church is all about; their Christianity may begin at home but it no longer ends there.

NEW THINGS HAPPEN

Local ministry invariably means that more things are done locally and more projects are undertaken and successfully concluded. Dodford is a market town with its team still in training and where

> . . . *the team has maintained the ongoing ministries. The visitor group has had another busy year and plans further training in September. The intercessors have enjoyed top-up training and have recruited new members. Welcome leaflets and church-history leaflets have proved popular with our many visitors. The ministry to children has continued to run very successful holiday clubs and has started an after-school Bible club at the primary school.*

In the large suburban parish of Bunton the team have helped to develop a scheme for baptism preparation and follow-up, a scheme for welcoming newcomers and a revamping of children's worship. In a city parish in Lorton the team were the inspiration behind the reordering of the church, the formation of a prayer and healing group, and the reorganization of the services. In the four-village benefice centred around Ederton the team now ensure that there is a regular family service in each church, a pastoral visiting scheme is in place, there is a regular healing service and the benefice has held a successful Alpha Course. The team at Fulford write:

The work the team is doing to develop the ministry of the benefice has itself many implications for the wider participation of our communities. Our first step was to draw the worshipping community together in a common prayer, the Benefice Prayer, which is becoming widely used, and to encourage the use of prayer books for intercession requests in our four churches. Praying together for those in our communities is a vital part of our shared ministry. Part of growing in confidence comes from exploring our faith together and sharing it with others, and the team, with the authority of four PCCs, is developing an Emmaus programme which, whilst including a beginners' course for new Christians and enquirers, has at its heart the vision of us on an Emmaus road journey of faith together, supporting and encouraging one another on that journey. A pilot course is now underway to develop a small number of potential leaders for the first actual courses which we hope will be beginning later this year, and the team is working on a new baptism policy for the benefice which will draw members of our worshipping communities in increasing numbers into helping prepare individuals or families for baptism, and developing a longer-term role as friends and companions on the journey of faith.

SOCIAL INVOLVEMENT

Nor do the team just devise new church activities. The team in Ederton now put a high priority on supporting church members who serve on parish councils and village hall committees. The parish also help with a local Riding for the Disabled group. At Topton the team have helped to establish a weekly coffee morning in the local Scout headquarters. This has the triple benefit of providing an occasion when local people can meet on neutral ground, of linking 'the village' with the Scouts and of providing an occasion when the incumbent – who lives two villages down the valley – can see and be seen locally.

The incumbent of the suburban city parish of Turton writes:

We have tried to develop our underlying roles of leading, co-ordinating and encouraging and, at the same time, give energy and direction to specific projects. Two of the team are working with teenagers and parents from the next parish and the Methodist church on the estate to get joint youth activities going again. One team member has taken responsibility for our administration so we have clear action notes and good communication. Unexpectedly, an idea came from the lunch club about a Good Neighbour Scheme. It seemed to fit in with our parish vision and to be a good way of increasing our community links. Now one team member, six others from the congregation and eight people from the wider community, for example, collect prescriptions, offer lifts and a 'sitting service' to give carers time off. The work/faith group has had to split into two because so many people were coming. It has members like a teacher, several managers, a nurse, a car salesman, who meet together to support each other and talk about what they face at work – like sacking people, employment contracts, commission, discrimination, death and dying. Our reader works closely with the bereavement group and is being asked to take some local funerals because people know her and some of the bereavement group through the lunch club and the Good Neighbour Scheme.

Our hopes for the future? The development of our community links has been amazing; we want to be able to open the church centre every day to support more community work. Every time we think we are getting closer to the sort of church we thought God was calling us to be something more seems to open up. It's exciting and it's not just the vicar any more – we really do seem to be 'better together'.

Two individual team members sum it up well. 'It lets us take the church out into the parish more to let them know the church is active and cares.' Even more significantly 'Local ministry has changed the way I see my work. I am serving God at work; not just when I am in church or doing something for the church.'

INDIVIDUALS GROW IN SPIRITUAL STATURE

As is evident from much of what has been written, local ministry often leads to astonishing spiritual growth for team members. Let them speak for themselves.

Local ministry training and the practice of ministry have been for me an exciting and challenging time of self-discovery, a re-establishing of self-worth and a growing acceptance that all my talents and abilities as well as my personality can be used in God's service. It has sometimes meant painful growth, it has led to sacrifice but, above and beyond all, it has given me joy beyond measure.

Local ministry has reinforced and deepened our commitment both to our faith and our church.

I have far more confidence now, even though I am not terribly certain of my own depth of knowledge. It's all been helpful, right from the word go.

The local ministry course grounds collaborative ministry in theological training at a level at which ordinary people can relate. In many cases it has led to nothing short of a miraculous discovery and development of personal skills in ministry and mission which would otherwise have remained hidden.

Jesus said he came to serve, not to be served. To me, this applies to all Christians, and local ministry is one way that makes it possible for us to serve. The bad news is that the course is hard work, time consuming and demanding. The good news is that it's worth every minute; you'll emerge with a strength and depth of character you didn't think you had. Local ministry is for local people with a desire to do more than sit in a pew on a Sunday. Give it a go, you've nothing to lose and everything to gain.

At the General Synod debate on *Stranger in the Wings*, a member from Hereford said:

I am a member of a team which is going to be mandated next week. We were terrified when we started, but actually it has been wonderful. I hope I can convey something of our excitement.

THE CHALLENGE TO BE THE BODY OF CHRIST

Teamwork is never easy and not every local ministry team really becomes a team. Nevertheless, the challenge of forming a team does mean that parishes are beginning to grapple with what *koinonia* means in practice, with the creaks and groans and rubs which are the concomitant of really being the body of Christ. But, after all, the battle to become a community is surely at the very heart of the Christian enterprise. The incumbent of Turton writes:

We hadn't realized how deep the adjustments were that we would all need to make if we are to work together in new ways. The clergy and lay members of the team have found it hard in different ways and we've had to look hard at leadership and authority. What is important for us is thinking of ourselves as a team; as there to support the ministry and mission of all the people – not to be managers and not to do it all ourselves. We have found out how different we all are and what amazing gifts we all have if we take the trouble to help each other look and explore and take risks.

4

೫

The Priests' Tale

The Ordained Local Ministers' Tale

This chapter weaves together the stories of a large number of ordained local ministers and incumbents in the common vision of local ministry. It tells of the way that OLMs have experienced call and had their vocation tested. It tells of their training and the way in which ordination has enabled them to express priesthood in their community, their church and their place of work. It also tells the story of some of those incumbents who have worked to promote local ministry in their parishes, engaging with diocesan schemes and working with local ministry teams. Taken together, these stories raise questions and identify issues for the future ministry of the Church.

HEARING THE CALL

Diane was shocked and amazed when her local church suggested that she might have a vocation to ordained local ministry. Brian had felt a strong sense of vocation to priesthood since he was a boy and John had come to ordination after many years as a reader. All three are living proof that ordained local ministry has brought a new dynamic to the process of ministerial discernment and selection.

Church of England bishops have always reserved the right to ordain people of their own choice though they all take serious note of the recommendations that come from the Advisory Board for Ministry and the bishop's selection procedure that they currently oversee. This procedure has traditionally identified candidates through national residential selection conferences, and the ABM has always recognized the need for candidates for ordained local ministry to undertake national selection and to attend such selection conferences.

The importance of the local contract

Alongside national recognition, vocation which emerges from the local church to serve the local community has needed to take the contribution of the local church very seriously as a key element in the process. There is indeed ample evidence from OLM schemes to suggest that the local community and parish priests have a key contribution to make in the initial identification and nurture of the vocations of many OLMs. Although the individual will need to make this calling their own for it ultimately to bear fruit, it may well be a vocation stimulated by the prayer of the local church community.

As Diane never tires of saying, the idea that she should become an ordained local minister had never once entered her head. She had been a Christian for many years and had always helped out in the local church when her demanding job at the local school had allowed. The new vicar had come to the parish with a real desire to promote the ministry of the whole church in that place and had given real opportunities to a wide variety of people to use their gifts in new and exciting ways. She had been involved with 'family worship' for some time and had given the odd 'address' at informal services but she readily took the opportunity to join the newly formed 'pastoral team'. Diane was in fact a well-known figure in the small market town in which she lived and there were many pupils and parents who were grateful for the time and care that she had lavished on them through the years.

The call from the local church community had come at the moment in which Diane had been contemplating early retirement and a new challenge in her life, but she had struggled with the way that other people saw her and initially found it very difficult to make this calling her own. However, conversations with her local parish priest and the Diocesan Director of Ordinands had helped her to identify a deep lack of confidence and sense of unworthiness which would have disabled her from recognizing this calling in herself. As it was, the community had seen what she could not and, after much prayer and soul-searching, she was able to acknowledge this calling and go on to an ABM selection conference to be considered for ordained local ministry. She has been ordained now for five years.

Brian had worked for most of his adult life in the local engineering factory where he had become a respected colleague and union representative. He had made his sense of vocation known to his parish priest in the past but had received a somewhat lukewarm reaction. He had seen the Diocesan Director of Ordinands who had advised him that his lack of academic qualifications would make him a doubtful starter for priesthood, so he regretfully gave up. However, with the introduction of ordained local ministry, Brian felt that the Lord could well be offering him another opportunity to explore this vocation. As he was to find out, training for OLM was to be rigorous and very hard work. It was to stretch him personally, spiritually and academically and he realized, once he had started the training, that he should not have been so easily discouraged in the past by his lack of paper qualifications. Indeed, Brian found in ordained local ministry the fulfilment of a vocation that had been with him since his youth. It also gave him an opportunity to express this ministry in his local church, his home community and his place of work.

John had been a reader for many years. The parish in which he lived had been joined to two others to form a three-parish benefice ten years previously and had been joined to a neighbouring benefice when both had become vacant two years previously. It had been a long time since a priest had lived in his village and the new benefice house was seven miles away. People had therefore got used to treating John as their vicar. He couldn't take communion or baptize their infants but, to all intents and purposes, he was the person that his community looked to as the public face of the church in that place. In many ways John was comfortable with his ministry. It would have been nice to be able to celebrate communion, baptize and marry the people to whom he ministered but, for John, those would be functions that would be added to a role that he already exercised. It was, therefore, hard for John to see the boundary between his reader ministry and that of priesthood other than in these functional terms. He knew also that the church was suspicious of people who appeared to be treating reader ministry as a stepping-stone to ordination.

However, with help from the DDO, he was able to recognize that, in his case, becoming an ordained local minister would both confirm and develop a ministry that he had been exercising for many years.

Jane worked as an administrator in the health service. Her call came initially through a conversation with her parish priest. He had been working in the parish for three years to support and encourage the ministry of the local church through the development of a ministry team. She had joined the team a year ago and had become involved with leading worship and pastoral visiting. The church served a large urban housing estate and needed to develop a variety of new ministries to support its mission. Jane was initially challenged to consider ordained local ministry by her parish priest, although this was later confirmed by the local church before being tested by ABM and supported by the bishop.

In the ordained local minister's vocation there exists a key relationship between a locally emerging ministry and the needs of that local context. He or she is ordained to be priest in that place and so the content of their ministry must reflect the needs of the community which they are called to serve. In many dioceses, candidates emerge from a team of ministers who have been called together to explore ministry or to form local ministry teams. In other dioceses, OLMs are selected individually and a group is formed to support their training. In every diocese, candidates for ordained local ministry attend a selection conference with the support of their PCC and take with them a 'parish profile' and a 'job description'. At the selection conference, the wider church then tests the call using criteria acceptable to the whole church. In this way the ministry of the individual is not separated from the vision of the local church.

Job descriptions

Diane's job description reflected her growing interest in pastoral care. In collaboration with her local church, she was able to identify the areas that she could explore and develop when she was ordained. Consequently, she now heads up a team of people in the parish who provide 'good neighbour' support to the elderly and housebound and lead worship in three sheltered-housing complexes. She still retains links with the young families of the parish and is welcomed into the school to lead assemblies and, together with leaders from other local religious communities, supports the work of Religious Education.

John's job description reflected his position as a long standing reader. It was really a matter of 'more of the same' with additional but very significant responsibilities. To his joy, John was now able to baptize the children of his local area, take the marriages and, best of all for him, celebrate a weekly communion at his local church. He is part of the benefice ministry team which studies and prays together and supports the diverse ministry of each of its members.

Brian's job description provided opportunities for the administration of the sacraments as well as teaching and pastoral care within his local church and community but he was adamant from the first that the engineering works would provide one key area of his ministry. Although emerging from the local church to work in the community in which he lived, Brian argued that he had always exercised a Christian ministry of care and support in the workplace that was bound to be enhanced by his ordination. Everybody would know that he had become a priest because many of the people who lived in the parish worked at the factory. In any case, Brian wanted his work acknowledged and valued by the Church as part of his vocation and as a legitimate arena for his ministry.

Jane's PCC had made the decision to plant a new church on the local housing estate. This would be initially housed in the hall of the local primary school and Jane had been identified as one of the members of the team that would take responsibility for this process. Jane's involvement would ensure a sacramental ministry within the new community although she still retained links with the parish church and led worship there.

Local and Catholic

Brian, Jane, John and Diane were supported and enabled by their local church community. Their priesthood emerged from that place to be used in its service. But this is such a new process that there is still room for misunderstanding and confusion. Although local churches knew that they were not being asked to discern their vocation or to select them for priesthood, it was not always clear to them precisely what they were being asked to do. There can be tension between the local church and the diocese, especially when a candidate that has been identified by and through a local church is not selected by an ABM conference. Bishops are often suspicious that local churches want to usurp their role in discerning vocation and selecting candidates and, in their turn, local churches are often suspicious that the processes which they are asked to undertake make little difference to the decision to sponsor or ultimately select a candidate.

One diocese has recently attempted to address this situation by clarifying the role that each individual or group plays in the process they have developed. A candidate for ordained local ministry emerges in this diocese from a group that has spent a year in study and ministerial exploration. This group explores 'possibility'. Some individuals join the group with a clear under-standing of their calling but, for many, this first year is of real significance. Given an opportunity to study, pray and explore, many grow in confidence and uncover a vocation that surprises them. Often it is other members of the group who spot the way forward for them. And this group does not work in isolation. Other members of the local church, as well as the clergy, will be involved in this initial process of deciding possibility.

The local church council then identifies its own ministerial needs, constructs a 'job description' with the candidate and decides 'acceptability'. The question faced by the PCC is quite clearly framed. If the person is discerned by the broader church to have a vocation to priestly ministry, would you find the ministry of that person acceptable, and is there a job for him or her to do in that place? The DDO is present at this meeting to help frame the questions and act as a resource to the council.

The DDO then explores 'suitability'. By meeting with the candidates, the DDO can discover how the vocation to OLM has emerged, the extent to which the person has made that vocation their own and whether or not the person can talk about it in a reasonably articulate way. It may be that the DDO recognizes that the candidate is ready to go to a selection conference straight away or that he or she needs further time for prayer and reflec-tion. In the case of candidates where the DDO has serious doubts or questions he may well need to open up a discussion with the

PCC and the bishop about the advisability of proceeding further.

The bishop then decides 'sponsorability', whether or not he is prepared to sponsor the candidate for a selection conference. The bishop will interview every candidate and read reports from the DDO and the local church before coming to a decision. The selection conference then decides 'recommendability', whether or not to recommend to the bishop that the candidate goes forward for training. The bishop then decides whether or not to recommend candidates for training.

The words 'possibility', 'acceptability', 'suitability', 'sponsorability' and 'recommendability' have proved enormously helpful in devising the roles that individuals and groups may play when the discernment of vocation is a process that engages the individual, the local church, the diocese and the broader Church of England. The system that has evolved in this one diocese has been criticized for reducing the power of the local church to discern and manage its own ministry. However, this has been designed to give due weight to each constituent part of a process designed to test vocations which have both local and broader 'Catholic' dimensions, and to do so with clarity, integrity and rigour.

Alex has newly emerged as a candidate for ordained local ministry and has recently been selected by an ABM conference for training for ordination. He found the process both demanding and difficult because he had to face his peers, as well as the DDO, the bishop and ABM selectors before his vocation to ordained local ministry could be established. However, he feels now that the process was worthwhile because his ministry is supported and owned by the local church and diocese, and his priesthood is a genuinely 'Catholic' ministry.

The language of vocation

Michael also felt that the process was worthwhile but suffered from a difficulty that he feels affects others. He realized that the way he was articulating his calling to priesthood and the language that he was using was perplexing the DDO and was likely to do the same with the ABM selectors. He had emerged from a parish that would happily identify itself as evangelical/charismatic and he had been part of a large leadership team. There was a strong commitment to all-member ministry and the priesthood of all believers, and a strong sense of being gifted by the Holy Spirit for ministry in the Church and world. Although it was recognized that different people should undertake different tasks and use their gifts in different areas, there was no formal leadership structure within the group and, when they were together, worship would be led spontaneously by any member present. The vicar was a keen advocate of shared ministry and operated as the boundary keeper and overseer of this lay team. Some team members openly advocated lay celebration of the eucharist because they felt that it made little difference which of them was moved by the Spirit to take that role. This dynamic process of shared leadership made it difficult for Michael to give a clear shape to his sense of calling to priesthood.

It was made even more difficult by the growing recognition that his local church sat uneasily within Anglicanism, gaining its inspiration and church models from some of the large, non-episcopal churches in the United States rather than the Church of England. It was suggested to Michael that he undertook a placement within a more conventional parish as part of the process of having his vocation tested. He agreed rather doubtfully but was surprised by the extent to which he warmed to its rootedness within the community that it served and its sense of tradition.

Michael grew to recognize that his vocation to priesthood would place him on the edge of the lay leadership team in his local church. His priesthood would represent and focus a ministry that both the parish and the church congregation could recognize as distinctively Church of England while acknowledging the ministry of lay people. Indeed, it might help him to minister to those who felt uncomfortable with the way their local church was developing.

Jean found herself with a similar problem but from a completely different context. She had emerged from what her own PCC described as a 'middle of the road' Church of England benefice on the edge of a large town. The vicar had been promoting what she variously called 'shared' or 'collaborative' ministry throughout the six years that she had spent there and she had seen a positive response from many of the growing congregation. Jean had begun a year of study and exploration with very little expectation of discovering a vocation to priest-hood. However, her group had seen the potential for ordained local ministry in her and asked her to consider this possibility. Her vicar had been tremendously supportive but Jean was struggling to make this vocation her own. She recognized that she still lacked confidence and that she was worried about how she might cope with study if selected for training. However, her real problem was that she could not picture herself in the role of priest or find the language to express her vocation. Although she had tremendous respect for her vicar and for another member of the group that had been selected for ordained local ministry, she realized that she could not be like them and express priesthood in the way that they did.

She found that the Ordinal did not help her much either. For a start, the language of the ASB assumed the priest would be male. She knew that the bishop made the language inclusive when he did the service but it was not just the use of 'he' and 'him' that gave her that impression. The Ordinal identifies the role of the priest, together with the bishop and other fellow priests, as 'servant and shepherd'. They are called to be 'messengers, watchers and stewards of the Lord', ordained to 'proclaim the word of the Lord, to call his hearers to repentance, and in Christ's name to absolve, and to declare the forgiveness of sins. He is to preside at the celebration of the Holy Communion' and to 'lead . . ., intercede . . ., bless . . ., teach . . . and encourage . . .'. She was aware that the Church of England has a rich story to tell about the way in which the 'vicar' has undertaken the work of ministry in urban and rural environments over many years. But these were all essentially images of individual leadership and ministry, fitting models of male leadership very snugly, designed to do things 'to', 'for' and 'on behalf of' the congregation, and they were images that she struggled to apply to her own situation and to that of her church.

She was also conscious of the diversity of thinking that now exists within the church. The old adage, 'one Dutchman one church, two Dutchmen two churches' could be typically applied to the clergy's view of priesthood. 'Six clergy, six views of priesthood' was not uncommon. She understood that there had been different emphases in the past between evangelical and Anglo-Catholic clergy, but the new emphasis on the priesthood of the Church and the ministry of all baptized Christians had made the use of traditional language quite difficult.

In the end it helped Jean to realize that God was calling her to be herself in the priesthood, to use her gifts in liturgy and pastoral care to focus the work of the church in the place that she lived and to represent the public face of the church in a variety of situations. She recognized that being herself, rooted in her community, known already and trusted by church and parish was what God was calling her to be. He was not wanting to recast her in somebody else's image or seek that she change to be accommodated in some kind of holy professional group. She also recognized that, if she waited until she was ready or became confident enough or thought herself sufficiently good to undertake the role, then she would never come to terms with what God was calling her to do or be. Perhaps it was what she had identified as her 'ordinariness' that God wanted to use in that place at that time to represent his Church.

It still felt a little scary to Jean because she was still conscious of the difference between herself and what she had always imagined clergy to be and still found it difficult to express how she saw her vocation in language that she felt might be convincing to the wider Church. However, she was encouraged to recognize that to see priesthood taking different forms in the lives of a variety of local Christians with different strengths and personalities might well be a strength of ordained local ministry.

Too good to be an ordained local minister?

Ralph's experience was different again. The catholic tradition from which he came gave him a way of expressing his priesthood in language that could be readily identified and supported. His own sense of call had been overwhelmingly supported by the local church, the DDO, the bishop and the selectors at his ABM conference. Indeed, such was their support that he was puzzled to be told by one selector that, in his view, he was 'too good' to be an OLM and would have easily been selected as an non-stipendiary minister, an NSM.

Ralph was surprised by this for several reasons. He knew that priesthood could be expressed in the diocese in three ways. He could have put himself forward for stipendiary ministry, to be a full-time clergyman. He could also have put himself forward as an NSM, which, in his diocese, would have meant that he would have committed himself to be deployable, ready to express his priesthood wherever that might be needed in the diocese and to take responsibility for the leadership of a benefice in certain circumstances. He did not do this for one very good reason. He wanted to express his priesthood in the place in which he lived and among the people who had affirmed his vocation. He therefore chose the third option, to go forward into ordained local ministry.

He was incensed that this option should have been considered some kind of lesser role. He was old enough to remember the eleven-plus selection procedure and an educational system that divided pupils according to their IQ ratings into schools that catered for either academic excellence or teaching in more practical skills. He'd hated such systems then and wasn't happy that similar assumptions were operating in theological education. He had a degree and felt himself quite capable of going to theological college if that had been appropriate. He also remembered other candidates in his year. There was one student with an MA in theology who was currently training for ordained local ministry and was being stretched by the experience. There were, of course, others with no formal educational qualifications and he rejoiced in that as well.

He was an OLM because that was what he felt called to be and not because he wasn't capable of being anything else. He was sorry that wasn't recognized more broadly in the Church, but realized that new forms of ministry always took time to find universal acceptance. However, he was surprised to hear such a comment from the lips of an ABM selector!

TRAINING FOR ORDAINED LOCAL MINISTRY

Finding the time

Sarah's most vivid memory of her training was the time that she cried her eyes out over an assignment. It seemed silly afterwards but at the time it helped release of a lot of tension, anger and frustration. It was partly her own fault. The principal of her diocesan scheme had come to visit her and her vicar – she remembered that they had met in the church vestry – and had worked through a training agreement with them. He had tried to explain to her that there was a natural rhythm in the training process.

Because students were unable to 'go away' to do their training it was important that they were able to manage their training while retaining their links with the local church. This has two aspects. The first is the need to withdraw from the roles that they have been undertaking when the training gets underway. Sarah had seen the point of this but knew that it wouldn't be easy. She had been churchwarden of a small village church for the past five years which only attracted about fifteen regular worshippers on a Sunday. The problem was that there were not many active people to keep the church's ministry alive in that place. That is why she had been called upon to undertake many practical and administrative tasks as well as organize worship and take morning and evening prayer once a month. Indeed, people had begun to say that they associated her with the church and didn't know what they would do without her. She had been initially flattered and had failed to spot the danger in this.

Rather predictably, when she said that she would need to give these duties up, nobody had come forward to fill her shoes. The result was that she had been persuaded to keep the role going for another year alongside her training. Actually, she reflected afterwards, her parish priest should have taken a stronger line with her and the congregation but, in truth, he was under tremendous pressure himself and had rather relied upon Sarah to keep things going in her part of the benefice while he concentrated on some rather tricky problems elsewhere.

The principal had also said that, while initially giving up many of those tasks that relate to the ministry that each individual has been exercising, it is necessary, as the training progresses, to undertake many of those duties that priesthood will demand. During the latter part of the training, undertaking these tasks as an 'ordinand' would assist in the development of the new identity in the local church.

The second aspect of this training management was a need for students to create space for study. At their meeting, Sarah had been encouraged to reflect upon every aspect of her life to enable specific time to be found for working on this very demanding course. She had been encouraged to preserve family and leisure time and to find space for training from the time that she currently spent on church matters. And this had been what had led her to those tears of anger and frustration. She had failed to give up the work in her local church and had found the study had disrupted her family life. Her husband Bob was normally very helpful. He did not go to church himself but was happy to support her in her church work. Normally very easygoing, they had rowed about her inability to give him the time that he thought was appropriate. She also felt, on reflection, that her coursework had taken the pleasure out of her church work and had eaten into her prayer time. She commented afterwards that she didn't feel that she had the time or the space to grow or to change. In fairness, she didn't blame the course. She thought she could manage without hurting anybody's feelings in the local church.

Robert had similar concerns but had dealt with them rather differently. He also was a key person in his local church, used to taking on all sorts of responsibility and many different jobs. But he had given these up at the start of his training. There had been prophecies of doom from his small congregation. Nobody would take on these jobs. The church would be in disarray, indeed it may have to close if nobody would step into the breach. But Robert was adamant that his ministry as an ordained local priest in that benefice was not going to be as a maintenance man. He felt that it was time that the church faced up to the fact that it was not just a human institution fighting for survival in the village but had been placed there by God to bear witness to his Kingdom. Perhaps they should pray about their future within the benefice and within the village and put their trust in God to preserve what he wanted and lose what was not needful for his purpose. His parish priest backed his stand and Robert was delighted that the church members began to think and pray about their role and purpose in that place and the way that they could serve the community in ways that were appropriate without Robert's short-time help.

Robert admits that it was still not easy to train for the priesthood without leaving his community but he was grateful for the way that they learned to give him the space that he needed to grow into his new role among them and other members of the benefice.

Cloning the vicar

Alan admits to a different problem that dogged his training. His parish priest had been the first to spot his vocation and had rejoiced when he had been selected for training as an OLM. A big man with a strong personality, this vicar had very clear views on how things should be done. Alan felt from the very beginning that his priesthood was being cast in his parish priest's image and that he was expecting him to be a colleague and clone in the local church. Much of the training that the diocese offered challenged the presuppositions of his parish and provided alternative views of ministry that Alan found interesting and attractive. However, he soon found that it was unwise to say too much about this because there was already a degree of tension between the diocesan staff and his parish priest about the content and nature of the course. His vicar would certainly have done the training differently if he'd been asked and had scant respects for 'the idiots' who worked for the Ministry scheme.

Alan had recognized this clearly when he had been on a 'preaching weekend'. The speaker had been talking about 'preaching parents', and had suggested that those who had experienced good preaching could learn good habits or, in certain circumstances, be disabled by such a person when they came to preach themselves. Similarly, bad 'preaching parents' could teach the beginner bad habits but was more likely to help them to avoid similar mistakes themselves. Both kinds of parents could be ghosts or grace to the preacher. The discussion over dinner afterwards was not of 'preaching parents' but of clergy. Alan shared some of the problems he was facing and was amazed to learn that he was not alone. Certainly each situation was different. Some parish priests seemed too busy to give their students adequate time and some tended, like his own vicar, to be prescriptive. However, he particularly remembered the words of a student who sat opposite him ruminating over his rhubarb crumble, 'My parish priest needs to realize that I want to learn *from* him. I don't want to learn to *be* him.'

A partnership

Many OLM schemes operate a partnership between training that happens in diocesan groups and training that happens locally.

The parish priest will always be a key figure in the training process because it will be he or she who supports the ordinand as they undertake practical work in the parish or benefice. However, it is not only parish priests who can sometimes prove problematic to a student in training. The new ideas provided by schemes at diocesan level are not always welcomed with open arms, especially in the first months of training. Most diocesan schemes understand their role as both supporting and challenging the ways of thinking that are prevalent in parishes of different churchmanship and orientation. All insist on a level of critical encounter with scripture, Church and world which can prove an uncomfortable experience for many who have accepted the teaching of their church for many years without subjecting it to careful thought and analysis.

The placement

One of the ways in which students experience a broader understanding of Church and ministry is when they are sent on a placement to another church for a six-week period, as happens on a number of training schemes. Jill had lived in her local community for many years and found her placement an extremely uncomfortable experience. She pined for her parish and her team and was devastated not to be allowed to attend her local church for nearly two months. The priest at the placement church expected worship to be undertaken with punctilious accuracy and maintained a close control of the parish and its life. She had no experience of high-church tradition which seemed a million miles away from her friendly village church. Nevertheless, in the course of the placement she came to realize that she could successfully take a service in a big church of another tradition, that this strange congregation really did like her as a person, that there were advantages in a well-organized teaching programme and that being ordained entailed being 'professional' about what you did. Her write-up of the project was humble and moving.

Sonia is a young mother with two children at school who lives on a city estate. She is a lively, exciting person who is 'chaplain' to the parish drop-in centre. A few years ago she rarely went to church and found it difficult to relate to the formal Church of England. For her a placement in an old-fashioned market town was a revelation. She found the members of the congregation disarmingly friendly to her and her family, and she was surprised to find that people in this parish had much the same problems and pressures that she experienced on her own urban estate. In fact the 'rural idyll' was little more than a mask. The services were much more formal than she was used to but when she attended the house group she began to realize that behind the formality lay a genuine holiness and wisdom. This was certainly true of the incumbent, despite his black suit and two-inch-high dog-collar. A bit of a rebel at heart, Sonia had to admit that the conventional C of E wasn't as hollow as she had secretly supposed. Partly as a result of her experience, Sonia feels that placements should be a regular feature of OLM in-service training.

All OLMs recognize that training away from the home path is not without tensions. It is not always easy to be true to the traditions of the local church while encountering the challenge of new ideas and new ways of thinking from a broader context. To find the time and the space to undertake this training is critical and to have the faith to go where God in Christ calls is essential.

Training with NSM and reader candidates

Many training courses make provision for some elements of the training to be undertaken with candidates for stipendiary and non-stipendiary ministry. Often candidates for ordained local ministry are wary of these occasions because they know that stipendiary and NSM candidates can view the training offered for ordained local ministry as 'inferior', the selection procedures 'an easy option', and the candidates as 'second-class priests'. This can lead to real hurt when they meet together for training

Bertha and Donald were extremely apprehensive about going on their first summer residential and their worst fears were realized when, on the first morning, they were asked to study and discuss the nature of priesthood. They were left in no doubt that some of the ordinands in their group regarded them as interlopers who weren't going to be 'proper' priests at all. At that stage they were far too apprehensive to cross swords in debate with third-year students who seemed to know everything. The course director was covered in confusion when he heard about it and promised that 'it wouldn't happen again' but, in the present climate of opinion, such encounters are sadly inevitable.

In contrast, John is confident in the group with which he trains. He is studying on a course with NSM and stipendiary candidates and is clearly as able as they are. His decision to train for ordained local ministry was based on a deep-seated feeling that God was calling him to work in his local church and this had been accepted by the community and the diocese. He fears, however, that others will judge his ability on the basis that he will 'only' have a local licence and this upsets him.

Deborah, Alex and five other candidates for OLM are studying on a training course with readers and this too sets up its own special dynamic. Many schemes provide integrated training at diocesan level and train OLMs, readers and other lay ministries on one basic course. The issue of vocation to OLM or reader ministry inevitably comes up at an early stage and, while it has helped OLMs to clarify their priestly calling, working with readers has also helped them to keep alive their sense of being first and foremost baptized Christians and has enabled them to develop collaborative patterns of ministry.

In some dioceses the local lay team plays a major part in the training of the OLM. Mary goes to seminars with other trainees, and then has to pass on what she has learned to her local training group. Her tutor helps her to prepare her presentation and talks it over with her after the event. Mary remembers how fired up she was by the seminars on worship and yet how hard she found it to channel her zeal into a coherent presentation to the group. With the tutor's help, she managed to cut down her prepared script by two-thirds and, in the event, the group seemed really enthusiastic, even though it was 2.30 on a summer's afternoon!

James, who comes from another diocese, is required to attend extremely high-powered lectures with other OLM and NSM candidates. He reckons that he needs his sessions with his tutor to make sure that he has got hold of the right end of the stick. He finds it a real challenge to hook the pure theology of the classroom on to the real-life experiences of his education group. But, like Mary, he has found that the challenge has drawn him into a deeper understanding of priesthood.

Wanting to be ordained with the team

The Ordinal and the 'normal' ordination service do not always seem to fit the OLM context, especially for those trained as part of ministry teams. Where the vocation is essentially personal, the celebration seems to demand the gathering of personal friends. Where the vocation is essentially congregational, something rather different would seem natural.

Sarah would certainly not have offered for ordination unless the congregation had suggested the idea and the team supported her training all the way through. She was therefore upset and surprised when she discovered that not only were the team uninvolved in the ceremony, they were not even going to be allocated tickets. To be fair, the bishop's staff did appreciate her point of view and seats were found, but this incident illustrates how OLM is bound to question practices which we have formerly taken for granted. Some dioceses routinely ordain OLMs with NSMs and stipendiaries, and in this circumstance it is difficult to reflect the local as well as the catholic nature of the occasion for the OLMs. However, those dioceses with larger numbers of OLMs do have the opportunity to organize separate occasions and try to reflect the unique nature of the OLM experience through the active participation of the local.

REJOICING IN A NEW ROLE

A new relationship with the local community

Joyce had been unable to envisage what it would be like to be a priest. She had tried to prepare herself for the new role that she would be undertaking but it was not until the bishop laid hands upon her that she fully understood what had been happening to her. The ordination itself was impressive. She remembered being made deacon in the cathedral and then being priested in her own parish church. She knew this was unusual and felt that it was a great privilege because, together, the ordinations seemed to speak eloquently of what it means to be a priest in the 'Catholic' and universal Church with a special relationship to the local. Her parish priest talked of the 'grace' of ordination and she now knew what that meant. It was a key moment in her life when she felt that God blessed her and set her aside for the role that she was fulfilling in his name.

It took her some time to gauge the effect that wearing a dog-collar had on people. At first it seemed as if a tiny barrier had been erected between her and the people in her church and community. Even her best friends treated her slightly differently than before and she was to learn that the relationships she had with so many people in the local church had changed forever.

This came home to her very clearly a few weeks after she had been ordained as a deacon. She had arranged with her parish priest and the PCC to have Mondays off. When the phone rang on Monday evening it was Julie, a long-standing friend and church member, who wanted to speak to her about a pastoral problem that had been troubling the whole church for some time. Joyce talked for a while and then gently mentioned that it was her day off and would it be possible if they could continue the conversation tomorrow, perhaps over a cup of coffee. Julie seemed a little nonplussed by this and reminded Joyce that she wasn't a parishioner but a friend. They did not argue but Julie was quick to point out that lay people weren't given days off from the church and that surely friendship should outweigh such considerations. Joyce felt upset when she put the phone down and for the first time recognized that being ordained could sometimes be a lonely experience, even in the midst of a ministry team.

To manage such a significant change of role from congregation member to priest is often very difficult. Tim found himself greeted with the words, 'Hello dear, couldn't the rector come himself?' when he visited one of the elderly members of the congregation after his ordination. The rector laughed and said that that was a common experience for curates and he would soon get used to it from certain of the more traditional members of the church. However, it was important for both of them to take a stand against the implications of this kind of comment. The church needed to know that a visit from either one of them was a visit from a priest and that Tim would not be visiting on behalf of the rector but on behalf of Christ and his Church. In the event, this did not cause a problem and many warmed to Tim and preferred the man that they had known since a boy. Nevertheless, it had to be made clear that there were to be no first-class and second-class priests in the parish.

Not only Tim but other OLM colleagues throughout the country find a ready acceptance in the churches from which they have emerged and in which they minister. That is not surprising as they have been, in a very important sense, 'home-grown'. Outside the Church, their acceptance has yet to be an issue. In communities in which the OLMs are known by a large number of the residents, acceptance has followed the pattern within the Church. Their priesthood is acknowledged and accepted and they are often especially requested to take marriages and baptisms because of their special relationship with the community. Where they encounter people who do not know them, they are treated as people would treat any clergyman or woman they encountered.

A new relationship with the workplace

Work is a trickier environment. Many OLMs have found their ministry welcomed and supported in church and parish but have struggled in their work environment. Without being overtly hostile, many companies discourage employees from engaging in activities that might compromise their loyalty to company policy or lessen their energy and commitment to their careers. Large companies do not like to favour one religious community over another and find the presence of a Christian priest in the workplace a matter of concern. William left the company that he worked for after his ordination because he felt uneasy with the way that they treated their staff. He was lucky to be in a career where he could find other employment relatively easily. Others are not so lucky and find that they need to be very careful in the way that they express their priesthood in the workplace.

Some, though, find that their priesthood is encouraged. We heard earlier that Brian was keen to express his priesthood in the local engineering works, and colleagues and management in that instance were supportive. Graham, a self-employed horticulturist, is quite open about his priesthood and finds customers happy with the notion that they are having their grass mown by an ordained local minister!

However, all of these ordained local ministers believe that the primary focus of their priesthood is within the community and church that gave shape to their vocation. They are not primarily 'Ministers in Secular Employment' (MSEs) who feel called to exercise the main thrust of their priesthood in their place of work, often in more formal arrangements between church and employer. But nor do they close the door on opportunities to represent the public face of the Church and to respond to pastoral need in any situation in which they find themselves.

Being local

Ordination has given to ordained local ministers a Catholic ministry of priesthood in the service of the local church. Some balance the demands of job and family with a ministry in church and parish, some are early retired who have considerable time to give to their new vocation. All have a particular area of work that defines what it means to be local but this differs hugely from OLM to OLM and from diocese to diocese. Some OLMs focus the work of the church in one small village. Some share the work of priesthood in large urban parishes. Others work in teams in benefices which contain a large number of tiny parishes, while others again work in small rural towns. For each OLM what it means to be local is slightly different, but for each it is key to their ministry.

Edna works in the depth of the country. She lives in a tiny hamlet with a few houses, a farm and a church. The benefice contains eight such hamlets clustered around a medium-sized village. Without local ministry the presence of the Church would have been severely restricted long ago. The rector had been in the parish for eight years and had come with the specific task of developing a local ministry that was appropriate to that place. There had been a lively debate about the viability of the benefice and the rector's appointment had been a compromise between the parishes that wanted to maintain and develop a presence throughout the area and the Archdeacon who favoured a degree of rationalization, the closure of some of the outlying churches and the concentration of the ministry around the village church.

A key question for the benefice was the way that the development of a ministry team could support the work of the church in such an area. An important piece of work took place shortly after the rector arrived. It started as a process he identified as 'audit' but quickly fuelled the imagination of a number of parishioners. The exercise was designed to investigate the nature and extent of the social networks that existed in the benefice. Clearly the housing had been designed to support a series of small farming communities. However, most of the land had long since been owned and farmed by a Dutch company who employed local managers and men, most of whom came from outside the benefice. There was a primary school in the village but when they reached eleven, children were bussed from the village to the high school in the town. Transport emerged as a key issue because the local bus service to half of the benefice had long been discontinued and only provided the other half with a once-daily return trip to the town.

After a considerable amount of research had been done, the churchwardens from the benefice sat and looked at a map. They discovered that many of the social networks and key structures like health, education, employment and local government converged in centres that were outside the benefice. It showed up the way that many people lived their lives within the benefice in a series of social and employment networks but it also showed up a huge level of deprivation and poverty around the elderly, the car-less and the unemployed. This led to a constructive debate about the role that the church should play in the benefice. One factor emerged that was to affect the way that Edna worked. To minister in such a parish required that ministers worked with the networks rather than in geographical areas. Therefore, to be an effective 'local minister' would require Edna to work across the benefice developing areas of work and taking responsibility for some of the strands that would make up the church's work in that place.

Edna's job description therefore required that she had a car. Churches in the benefice were organized into three 'clusters' for Sunday worship and Edna was the priest for her cluster. These clusters did not reflect the previous parish system but rather the social patterns now prevalent in the benefice. However, her pastoral ministry operated across these clusters to provide practical care and support for the elderly and housebound within the benefice as a whole. Her 'local' ministry was therefore designed around the social networks of the benefice and not on strictly geographical grounds.

The geographical area in which Jane operated was not in doubt. She was licensed to a large urban parish and her job description involved her in working as one of a team that was planting a new church on the local housing estate. Although the new church was to meet in the local school, Jane lived on the estate and recognized that her home would also form a focus for this new venture. For Jane, although retaining links with the parish church, local meant the estate on which she lived, clearly bounded by two main roads, a canal and a railway line. She was a working mother with two teenage children. Her husband was a practising member of the church and was enthusiastic about the project. However, both lived busy and demanding lives so it was essential that their part in the team that was planting the church needed to be clear and well defined and their time well used.

For Ben, local is also, at least partly, geographical. His benefice includes three villages of about equal size in a rural part of England and the ministry team recognizes his initial responsibility for one of these. Ben is unusual, although not unique, inasmuch as he is an American by origin. He is also black. He has lived for many years in this part of England. Initially he worked on the local American base and then, having married a local girl, he settled down in the village. He still works on the base but is no longer an American serviceman.

Ben was supported by his local church who felt that he was the right person to be their priest. Although supported by a benefice team of ministers, the ministry has been divided along the traditional parish boundaries. The team of accredited ministers comprises the rector, two OLMs, each with responsibility for one of the villages, and two readers. Other members of the team include those supporting youth and children's work and pastoral care. Ben is obviously not indigenous to the area in which he works but vigorously defends his ability to be and represent the local. In this respect, however, Ben is typical. Very few OLMs currently ordained in England are strictly indigenous. Most have come to settle in the places in which they now minister but all have been affirmed by their local church to work among them and focus the priesthood of God's people in that place.

Working in teams

Edna, Jane and Ben have key things in common. They all work with others in ministry teams or groups which express the collaborative, shared nature of the Church's ministry. Not only do they share ministry with other team members but they also work to support and enable the ministry of all God's people in their churches. All are aware that to fail to support and enable the ministry of others is to endow the church with a ministerial elite – six vicars instead of one to do all the work and make all the decisions.

They are all assistant priests. All felt called to local ministry and all are comfortable to work under the leadership of the stipendiary priest. Although Edna, Jane and Ben have been allocated areas of responsibility within the benefice, and charged with the development of new pieces of work, they are not given responsibility for managing the whole. In this context they are team members, giving their time and energy in clearly defined ways but leaving the overall leadership to their stipendiary colleague.

They all have working job descriptions. One of the strengths of ordained local ministry is the diversity of the work and the range of the people called to do it. Local can mean different things in different situations, and the range of sacramental and pastoral work can be extensive. However, each OLM has a clear job description which has emerged with them through the early years when their vocation was tested and has gone on to inform their working ministry. This job description or working agreement has also changed with them as they and their work have changed but, in cases of best practice, it has never lost its clarity and its sensitivity to the needs of both parish and minister.

The Incumbents' Tale

WORKING WITH THE DIOCESE

David had been involving lay people in ministry since his ordination in the 1970s. When he was asked whether his parish would be prepared to be part of a pilot scheme for local ministry he couldn't initially work out how this would be different to what he had always done. Surely it didn't need a diocesan scheme to develop the ministry of lay people in a parish? Surely that was something that could be safely left in the hands of parish priests?

However, David was to change his mind for three important reasons. Firstly, he had underestimated the extra weight that a scheme which was supported by the bishop could give to the project. It certainly helped convince the less enthusiastic members of the church that this was something more than the idiosyncratic whim of the present incumbent. It also had, even from the beginning, a rigour and a depth of education and training that could not easily be reproduced at parish level. Secondly, the scheme promised continuity. David looked back to his previous parish and had to concede that the clergyman who had followed him had quickly dismantled the teams he had painstakingly assembled to lead worship and support the work of pastoral care. The bishop had committed the diocese to the maintenance of those local ministry teams that were formed as part of the scheme. He had agreed to appoint to those benefices involved only clergy who would be prepared to work with them. Thirdly, it had helped him to develop his vision of Church and ministry. He had certainly recognized the need for lay people to help in the ministry of the Church. He had recognised that ministry did not belong to him as a priest, and understood that it would be richer and more effective if more people were involved in it. However, he had not seen the full implications of working in and with a church in which ministry was shared out among people who were empowered by the Holy Spirit to do God's work in Christ in a whole variety of ways and in any number of places.

Looking back on the experience of those days, David recognized that it changed both him and the church. It nurtured faith and personal development among individual members and stimulated a growth in the numerical strength of the church. It was a time of renewal for him and the church as the local congregation struggled with what it might mean to work with a style of ministry that he believed to be grounded in the New Testament and to explore the church as the 'body of Christ', the 'fellowship of the Spirit' and a 'royal priesthood'. It also required that David change his understanding of his own ministry and the way that he worked in the parish.

Before the scheme, David had not realized how much the parish relied on him for its vision, its life and its care. He had always encouraged a broad level of decision making within the parish and had used the PCC to discuss and decide upon issues of policy and practice. As with his previous parish, he had begun the process of involving members of the congregation in leading worship and undertaking pastoral care but it was still true that nothing ever really happened without his say so or without his energy and commitment. Looking back he could see how he had gradually needed to make changes in his own leadership style to accommodate the growingly effective ministry of other ministry team members. He had always been a practitioner of ministry himself, particularly gifted in pastoral care, and this had never and would never stop. However, his ministry had required that he give more serious thought to the way that the parish was managed so that the different ministries could flourish and grow in an integrated way. Less an individual practitioner, more an enabler, encourager and supporter of others, he nevertheless found the experience enriching and motivating.

MAKING IT WORK

Paul's experience was similar although he worked in another diocese. It had become clear to him that the role of the stipendiary priest must change as benefices grew in size throughout the countryside and paid clergy continued to decrease in numbers. Faced with parishes and benefices of ever-increasing size, it would become necessary, especially in the countryside, for stipendiary clergy to change their traditional models of practice and to develop ministries that could encourage, support and oversee the work of others. The development of groups and teams of ministers drawn from their local churches therefore seemed to him to be essential if the church was to maintain a presence, let alone engage in mission. Rather like the bishop in his diocese, he felt that stipendiary clergy were increasingly asked to engage in a ministry that could be identified as 'episcopal'. He was worried that he and others had not been trained for such a ministry and were not necessarily gifted to undertake it. Many older colleagues had told him with some bewilderment that this was not what they had entered the ministry for, all those year ago. They had spent their lives being good parish priests but freely admitted that the idea of managing, supporting and enabling a large and diverse ministry team to operate across seven parishes in a rural benefice was a frightening prospect. Paul understood this and sympathized. He understood less well why the young curates, fresh from theological college, seemed to have little idea of this new role either. The fact that one told him that collaborative ministry had been the subject of a single session in the pastoral ministry module during his last term at college did little to lighten his mood.

Andrew worked in a busy parish on the edge of a large town. During that time he experienced the development of local ministry and took part in a pilot scheme run by his diocese. He now looks back on that initial experience as being crucial to the parish and to his own ministry. The previous incumbent had enjoyed the services of a curate and a retired priest and had maintained a traditional priest-centred ministry during his stay at the church. When Andrew went to work there he knew that there had to be change. As often happens the curate left, not to be replaced, and the retired priest was hospitalized within a few weeks of his arrival. The church, of Catholic persuasion, was used to regular eucharistic worship. Funerals in such a busy urban parish frequently ran at three a week and there were many people who wanted to have their children baptized or to be married in church. As is often the case, change was to be both vision and practice led. Andrew wanted to open up new horizons of Church and ministry but also desperately needed ministerial colleagues to support the ministry of the church in that place. Both were forthcoming in the pilot scheme that his diocese ran. However, the four years that elapsed before a new team of people emerged to support the work of ministry were hard for Andrew. Attempting to deal with the pressure of work demanded by the parish was difficult. However, he had to combine this with the need to sow new understandings of ministry among the congregation and the PCC while also helping them to identify and support the two ordained local ministers, the two readers and the five people with pastoral and educational gifts who were to emerge to train on the new diocesan pilot scheme.

Andrew is fond of recalling two incidents from that time that he thinks are significant. The first was the time that they painted the church. He had been tired of hearing that ministry was the job of the parish priest and, when mentioning the state that the church was in, that decorating the church was best left to the professionals. To subvert both pieces of thinking he had decided to persuade that PCC that they were capable of painting the interior of the church themselves and that it could be done for the price of paint, brushes and the hire of scaffolding towers. Everybody joined in and Andrew worked harder than most. The event eventually became a time when trust and teamwork were established and the first crack in the edifice of the sacred professional was effected.

He also remembers a moment, later in the process, that was also significant. His predecessor had been keen to use the vicarage for meetings and events, even though it was a new, quite small house next door to the church and church hall. All of the church equipment and duplicating facilities were kept in the study. It really hadn't occurred to Andrew that there was nowhere that other team members could work or use the church equipment apart from his house and study. It took another group of people with paint brushes to prepare a room in the church hall to be a parish office. For Andrew, the moment of moving the church's office equipment out of the study and into the church office was a kind of parable for what was happening in the church. A new centre was being created that all could share and it was being established outside the vicarage.

Andrew can also remember the first occasion on which one of the OLMs was asked to do the funeral of a significant church person. As the incumbent, he had often said, and truly believed, that there was somebody in his new team of ministers that could perform any aspect of ministerial practice at least as well as him, if not better. In truth he felt that he had an edge on preaching but he wasn't sure how long that would last. Generally he rejoiced in this, but on this particular occasion he felt strangely hurt. He had known the person in question. He was the vicar of the church and it hadn't occurred to him that anybody other than he would do the funeral. He could see why the OLM had been asked. He had known the person for many more years than Andrew. In the end he suggested that the OLM should preach and go to the cemetery for the committal and he would take other elements of the service. It was not, of course, the funeral itself that was the issue. It was the recognition that shared ministry meant letting go, and for each incumbent that proves hard in different ways and makes itself felt at different moments.

SETTING UP A LOCAL MINISTRY TEAM

Stephen, Martin, Eric and Adrian all worked in a diocese that was developing local ministry through the creation and maintenance of local ministry teams. Stephen had done a wonderful job in a very difficult parish. It was a small market town where everyone was aware of what everyone else thought so that no one would ever put their head above the parapet. 'We're right behind you vicar', said it all! On top of that, the church's cupboard positively rattled with skeletons of the misdeeds of past vicars. But Stephen wasn't a good organizer and, having called out and energized lots of really wonderful lay people he couldn't somehow get round to making the best use of them. The trouble was that his study was right at the centre of the spider's web and that was where all the wires got crossed.

A local ministry team seemed a possible way forward and so the idea was canvassed and got PCC support. True, the parish days were two months later than had originally been intended and, because of double bookings, few people came to both days, but at least when the nominations for team members came in there were lots of them. Stephen went through the list with the local ministry officer, then set off to invite people to join the team. This proved to be a very time-consuming business, especially since so many of those nominated said they just hadn't time to take it on. It was extremely depressing work and, as the date for the first meeting drew nearer, his stress level rose dangerously. At the very last moment, however, it all came together and, in the event, the team is a most interesting group who are all the better for not being the obvious choices.

The best thing for Stephen was that, at the team's first meeting, he suddenly realized that for the first time in years he was not expected to take the chair, provide input, take notes or act as secretary. He just had to be cheerful, prayerful and wise!

Martin had been a team vicar in a large urban parish in a diocese with no local ministry scheme. His team rector's style of leadership was very much modelled on the First World War

Officer Corps. He was inducted to a multi-parish benefice which has seven settlements, one of which had a well-established local ministry team. At the induction service he was mandated as a member of the team – an impressive ceremony of congregational collegiality set in a service which otherwise sounded loud and clear the message that the new vicar had arrived and the new vicar was in charge.

Having been a curate and a team vicar, he was raring to start running 'his' parish and clearly found the collaborative ethos of his new diocese extremely difficult to understand. He had asked both the local ministry officer and the team whether he was supposed to chair the team meetings and prepare the agenda. When told that chairmanship shifted depending on the subject being discussed, he seemed mystified. Fortunately he and the team are scheduled for a teamworking weekend in the autumn.

Eric was asked to take on a parish which already had a local ministry team. Being a traditional animal by nature he had managed to evade the missives about local ministry from bishops, archdeacons and officers which had dropped through his letter-box. But now he was caught. Originally, he imagined that he could continue to be the traditional parish priest he had always been in other places. But, overwhelmed by pressures of time and distance it soon dawned on him that he just couldn't perform there to a standard which would satisfy either himself or local people. Looking again at the team he had inherited, he realized that, at the very least, they could ensure that the parish enjoyed a basic level of pastoral care. He was, in fact, lucky to have them. Having decided to accept and use them, he came to realize that they had lots of valuable gifts to use in the service of the church and were also exercising an effective Christian ministry in their jobs as a small farmer, a nurse and a secretary. Since those early days, he has developed other projects in collaboration with the team and now Eric wants the other parishes in the benefice to develop similar teams.

MAKING TEAMS WORK

Leadership training for most clergy seems to comprise, at best, a few sessions on group dynamics. Unless they have worked in the world of business management, ideas about shifting chairmanship, Belbin tests or collaborative decision-making are foreign to them. Of course there are a host of books on the subject but the only sure way of learning these skills is through experience.

Adrian and his newly formed team were sent on a team building weekend. He was very tired indeed when he went and immediately took against the brash, simplistic lecture style of the person leading the event. When he was put into a group whose task was to produce as many booklets as possible in half an hour he was at boiling point. His temper was not improved when the group that he was with all started talking at once and simply refused to listen when he told them precisely how it could best be done. About halfway through it finally dawned on him that the task was rather more complicated than he had imagined and that the mousy young man, who was a mathematician, did have some good ideas, but everyone continued to butt in, trying to run the thing themselves. Eventually the group produced six rather tatty books.

The review session was even more uncomfortable and two or three group members actually accused him of looking like a brooding volcano, asking if he couldn't just smile occasionally and be a bit more encouraging. The conversion experience of the weekend for Adrian was when he was working with his own team and they had to make a model of a vicar out of paper and paste and a stapler in twenty minutes flat. Adrian could not draw and, when it came to craftwork, he had always been fingers and thumbs; after all, he was an ideas' person. But the parish secretary was just brilliant and soon got the rest of them organized. Within the allotted twenty minutes, under her direction, they had a wonderful vicar with a broad smile and bulging tummy. Discernment of gifts and shifting chairmanship suddenly made sense. He still occasionally finds himself slipping into old ways but Adrian is now a firm convert to collaborative ministry.

CHANGING ROLES

The incumbents mentioned above worked in different dioceses with different local ministry schemes. However, they all worked for a vision of Church and ministry that recognised the sharing out of gifts and roles among the members of the Church. To manage a local ministry church is to be committed to a way of being Church that subverts older attitudes and demands new working practices. It requires that the Church and the clergy let go of the myth of multi-competence, the individual priest who can do everything well and is the only person professionally competent to lead liturgy and undertake pastoral care.

All found that their roles and duties changed in the parish when others ministered in Christ's name but none gave up the practice of ministry to be 'mere managers' as some of their colleagues claimed they would. Neither did they fall into the trap of creating a new elite in the Church. Andrew, in particular, took care always to involve other church members in the tasks of ministry and to continue to provide opportunities for their ministry to develop.

All the incumbents also found that their parishes needed to be structured in such a way that there was real space and opportunity provided for others to minister. Organization and management were important, time for regular team meetings essential and the monthly service rota indispensable. Paul gave over the administration of his parish to a congregation member gifted in that way, but others felt comfortable with this role.

THE INTERREGNUM

Perhaps the biggest fear that all the incumbents and OLMs represented in this tale would have in common is that the work which they do together will be dismantled or destroyed when one incumbent leaves and another takes over the benefice. Most dioceses with local ministry schemes have solid processes in place that make it difficult for an inappropriate appointment to be made. However, as we have seen from previous tales, when proper arrangements are not in place there can be problems for vicar and parish. Most dioceses with local ministry schemes allow OLMs, readers and members of ministry teams to meet with a prospective incumbent before the appointment is ratified, and they ask new incumbents to commit themselves to the existing ministry of the church before they take over the parish or benefice. Some even ask candidates to make a five-minute presentation on collaborative ministry as this can be very revealing. Although not foolproof, meetings between existing ministry teams and new incumbents before appointments are made have facilitated some very good ongoing working relationships and avoided some disasters.

But even when the guidelines are followed to the letter, and when the new incumbent is truly a team player, integration is still a difficult process. Every time someone leaves or joins a team, the old team dies and a new one is born. This is even more significant when the new team member is also the stipendiary incumbent. Bernard arrived from another diocese to join a relatively young team. He did all the right things; he listened, he was humble, he was encouraging. But after six months he still could not grasp what his own role should be. It was only after he had been invited to sit in on the meeting of another team in order to see how that incumbent operated that he realized how he should fit into his own context. Since then the ministry of the team in the parish has gone from strength to strength.

The Priests' Tale

This priests' tale has woven together the stories of a large number of ordained local ministers and incumbents in the common vision of local ministry. Incumbents are called to oversee the life and work of the benefice and OLMs are called to develop appropriate areas of sacramental and pastoral ministry in the places from which they come and in which they serve. They are joined by the collegiate and catholic quality of priesthood yet meet to undertake their different roles within the local church. They are roles and expressions of priesthood that are complementary and are undertaken by people with a rich variety of gifts but a common calling to serve. They represent an important way forward for the Church.

5

⌀⌀⌀

The Officers' Tale

What Is an Officer?

Within the Church of England the word 'officer' or 'bishop's officer' is used to describe a person who is doing a particular piece of work for, or on behalf of, the bishop within the diocese. The post can be full time or joined with a parish responsibility and, in the case of local ministry, can have a wide variety of responsibilities and job descriptions depending on the diocese and circumstances. As different dioceses have different strategies for local ministry and operate a wide variety of schemes, local ministry officers can have responsibility for:

- helping parishes to set up and maintain local ministry teams
- the whole diocese or an area of it
- the oversight of the process of OLM selection
- training parish teams and/or accredited ministers like readers and OLMs
- the conditions of service of those they train, and their continuing ministerial education.

Indeed they can be responsible for one or all of these and they can be full or part time, male or female, lay or ordained. The stories that follow and the issues that they highlight will reflect the experience of those who work in different ways and with different responsibilities in the name of the bishop of their diocese.

Why Do They Do It?

Ask an officer why (s)he has become involved in local ministry and you may initially get a flippant response. Pursue the matter and there will be a firm commitment to a vision of Church, of ministry and of what it means to be a human being on God's earth that will share many values in common with colleagues around the world.

Paul would agree that he was something of a pioneer in the movement. Close to retirement now, he has been a parish priest for most of his adult life. It was back in the sixties that he had first become aware of the huge amount of talent that lay members of his church possessed and which the church was wasting. He was not a particularly humble man but he had learned early in his ministry that there were many jobs and responsibilities that the clergy had accrued to themselves over the years that would be better done by able lay people. Certainly in the parish in which he worked there were many aspects of church life and ministry that would be done much better if a more talented and able person was doing them. He smiled as he remembered one or two of the chapter meetings at that time. The clergy used to gather together for 'chapter' meetings (meetings of all the clergy who work in a deanery) on a Tuesday morning. They used to take it in turns to go round all the churches. The meetings always started with a eucharist in the church and then breakfast in the rectory and were followed by a discussion on some topic of interest and concern followed by a period when the rural dean would share any notices or matters of concern. The first time that he articulated his concerns about lay people the clergy listened to him with a cross between pity and friendly concern. The general consensus was that they wouldn't let 'their' people engage in work for which they were not trained and had no experience. One member announced that the laity were fully involved in his parish and it couldn't run without them. If the ladies didn't do the flowers and make the coffee after the service, and the men didn't look after the building and cut the grass in the churchyard, he wouldn't have time to do any ministry himself. Paul remembered that the conversation was diverted at this point as one of the elderly clergy nearly fainted away at the thought that coffee was served after church services. While still semi-conscious he denounced it as a dangerous modern habit that they would all come to regret.

However, Paul had persisted in his belief that the Church needed to take the ministry of lay people seriously and introduced the habit of having coffee after worship on a Sunday morning. He found, of course, that there were others who thought as he did and agreed that the system was making captives of ordinary church folk, even if many of them felt comfortable and safe in that role. Indeed 'lay ministry' became something of a crusade through the seventies and he felt that he had taken seriously the needs and talents of the people with whom he worked throughout that time.

Paul's other abiding interest had been in the field of adult Christian education. He had been a keen exponent of the need for lay Christians to learn more about their faith than could be gleaned from his Sunday sermons and the odd Lent group. He was therefore pleased to join a group in the diocese running a 'bishop's course' for lay Christians. The course was to be group-based, with a tutor facilitating the learning. Each member was to have a responsibility for his/her own learning and the learning of the group. For Paul this began to capture something of the vision of a church where lay Christians were freed to express and develop their faith and engage in theology together.

When, many years later, the diocese embraced local ministry and wanted to pilot a scheme for ordained local ministry, Paul was delighted to accept the bishop's invitation to create and manage the scheme, even though he was asked to do this together with the care of three semi-rural parishes.

Joyce had been in adult education all her life. She had been to church as a child but had left when she went to college and didn't resume her membership until her two boys had begun to attend Sunday school. She felt that the rector at that time was slightly intimidated by her, uncomfortable with the fact that a young, intelligent and able woman should feel that her best contribution to church life was not necessarily the Sunday school or the crèche even though she had two young boys and worked in education. In fact she was deeply concerned that Christians were not being fulfilled in their faith and that women had a particularly difficult task in expressing themselves outside the roles that the Church had provided for them. At this time the debate about women priests was dominating General Synod and polarizing the attitudes of clergy and people to the ministry of women.

Her diocese had embarked upon a scheme to develop local ministry teams and had asked her to work as a part-time officer to enable this development and provide some training for the teams. As her children were young and she was not in full-time employment she readily agreed. She still felt that many of the clergy were suspicious of her but she had a natural ability to inspire congregations to explore this brave new world. Conditions in the Church demanded that alternative strategies be developed, it having finally occurred to many people that one rector could not manage six country parishes in the same way that he had once managed one of them. New models needed to be found, and this one was worthy of attention.

As well as being motivated by a real desire to enable lay men and women to fulfil their potential in Christ, Joyce was also passionate about the need of the Church to engage much more successfully with the communities in which they were set and to recognize and support lay Christians in their worlds of work – a truly missionary Church. Joyce was certainly not interested in bolstering up a system which she felt was hierarchical and paternalistic and failing to provide channels for the Holy Spirit to renew both Church and world. She therefore insisted that the new ministry teams were developed in conjunction with the local communities that they were created to serve, involving non-church people in the nomination and support of team members. She was also concerned that the teams did not themselves become the new church hierarchy – six vicars instead of one. She also recognized at an early stage that the process that the diocese had begun would require a significant commitment of officer-time and money in the future.

For Tom, theology was a key to local ministry. He had been involved in Christian education since the beginning of his ministry as a stipendiary priest and was committed to the development of lay ministry within the Church. His particular concern had revolved around the way in which the study of theology could be made relevant in this process. For many priests, theology was what they did in college and would like to do more of now if they weren't so busy with parish work, and for many lay people it was an academic discipline that happened at university. For many, the study of theology was irrelevant to the development of their faith and discipleship, while for some it was even seen as a destructive force, questioning the firm foundations of belief. Tom had remembered the way in which a reader from his own parish had struggled to reconcile a simple but deeply held faith with the academic theology that he met when he had begun his training. However, this was some time ago now and Tom was aware that theology was undergoing change. It was still alive and well in universities where it had been traditionally strong and there were still people working away at biblical studies, church history and doctrine. But, in addition to this, in South America 'liberation' theology had developed as a tool to challenge the Church to work in the service of the poor and the oppressed in society, whilst feminist theology was critiquing the Church's scripture and traditions from the perspective offered by women's experience. Both demanded that theology take seriously the experience of ordinary Christians and the context in which they live and work. Both demanded that theology should work for practical outcomes that change the lives of those who are marginalized or oppressed.

Practical or contextual theology emerged from this new situation as a way of helping ordinary Christians to relate the scriptures and traditions of the church to their own situations of church, work and family life. To an extent, this is what Christians have always done throughout the centuries, but practical theology has emerged as a way of doing this critically and systematically. It therefore uses the insights of scholars who study scripture and church traditions, develops ways in which people can analyse the situations in which they live and work, and helps them to bring the story of the Church and of their lives into a new dynamic relationship. Equally important, practical theology demands an outcome. It is not an exercise in theory; it is a way of living theologically and working out discipleship and ministry through making appropriate decisions and undertaking appropriate action. Therefore, when Tom was appointed to be the principal of a local ministry scheme and invited to design an education programme that would train local ministry teams, he was excited by the prospect of putting practical theology at the heart of the enterprise.

For Sarah there is also an interest in theology but for a very different reason. She is an 'academic' who had spent much of her time teaching the Old Testament to university students. She noted that most of her colleagues were uncomfortable with the way that local ministry was developing and were concerned at what they considered to be the paucity of theological thought that underpinned it. For many in the parishes this was not a problem. They had felt the wind of the Spirit moving through their churches and had seen the integrity of the ministry that was emerging, but for Sarah there was a need to work with the theological academy to discuss the biblical, doctrinal and ecclesiological basis for local ordained and lay ministry and to provide a forum for serious and sustained debate. Not an 'officer' in the strict sense of the word, Sarah supports her diocesan scheme in any way that she can and has become a key theological resource.

Brian would see himself as an essentially practical man. He is a priest but had struggled at theological college to pass the necessary exams. Indeed, he had nearly not become a priest at all. When he had first felt a calling to the priesthood he had been told to go and see the Diocesan Director of Ordinands. Brian is proud of his working-class roots. His father worked in a foundry until he retired with ill health and died in his sixties not long afterwards. Going to the cathedral to see the DDO confirmed all the fears that Brian had. His local parish priest had supported him and his mother and father had agreed that he should explore this vocation. However, the world of the cathedral was very different and the interview was hard work. He can't remember what the DDO said, apart from the fact that he didn't think his qualifications were good enough to start immediate training. He remembered that the DDO was not unkind but had a tendency to patronize him. All in all, Brian was discouraged and came to the conclusion that he would be uncomfortable in the kind of world that the DDO lived in. Later, he was to have his vocation to the priesthood confirmed. He was to complete his studies and exercise a significant ministry in a variety of different parish settings. However, when asked to be the local ministry officer responsible for the selection of OLMs, Brian was to use his own initial experience to good effect. He knew that many felt excluded from exploring priesthood for one reason or another: their background, their education, their age, their sex, their self-esteem, divorce and remarriage. To see initial difficulties overcome and a vocation to ordained local ministry emerge in a person who the Church or society had marginalized for one reason or another was a constant joy to Brian. Not surprisingly, all the candidates valued his warmth, care and honesty through this difficult process.

Alec had worked all his ministry as a stipendiary priest in the inner city. He had contributed to the debate that had led to the report, *Faith in the City*, and was keenly involved with issues of community development. He had been aware of the previous experiment in ordained local ministry that had been initiated by Ted Roberts and fully understood the need for the ministry of the local inner-city church to be indigenous. During the working week, the community was full of experts who lived in the suburbs but travelled into the parish to teach in the schools, to provide social services and policing. He was the only professional who lived in the parish and he believed passionately that his job was not to be the professional priest and holy man, but to enable the local church to work for the Kingdom of God in that place. That meant that he must work *with* rather than *for* the church community in order that they could then work *with* rather than *for* the local community, providing a truly indigenous ministry that was yeast and salt to the people who lived in that place, striving with them for justice and peace. Alec was himself naturally suspicious of church hierarchy and dismissive of the expert culture that surrounded colleges and universities. When asked to work as the bishop's officer in his diocese to develop local ministry he insisted that a great deal of the decision making surrounding the selection and training of candidates should, where possible, remain with each local community. He resisted from the beginning procedures of training and assessment redolent of what he called 'the middle-class book culture' and set out to design a course that placed a great deal more emphasis on oral assessment and group presentations.

Adrian is a countryman born and bred and, having discovered his true vocation as a country priest, he has devoted himself to making sure that the suburban church remembers and learns to value rural ministry. His devout hope is that God will continue to be praised in our villages in the next millennium, just as he has been in the last. He has also yet to visit a settlement that is the better for not having a church building! At one stage it seemed possible to him that, with a bit of encouragement and goodwill, a version of the old system could survive. Then he read a paper by Nigel Robertson-Glasgow which set out in simple diagrammatic form the difference between a parish with a resident parson and a parish without one. It dawned on Adrian that, if a vicar is not resident, the traditional model for Anglican ministry collapses like a pack of cards. The only reasonable alternative is that local people in small villages should minister to each other. It was the germ of this idea that eventually led to the setting up of a local ministry scheme in his diocese, which has more than its fair share of tiny parishes.

So Adrian's original motivation for backing local ministry was essentially practical and conservative. He wanted to see the witness of the Church maintained in the villages. The educational and theological implications of the hare he started back in 1993 have, as it were, crept up on him unawares. He has therefore been a late recruit to the revolutionary cause, a development which has been greatly helped by being able to talk it all through with enthusiastic colleagues.

Each officer has become involved in local ministry training and development for a variety of reasons and from a variety of backgrounds. They all, however, share certain values in common even though each would put them in a different order of importance. Each is passionate in the belief that the Church will need to change radically if it is to meet the challenges of the new millennium. All believe that the Holy Spirit is leading the Church into new ways of working and new ways of understanding itself that are nevertheless deeply rooted in the scriptures and early life of the Church. All believe that human beings are called to grow into maturity in Christ Jesus and so be enabled to fulfil God's will for them. All believe that the Church is called to be a living body where the gifts of all are valued and used. All believe that the Church needs to repent of the way that it has robbed the baptized of the ministry that Christ has entrusted to his Church and put it into the hands of a professional ministerial caste of bishop, priest and deacon. All believe that the Church exists only for its mission to the world, to serve people in Christ's name and to witness to the salvation that he brings; and all believe that the way to achieve this is through unlocking the resources of the local church with the vision of local ministry.

From Pioneers to Specialists

Most of those who are involved in local ministry would recognize that they are pioneers. Many had been parish priests who recognized the need for change and welcomed the opportunity to help to bring this about. Most have skills in adult education and some have taught theology, but few have been specialists in theological education and all have had to learn as they go along. However, as diocesan schemes grow and mature, there is an increasing need for those who manage courses to have a degree of theological expertise and practical ministerial experience. They also need to have specialist knowledge and an understanding of education design, teaching and assessment strategies, and also, of course, accreditation, moderation and inspection procedures.

For many, the move that the local ministry officer is inevitably making from pioneer to specialist is both inevitable and welcome, but to others it is, by its very nature, inappropriate. The sense of riding this new animal by the seat of the pants is still exciting to many and they inevitably mourn its gradual passing. However, the need for guaranteed and consistent standards of selection and training is for others a sign that local ministry is itself maturing and gaining a wider acceptance. For some, the hallmark of local ministry is that it is an affirmation of the laity and life experience, and it helps to break the clerical mould. They are suspicious of the Ministry Division and fear yet another sell-out to the clerical bureaucracy. For others the challenge is precisely to use specialist education skills to promote and maintain the pristine vision of local ministry supported by theological and educational rigour and integrity.

What Kind of Training?

Many officers had begun planning courses for training individuals and teams for their new roles in local ministry with blank pieces of paper. The truth is that, in the early days, there was little experience to share and no established practice to follow. However, the values that officers brought to the task guaranteed that certain features soon emerged that were to be common to the courses that they eventually created. In most courses a significant element of the training would take place in the local context; courses would be designed so that they could utilize the experience that individuals brought to the training process; opportunity would be given for students to reflect upon the local context in which they operated; learning would take place in teams or groups and would be seen as a collaborative rather than an individualistic endeavour; students would be taught the practical tasks of ministry; and the syllabus would integrate areas of study that the traditional curriculum separated out into subject areas. Also, a greater emphasis was placed on students' ability to reflect upon themselves, their learning and their developing ministry. Many officers understood the educational process and were keen to design and operate courses that promoted local, practical, collaborative, contextual and reflective learning.

The problem that many faced at an early stage was how to provide quality theological input to these courses. It would probably be fair to say that many failed to do so convincingly. Some dioceses operated in areas that did not have university or college departments which could provide such expertise, and some that did have these found them unwilling to co-operate in these new and questionable enterprises.

Paul would admit that the pilot scheme for ordained local ministry that he designed for his diocese was a good piece of adult education. He believed that the experiential learning that the course enabled, and reflection on the nature of community church and the individual, prepared candidates very well for their new ministry while enabling parishes to build effective ministry teams. However, even though the material was integrated in an interdisciplinary way, he wondered if the knowledge and understanding that the students had gained of the Church's scripture, tradition, liturgy and pastoral practice was adequate. It had come, in the first instance, from his own learning and the learning of other parish priests in the diocese. It was, therefore, possible that it was incomplete and even out of date. He was stung by the comment of one academic who noted that she rarely saw a book in the clergy studies that she visited that was less than fifteen years old. He himself had few. However, it was difficult for Paul to give his students access to the latest thinking with the resources available to him and in a form that was acceptable.

The scheme in John's diocese was very different. It was not constructed to set up, train and support local ministry teams but was rather concerned with individuals who emerged from parishes to train as OLMs. John felt that it was essential that a local group be formed around the candidate to support their learning and provide a context for their reflection and study. However, he also felt that it was important to use the resources of the regional course which trained NSMs and stipendiary clergy. He therefore set his OLM scheme up in a different way. Students undertook their training in three different contexts. Some elements of the course were undertaken with NSMs and stipendiary clergy on the regional training course, some were undertaken with other members of the diocese on existing diocesan training courses and some were undertaken with other local people in a local training group. This gave students access to current theological thinking but proved very difficult to manage in practice. One of the problems was that each element of the training was undertaken in a different way so that students had to deal with very different teaching and learning strategies at very different standards in each part of their learning. Integrating these proved problematic.

When Graham took over from Paul, he set about providing the scheme with a more solid and up to date theological base. He developed a good relationship with the regional course and Federation of Theological Colleges, and they provided the course with academic consultants who helped the course staff to write, deliver and mark various elements of the syllabus. When Bill took over from John, he stopped using diocesan courses, developed the local training group and began to work more closely with the regional course. In this way he was able to provide a more co-ordinated package of learning for the students.

The main challenge for Kate was not training OLMs at all; it was training teams of lay people to share leadership of ministry with their incumbent. As a teacher herself she knew all about modern educational method and she recognized its value for the job in hand. Her problem was that the teaching material she had inherited was 'old style', and both her colleagues and most of the tutors available to help were used to 'old-style' methods of teaching. Over the years she has managed to rewrite most of the modules and to re-educate most of the tutors so that the course and the delivery are now pretty satisfactory.

But satisfactory for what? The aim of the course is to train local people to enable the ministry of the whole congregation. At bottom it aims to build up their confidence, to give them the experience of working as a team and to help them to mature spiritually. It is not a course in credal Christianity or in clerical formation but it is exactly what is needed for the job in hand. She would also maintain that it is, in fact, vital for the training of effective OLMs but her problem is to explain to the authorities how it meshes in with the more academic courses others have to study if they are to be ordained.

Do We Go for Course Accreditation?

From the beginning, courses have had to balance local learning with learning in a broader context. Both elements are important. Students need to be able to contextualize their learning and the local group supports this process. Equally, even those who are going to express their lay ministry or priesthood in the local context need to experience a broader vision. Work in regional or diocesan groups is also therefore important. Some courses were designed from the beginning to train local ministry teams. Some never envisaged ordained local ministry. Some train ordained local ministers with readers and those called to other forms of lay ministry. Other courses train individual OLMs who emerge from local parishes. In each case, provision is made for local and broader learning and experience. Because of the need for specialist theological knowledge to support good educational practice, many partnerships have developed between regional courses, theological colleges and university departments. Some have worked eagerly for such partnerships and others have shunned them. Two factors are often involved in these decisions. The first relates to the philosophy and practice of the courses and colleges in the different areas. Some embrace values consistent with local ministry and some do not. The second factor relates to the philosophy of the local ministry scheme. Some are open to exploration and some feel that the education for ministry that they are providing for local people could only be disrupted and damaged by the involvement of academic institutions.

After several years developing local ministry in the inner city,

Alec still feels this way. Like the authors of *Stranger in the Wings* he wants to stress the particularity of the vocation to OLM and to insist that it be collaborative and open to everyone whatever their educational background. In fact, he feels passionately that OLM must not be allowed to be emasculated by 'the system'. He points out that even without academic accreditation it is difficult enough to defend the 'ministerial virginity' of OLMs against the pressures on them to become clerics and he vividly remembers how the OLM candidates were treated by the stipendiaries on their first residential. He is, therefore, deeply suspicious of the temptations offered by academic bits of paper and agrees with *Stranger in the Wings* that a key issue is what level of validation is envisaged. If it is too high you are excluding the people you most want to keep, and if it is too low it is not worth the effort anyway.

Graham has taken a very different view. Having established a good working arrangement between his scheme and the regional course and theological colleges, he explored the possibility of university accreditation at Dip HE level. He felt that this would add rigour to the course while helping the diocese and his students to recognize that the course they were undertaking was of a similar basic standard to that required in other forms of initial clergy training. He found a well-established and respected university that was prepared to accredit the course which the diocese operated without making fundamental changes to its modules, its teaching strategies and its assessment procedures. Indeed, the university was prepared to use its resources to develop new procedures in line with the values of the course, helping the course to assess local, collaborative, reflective learning with rigour and to a recognized academic standard. To date, Graham would argue that the course has not become 'more academic' and is still being successfully completed by people without traditional qualifications or significant prior learning. He is thrilled with the process and feels it is a way forward for many schemes.

Ministry Division Inspections

Schemes are not left to their own devices. The occasional paper 'ACCM 22' preceded the widespread accreditation of OLM schemes. It sought to bring clarity and consistency to the training offered by colleges and regional courses through a process of accreditation which values the diversity of approach offered by different institutions while demanding consistent standards of ministerial education and formation. 'ACCM 22' was, and still is, a remarkable document which sought (p. 9) 'a unifying purpose, content and style for ministerial training which is rooted in the mission of the Church to the world'. When OLM schemes were accredited by the House of Bishops, the ACCM 22 procedure was adopted for them. All colleges, courses and schemes are therefore accredited every five years using the same basic process.

The Ministry Division is charged with the responsibility for accrediting and monitoring OLM Schemes. Schemes that train OLMs are asked to submit accreditation documents against three questions that were originally outlined in ACCM 22. The questions are:

- What ordained ministry does the Church of England require?
- What is the shape of the education programme best suited for equipping people to exercise this ministry?
- What are the appropriate means of assessing suitability for the exercise of this ministry?

These are pretty searching questions which are not going to be answered in five minutes! Those schemes which also train readers are subject to reader moderation, and many principals of theological colleges and regional courses have university accreditation and moderation to manage as well. Given these demands, it is hardly surprising that many officers feel that their work is becoming more 'specialist', and they are seriously worried that the demands of the Ministry Division are becoming increasingly difficult for schemes to meet. While some would see this as a guarantee that OLM schemes do not offer 'second rate' courses with questionable standards, all acknowledge that the limited resources available make the process particularly difficult.

This is exacerbated by the requirement that colleges, courses and schemes should be inspected by the House of Bishops' inspectorate at five yearly intervals. These are now timed to coincide with a new submission, so that an inspection will occur at the end of a five-year period and the results of the inspection will be fed into the new submission. Even colleges and courses find that this process is time consuming and demanding of staff resources, but schemes are rarely staffed sufficiently to account for such demands, and this adds considerably to the difficulties.

Jim does not conceal the fact that the Ministry Division inspection was a nerve-racking experience. It involved filling in a 32 page questionnaire with 256 questions. He says that the inspection dominated the life of the scheme for a year – and they were lucky; it could have taken two years! He says that you have to make sure that the inspectors fully get linked into the life of the scheme or they won't really understand what they see. He also advises that it is best to keep a diary of events as an insurance policy against unjustified calumnies! When the draft report arrives, officers have to drop everything and respond at once. Despite all this, he says it was good for the scheme because it made them revisit the fundamentals but he admits that the officer-hours involved in the process were incalculable.

Jim is responsible for a scheme which is largely to do with training OLMs. Kate runs a scheme which on average trains only three OLMs a year as against forty lay team members. So far she has only had to resubmit for the ACCM 22 and, like Jim, she says that it was a valuable experience which helped the diocese to iron out a number of serious problems that had been shelved for far too long. On the other hand, she came close to having a breakdown – and her colleagues did not enjoy the experience either! It is no exaggeration to say that the ACCM 22 nearly brought a thriving scheme to a standstill. It involved hundreds of officer hours and meant that a raft of important things were left undone, all for the sake of three candidates a year. For a diocese which sees local ministry as first and foremost a means of shifting the church towards all-member ministry it has to be asked whether the OLM 'add-on' is worth the effort involved.

The Officer and the Diocese

RESOURCING LOCAL MINISTRY

Perhaps at the heart of the resource problem is the question of ownership. Inevitably, local ministry must be owned by local churches and the diocese that supports and enables them. Each local ministry scheme is a diocesan scheme. Many train OLMs, readers and other local lay ministers and are therefore account-able to the national structures which support and moderate OLM and reader training as well as to the bishop in his diocese. Schemes are new and, therefore, nobody as yet agrees how they should be staffed and financed. The Ministry Division recom-mend a teaching ratio of one staff member to six students in theological colleges and one staff member to fifteen on regional courses. Graham has 210 students on his local ministry scheme, 24 of whom are OLM candidates, 20 reader candidates, 12 awaiting a selection conference and 80 still working on the first year of the course prior to selection. He has, until recently, worked as a full-time officer with the help of a secretary/adminis-trator and two other part-time staff members. Like other local ministry courses, he covets the considerably higher grants made to colleges and courses and the staffing that they can employ as a result.

In truth, dioceses do not understand the need for staffing. Bishops still believe that OLM courses can be run by one officer who is also required to run three small country parishes. They fail to recognize the levels of expertise required by officers and tend to compare schemes with courses run by other diocesan officers rather than with those run by regional schemes or col-leges. By and large, they are still failing to recognize that schemes cannot be run to the high standards demanded of the Ministry Division without proper resourcing. Graham has survived due to the goodwill of his regional course and college colleagues and the endless goodwill of the parochial clergy who support the course at every opportunity. He is also getting a full-time colleague in the near future but is still concerned that schemes are being squeezed between the growing demands of moderation and inspection and the poor resourcing by dioceses. He fears that this may lead to the demise of many schemes and may hinder the development of ordained local ministry in England.

MATCHING LOCAL MINISTRY TO THE CONTEXT

The churches have been gestating local ministry for a generation and, as we have seen, it is emerging in a whole variety of different forms, depending on what has gone before. In Lincoln and Gloucester dioceses, local ministry was initially driven by the needs of rural parishes. In Manchester and Southwark dioceses, it evolved to meet the felt need of inner-city parishes for indigenous priesthood. In Nebraska and Michigan, USA, and in a number of dioceses in New Zealand and Australia, the Church could no longer support financially small, usually rural, congregations, sometimes hundreds of miles apart, who were a constant drain on increasingly scarce resources. For them it was a question of local ministry or closure. In Salisbury and Winchester dioceses, with their well-developed schemes for lay pastoral assistants, local ministry when it comes is bound to be coloured by the structures already in operation. This illustrates how important it is for the officer to sort out where local ministry fits into the diocesan strategy.

The first duty of local ministry officers is, therefore, to catch hold of a vision appropriate to the needs of their particular diocese and to make it their own. The second duty, however, is not to make the vision so possessively their own that they cannot respond flexibly to changing needs. In New Zealand, local ministry is seen as response to the needs of small congregations. Theologically it is just as appropriate a model for large congregations but it will need a good deal of lateral thinking on the part of diocesan officers if they are to adapt their existing schemes to a different context. Similarly, in Gloucester Diocese the original scheme had to go back into the melting-pot and be recast in a variety of moulds before being flexible enough to meet the needs of large urban parishes.

Local ministry is such a new invention that diocesan officers usually have to start from scratch. In a number of cases they have never worked a local ministry parish themselves before they start telling others how to do it! Ian had experience in the field of adult education. His plans for training local ministry teams were excellent and the training modules were exemplary. He was given the job of introducing local ministry into the diocese and he visited a number of other schemes elsewhere. But he hadn't ever worked as a sole incumbent or as a rural parish priest and so his expectations of both clergy and lay volunteers were spectacularly unrealistic. Partly because of his optimistic advice, the scheme was grossly under-resourced and, without adequate support, parishes ran into trouble, felt abandoned and became disillusioned. Nothing fails like failure.

Richard was trained as an industrial chaplain. He was therefore very up in 'contacts', 'structures' and 'business management techniques'. Given the job of establishing a team in every parish by the year 2000, he set to with a will only to find that, if local is to mean anything, congregations will want to work in the way that suits them, whatever the diocesan blueprint may decree.

Bill was a rural dean and was regarded as something of a revolutionary back in his home diocese; but then 'home' had turned its face against any radical change for a generation. He moved to a new diocese to join the diocesan local ministry team which was already way down the continuum line towards all-member ministry. No dog-collars in sight! It took him two years to assimilate the new context and one of the things he quickly discovered was that his own view of ministry was distinctly conservative. He sometimes caught himself wondering whether he wasn't, at heart, a dyed-in-the-wool cleric!

Jane and Stephen had some hands-on experience of local ministry in one diocese but, on transfer to another diocese, they soon found themselves at sea. The structures were more flexible (or wishy-washy), teaching methods were so interactive that the links with the set module often seemed hazy in the extreme, and the role of the clergy was definitely relegated to the back boiler. Even key words like 'facilitate', 'tutor', 'business meeting' meant something significantly different. It was almost as difficult to unlearn old ways as it was to learn new ones.

RELATIONS WITH THE BISHOP

One of the ironies is that 'local' ministry has to depend on the diocese. People at grassroots' level may have bright ideas but they are unlikely to survive the first winter without the enthusiastic support of the bishop and his staff. And, as with all diocesan policy, the nature of the local ministry 'vision' in a particular diocese depends a great deal on the views (some would say prejudices!) of the bishop and his staff. This is right and proper, since at the core of local ministry is the assumption that the OLM and team will be formally authorized by the bishop. (In a number of New Zealand dioceses one way of expressing this close connection is to say that the bishop is an ex officio member of all local teams.)

As we have seen, there are a number of options open to a bishop. Local ministry can be seen as a strategy for survival which bolsters up the status quo or it can be seen as a radical challenge to existing structures. It can be adopted as just another stage in the move from stipendiary to non-stipendiary ministry or it can be adopted as a way of breaking the clerical mould.

Local ministry officers, who have plenty of time to think about it, are likely to veer to the radical end of the spectrum, or will at least have a clear idea of what *they* think local ministry should be about. The bishop and his staff, on the other hand, have a much wider agenda and are unlikely to see things with the same clarity as the officers. And yet the officers can only operate that model of local ministry which is supported by the bishop. It is fertile soil for frustration and the problem is compounded when bishops move.

In one very large diocese, the complexity of theory, theology and personality are such that there are no less than three schemes, each with its own set of rules; and, in practice, there is a fourth scheme administered by the very able (and very determined) director of the local ordination course! In another diocese, with a long history of local ministry, the arrival of a new bishop who was not afraid to ask difficult questions and who could easily match the officers intellectually has led ultimately to a complete revision of the course and to the departure of the director of the scheme. In another diocese, the arrival of a new diocesan bishop swiftly led to a serious confrontation and, though heads have not ultimately rolled, the scheme has been completely revised to meet the concerns of the bishop. In a fourth diocese, it was the bishop and archdeacon who moved elsewhere in quick succession and who took the vision with them, leaving a vacuum which newly imported officers have had to try to fill. In yet another case, where the bishop and his staff have put local ministry firmly at the centre of diocesan strategy, the officers still struggle to 'educate' the senior staff both in the theory and the implications of adopting it. Episcopal sermons, articles in the magazine, speeches at synod, are scanned to see how well the educational process is going!

It is, therefore, very important indeed for the officer to ensure full and frank discussion with the bishop and his staff about what exactly they are being asked to deliver. It is also important that whatever decisions are reached are properly costed and accepted by the Board of Finance. As we have seen, the cost of training OLM is usually grossly underestimated and the same is often true for the training and maintaining of local ministry teams. Not only does Kate have to persuade the bishop of what she is about, she also has to watch her back in relation to the Budget Review Committee and to defend the cost of the enterprise in the face of the 'jealousy' of other budget holders. It is amazing how much officer-time at ten pounds an hour can be spent on trying to reduce the telephone bill by five pounds a quarter!

The Officer at Work

HOOKING THE INCUMBENT

When things go well it is very exciting indeed to be a local ministry officer. Serious work begins with a visit to an incumbent. Sometimes it is a matter of pushing on an open door. Robin and James were both fully convinced that the Holy Spirit was urging the Church towards collaborative ministry and they were both determined that by the time they retired, their parishes would be on board. The job of the officer was more to temper their enthusiasm than to kindle it. Emma, on the other hand, needed to be assured that going for a team would not devalue the work already being done by a variety of people in the parish. Kevin seemed exhausted and was clearly longing for help in what he saw as an impossible job; in his case it was the clarity of vision and enthusiasm of the churchwardens which persuaded the officer that the idea was worth pursuing in the parish.

THE PARISH AUDIT

If, and only if, the incumbent is persuaded, will the officer consider making a presentation to the parish about local ministry. As with all presentations, the experience can be painful or it can be thrilling. The parish of Monkton had just been delivered from a thirty-five-year incumbency. Faithful survivors and enthusiastic newcomers alike were raring to go. The audience listened with rapt attention, the questions came thick and fast and were virtually all positive. Officer and vicar went home very elated.

Five meetings with the enthusiastic incumbent, the churchwardens and the key PCC members of Browton seemed to have laid the foundations for a major approach to the whole congregation. This was to take the form of evening meetings during Lent. Six people came to the first meeting and eight to the second. Back to the drawing board!

The benefice of Waterwell put on two parish days to try to get a feel for where God had used them in the past, how he was using them now and where he might be calling them to go in the next century; and would local ministry help them to get there? Lots of people came along, and a good time was had by all. Not everyone was in favour but there was a good clean fight, and the best thing was that people's minds were changed – the Holy Spirit was at work revealing himself to his people. A couple of key moments stand out. There were two distinct views within the parishes of what had happened in the past. A 'time line' was used and, as people silently pondered what they had written, the past was affirmed, the disagreements were seen to be less important than had been thought, and one could sense 'the past' beginning to become 'history'. The other key moment was when the incumbent, a dual-role officer, was induced by the use of role-play to pour out her frustrations concerning an impossible job and, for the first time, the laity perceived the loneliness of the clerical pedestal and resolved to do something practical about it.

But there is pain and worry too. The powerful young incumbent of Under-edge was determined that everyone in the benefice – and that meant everyone – was going to be 100 per cent in favour of local ministry. During the parish audit days it became crystal clear to the officer that, while one parish was in favour and one would go along with it, the third just didn't feel comfortable with the idea at all. It wasn't that they were articulately and determinedly opposed, just that they had only recently lost their resident vicar and were still in mourning for a past era. But they were not allowed to mourn. Whenever they tried to express their hesitation they were 'suppressed' and even their (divided) vote at the end of the day was manipulated so that it seemed to express an enthusiasm which was certainly not there. The officer remonstrated with the incumbent and was so worried about the situation that he seriously considered recommending to the bishop that the parish should not be allowed to choose a team. After protracted consultation with other officers, the decision was taken not to intervene and the good thing is that the incumbent has become a firm friend of the local ministry enterprise; he is even beginning to listen and learn! Only time will tell whether the third parish remains a 'thorn in the flesh' or is transfigured into 'an angel unawares'.

THE PCC DECISION

No parish should take on local ministry 'unadvisedly, lightly or wantonly, but in the fear of God'. Hence the final debate in the PCC about whether it should or shouldn't be embraced is rightly serious and tense, and can go either way. At Castleton, the debate had reached an impasse and, after months of preparation, it seemed that the misunderstandings of a few would frustrate the aspirations of the many. A reader, who had taken very little part in the preparatory meetings but who was highly respected for his sound common sense, broke the frustrated silence. 'Here is the diocese offering us what is, in effect, thousands of pounds worth of training and help for free. I think we'd be mad to turn it down.' He carried the day. At Riverside, on the other hand, a small minority were angry and frightened. Deeply hurt that they no longer had 'a vicar of their own', they believed that local ministry was part of a devious plan by the diocese to deprive them of all clerical and pastoral care. They boycotted the very encouraging public meetings but came in force to the PCC which had to make the decision. They persuaded other members and the motion to proceed was defeated by eight votes to six. Not surprisingly, it was a very distressing evening for the officer and the incumbent.

After six months working with the incumbent and the PCC steering group of the parish of Underdown the officer came to the last major meeting at which the great decision was to be taken. All seemed to be going well and even the most searching questions seemed to have been answered satisfactorily until, at the very last minute, the incumbent intervened to say that he felt that the scheme was inappropriate for their situation and he could not recommend that the PCC say yes to it.

CHOOSING THE TEAM

If the scheme is one which involves a leadership or an education team the next stage is to identify the right candidates. Choosing the team is always an exciting time, and a frightening one. Usually there seems at first to be a wide field of choice but it soon becomes apparent that, though everyone is in favour, everyone imagines that someone else is going to do it. The officer has to be as calm and collected as the father of the bride on her wedding day, with a steady faith that it will all come together eventually. At Bridgetown, there had been over fifty people nominated but, with two hours to go to the first meeting of the team, there were still two vacancies to be filled. Should the incumbent invite the Free Church minister (who had been nominated) to be a member of the team, or should he not?

In considerable trepidation, with considerable reservations and with a liberal use of arrow prayer, the incumbent and the officer together called on the minister. Within ten minutes all was settled and the team was complete. True, it was not the team they had planned. Instead of being an Anglican team it had become a Christian team, and one could only guess at the joy in heaven. Instead of assembling for a requiem, an hour later everyone was celebrating a miracle!

TRAINING THE TEAM

If a team is formed, the officer is immediately involved in a round of negotiations, plans and compromises. Training usually has a local and a diocesan component. The diocesan component should be easy enough because the dates have been fixed well in advance. The trouble is that you can be sure some members of the team will already have something else in their diaries. For a year the new team at Dowton tiptoed around each other and could not seem to arrive at a working arrangement. They had missed their team-building weekend, diaries being full, and it was only a year later – when they genuinely had no excuse – that they managed that particular residential. Everything immediately slotted into place! Getting dates in the diary is a perennial problem. On one occasion at Castleton it took twenty-five minutes to engineer agreement about six sessions, and then these were spread over four months.

The local element of the course is usually delivered in the parish by a tutor coming from outside. Valleytown worked through their modules well enough but by the time they had experienced four different tutors with four different teaching styles they went on strike. Stanbury, by contrast, had the same tutor throughout and they complained that the teaching was 'rather thin in places'. At Olderton, the tutor had a major fall-out with the vicar. Sorting out what module comes next, letting the office know, ensuring that the book-box has arrived before the last session and finding a tutor who 'fits' and is happy in their work, is all ultimately the responsibility of the officer. It is a job which requires the wisdom of Solomon and the patience of Job.

The officer will also usually be responsible, with the incumbent, for the nurturing of team members. They invariably also find that they will need to support the incumbent who, after the first flush of enthusiasm, tends to be a bit aghast at what he or she has let themselves in for. At Kingsley, where two clergy were involved, the officer decided to have a working lunch with the tutor and the clergy at the end of each module. It was expensive in terms of time and petrol but it headed off two major crises within the first year and was rewarding at a deep level.

Local teams inevitably begin to form a relationship of trust with the officer, which develops if part of the process includes a yearly personal review. This is fine, but the officer does need to be aware that there are dangers. The job of the officer is to facilitate the birth of local ministry, not to act as nanny to the team. It can be extremely difficult to allow the team the freedom to make mistakes. The team at Valleytown had been mandated for a year. Its members had made the most of their training and were devastated when it finished; so devastated that they couldn't seem to galvanize themselves into going it alone. One minister left and the other quietly returned to his old ways, as if the team did not exist. The instinct of the officer responsible was to bang on the table, call an immediate meeting and read the riot act. 'Nanny' to the rescue! He was saved from this by the arrival of a new minister who needed to be 'joined' to the team. Everyone saw the point of having a meeting and of inviting the officer to come too. The 'innocent' questions of the new minister soon revealed that this particular emperor sported only the scantiest underwear and the officer was able to step in with the flip-chart and help to facilitate a new beginning from the sidelines.

A JOB WITH NO BOUNDARIES

Of course you don't get the view from the top of the mountain without a hard climb. Not only do officers have to run teams and nurture them, discover OLMs and train them, there are also all the other back-room jobs that need to be done if the summit is to be reached. Someone has to run the study days and residentials, create and monitor new modules, plan, chase and organise, and sit on the relevant diocesan committees. Above all, everyone needs to meet each other, make plans with each other and care for each other so that we may all journey in the same direction.

The officer's job is like quicksilver – ungraspable. No sooner is one door bolted and barred than another flies open. Five years ago, one diocese launched their scheme with a flourish. Having borrowed their training material from Lincoln, it seemed to them, in their naiveté, that all they had to do was drum up custom and then deliver the goods. Instead, they have needed to:

- recruit good office staff and set up an efficient office
- recruit tutors and train them
- revise the module material
- develop material on team working
- organize and develop study days and residentials
- devise a sophisticated system for testing whether parishes are truly ready for local ministry
- assess members and prepare teams for episcopal mandating
- invent a mandating service and ensure that it is a BIG event
- develop the job of team facilitator
- nearly go potty trying to rewrite their ACCM 22
- train their first raft of OLMs.

Now, having somehow, against all the odds, got the show on the road, it's time for the whole thing to start again. Teams need to add new members, the earliest ones are coming up for reinspection and remandating and, next year, there will be a full-scale Ministry Division inspection. How rightly we speak of 'the pilgrimage' of a scheme, for none has yet arrived.

The huffing-and-puffing race against time to do a job which is undoable is not helped if the officer happens to be exercising a dual-role ministry. Most dual-role officers are schizophrenic in that they spend half their time complaining about the frustration of not being able to do either job properly and the other half on an emotional high because the one job so obviously complements the other.

Nor is it easy for those who have to work with them. Both full-time officers and local teams find it frustrating having to deal with these Cheshire cat-like creatures who, whenever you really want them, seem to be off taking funerals. On the other hand, they do find it reassuring to be dealing with people who have hands-on experience of parish life.

THE AWESOME RESPONSIBILITY OF IT ALL

At some stage, most officers are filled with a sense of awe about what they are doing. They are in the business of rubbishing an old and tried model of ministry which has been exercised by faithful priests and congregations for a century and which has been remarkably successful in 'keeping alive the rumour of God in a godless generation'. They recommend replacing it with a model which, while it is strong on theory and even theology, is very short on practical experience. Local ministry could be the salvation of the Church, but then it could herald a return of self-destructive congregationalism.

Officers are also in the business of gambling with people's lives. They are challenging individuals to give up time and other commitments in pursuit of the crock of gold at the end of the rainbow. It is agonizing enough for the stipendiary clergy involved who have painfully to unlearn old ways, but at least they are paid for it and in the last resort can move back to pastures old and familiar. But, like Jesus himself, officers are also asking lay people to give up family and friends, spare time and hobbies, even wealth and alternative opportunities for the sake of a gospel which, though we believe it to be of the Holy Spirit, could conceivably be a figment of a lively human imagination.

There was no doubt that the enlarged parish of Valleyside could do with a local ministry team. There was a big pastoral job to be done and, on top of that, another start-again-from-scratch parish was added to the benefice. The incumbent was enthusiastic but not a very good organizer and, from the start, he was uncertain of his own role within the team. Sometimes he tended to dominate them, and sometimes he left them to their own devices. The preparation work for choosing the team was unfortunately left until the last minute and there were pitifully few nominations. Only four who were asked to join the team said yes. In retrospect, the officer should have stepped in at this stage to call a temporary halt but, after discussion, it was agreed to allow the commissioning to go ahead. For a year the team sacrificed time, energy and prayer to try to make the thing work. The officer, realizing what difficulties they were having, enlisted the support of a succession of experienced outside consultants to see if anything could be done, all to no avail. The most that was achieved was that, when the team finally dissolved, it was a matter of mutual agreement rather than a damaging volcanic eruption. For this parish, and for a group of committed Christians, local ministry had proved to be, not a path into the Promised Land, but a dead end.

But, despite all the problems, most officers thoroughly enjoy their job. They feel themselves to be at the cutting edge of the Church's ministry doing something really worthwhile. The best thing of all is to see lives change. Running a weekend on personal spirituality when 80 per cent of the evaluation sheets say that the last two days have been nothing short of a revelation, or leading a study day on the Bible which grapples with deep theological issues and begins to change inherited prejudices (and still they say it was really good!), or tutoring a module on worship when Anglicans and Free Church people speak openly to each other about what they do in church and, for the first time, glimpse the richness of diversity, or, most wonderful of all, seeing earthbound caterpillars turn into aerial butterflies, is a memorable experience!

6

⟳⟳⟳⟳⟳

The Bishops' Tale

This chapter tells of the way in which the bishops of the Church of England have engaged with local ministry. It acknowledges the challenge that faces bishops to express episcopacy in a collaborative way and recognizes the role that the national church plays in the development of OLM and reader ministry. It then charts the way in which various bishops have nurtured local ministry in a variety of different ways in their dioceses and the issues that they have encountered along the way.

An International Perspective

In February 1999, Burlingaine in California was the venue for an International Symposium on 'Local Collaborative Ministry'. Anglican dioceses from the United States, Canada, Australia, New Zealand, Kenya and England were all represented. It was interesting to note that the majority of dioceses outside England were represented by a team that included the diocesan bishop, whereas dioceses from England were, by and large, represented by diocesan officers. Only one suffragan bishop from England was present. This was partly due to the very different context in which Anglican dioceses operate and are resourced. Diocesan officers responsible for education and training rarely exist outside England where dioceses often cover huge geographical areas but contain significantly fewer church congregations. Consequently, those bishops who came from these dioceses had much more 'hands-on' responsibility for the way that ministry was developing and for the training that supported it. Most of those dioceses represented were comfortable to call themselves 'local ministry' dioceses and were committed to collaborative ministerial practice. Each had programmes in place to enable and support the development of local ministry within their various congregations and each included provision for what has, in England, become known as ordained local ministry.

During the symposium, the bishops were able to come together in a workshop environment to share some of the joys, difficulties and issues that surround the work of a bishop in a 'local ministry' diocese. Perhaps not surprisingly, many stories were told and, less surprisingly still, much of the conversation revolved around the role of a bishop. There was general agreement that the concept of collaborative ministry challenges what Stewart Zabriskie, present at the symposium and author of the book *Total Ministry* calls (Zabriskie, 1995, p. 38) the '"Star System" that has attended the selection and treatment of bishops over the generations: the raising up and setting apart that . . . deny the co-ordination of community'. If episcopacy can be freed from a traditional hierarchical concept, questions are raised about the way in which a ministry of leadership and oversight can best be expressed in a collaborative environment. If the role of the bishop is no longer to be the one who leads from the front and articulates the way that he wants the diocese to proceed, what alternatives are viable and productive? Where is the vision of the diocese located? And in what ways can a bishop express the traditional episcopal roles of 'defender of the faith' and disciplinarian? The question also surfaced about the role of the bishop in society. One of the bishop's traditional roles has been to focus the mission of the Church in society. Isn't it, therefore, still incumbent on a bishop to pursue a personal ministry in support of kingdom values among those who have influence and authority for social policy and government in society at large?

Although the workshop did not produce a consistent set of answers to these questions it was interesting to observe the way that the bishops were struggling with both language and structure. It was noteworthy, for example, that many insisted that people in their dioceses call them by their first or 'Christian' names, rather than by the title 'bishop'. They did this as a matter of policy because it was the name given to them at their baptism and represented the commonality that all share in Christ. They were

John, Brian or Stewart who had been called to episcopacy but who never lost the essential status that was the key to all ministry, being 'baptized into Christ Jesus'. This seemingly minor point seemed to represent a significant shift in the way that they understood their role and wanted to express it in the diocese.

Indeed, this was part of a process of exploring what it might mean to be a 'servant leader' and, in the sense that Jesus uses the term in St John's gospel, a 'friend' to the diocese. The friends of Jesus are called to work together in love and bear fruit for the kingdom. The bishop as 'friend' therefore shares a common status within the baptized community but acts, in role, as the focus of its accountability as a missionary, serving community. Such a servant-leader both listens to and holds up the vision of the diocese, enabling and supporting the full participation of every baptized person. Bishop Zabriskie has explored his role in the Nevada diocese as servant-leader and uses the symbol of yeast (that which enables the dough to rise up to its full potential) and gluten (that which binds the dough together into a whole) to describe his ministry. Such language is radically different to the parental and even princely images that have traditionally accompanied the episcopal role.

Key to these discussions was the way in which those present felt that they should exercise authority. It was clear to all that the bishop will always hold a pivotal position in the diocese, able to create an environment in which individuals can be enabled or disabled, encouraged or manipulated. Consecrated to be a focus of authority within the Church, those called to work in dioceses committed to collaborative ministerial practice were clearly searching for new ways to structure and manage their dioceses while remaining true to the values that they espoused. In order to be effective in a role which demands the oversight of the Christian community, the bishops inevitably looked for ways in which the burden and the joys of episcopacy could be shared with others. Indeed, there was a discussion at the symposium about the use of the term 'shared episcopacy'. Some felt the phrase was appropriate but others were uncomfortable with it because they felt that the concept of sharing retained the basic notion of individual ownership. Quite simply, something that is shared still belongs to the person who shares it and therefore can be taken back at any time. It is better to use the term 'extended episcopacy' to recognize that episcopacy can be expressed by others in the diocese with and on behalf of the bishop. In local ministry dioceses abroad, episcopacy is often extended to include stipendiary priests who have responsibility for certain geographical areas of the diocese. Indeed, it became clear in the symposium that the problems associated with the expression of episcopacy within local ministry dioceses are a larger version of those experienced by parish priests in their increasingly large and complex parishes or benefices. Expressing appropriate leadership, working with a shared vision, structuring church life to enable collaboration, being the centre of accountability, promoting the language of service are common issues to priest and bishop and can only be addressed when there is a common commitment within the diocese to work together to promote these values.

Local Ministry in the Church of England

The workshop on episcopacy within the San Francisco symposium was of great significance to the bishops' story within the Church of England because it was a way of identifying key issues that will always accompany the move from hierarchy to collaborative ministry for those called to leadership. It is also worth noting that the overseas dioceses represented in San Francisco were committed to a programme that included the establishment of ordained local ministry. Within England there has been development in the process of local ministry which in some dioceses has included the development of OLM and in other dioceses has excluded it. Some have concentrated on the development of local lay ministry teams, some on the development of ordained local ministry and some on schemes that combine the two.

A national consultation on the development of local ministry, sponsored by the Edward King Institute in October 1998, recognized the diverse way in which local ministry was expressed within different dioceses yet affirmed that it was a key strategy for mission and ministry for the Church of England as we approach the new millennium. It also recognized the need to develop constructive relationships between the local parish or benefice and the diocese. The diocese clearly has a responsibility to stimulate, encourage and resource local ministry. However, it is of critical importance that a great deal of the initiative and oversight of the process remains the responsibility of the local church. Most dioceses have struggled with this key relationship. Some bishops are concerned that, if they give too much authority and responsibility to the local church, they will foster congregationalism. Therefore, many parishes and benefices feel that they lack the freedom to develop in ways that they think is most appropriate. On the other hand, some bishops feel that it is right to give the local church as much freedom as possible to develop a ministry that is appropriate to the local context. There is inevitably the need for more diocesan oversight when local churches produce OLM or reader candidates because the training and selection of both is ultimately the responsibility of the bishop and requires accreditation by the Ministry Division of the House of Bishops. Those dioceses that have developed local ministry teams also recognize that there is need for a considerable amount of diocesan input to create and maintain them. It is, therefore, important that those who are responsible for the development of local ministry and those at the local level share and own a common vision for mission and ministry. It is also important that the local parish and the diocese should know what options are being offered, what role each must play at each stage in the process and where the responsibility for each element lies. The way in which a diocesan vision for local ministry is fostered, and appropriate procedures for selection and training are implemented, will be the responsibility of the diocesan bishop and part of the bishops' story.

The Bishops' Story?

It is well to note that the bishop's story will be very different in each diocese and important that we recognize the role that the national church plays in the case of ordained and reader ministry. It is also well to note that the vision which supports and enables local ministry will often find a focus in those officers that are appointed to promote and support it, the schemes that they run and the committees that manage their work. As diocesan officers, those responsible for the development of local ministry share in, or have the bishop's episcopacy extended to enable, the work that they do. The officers that are appointed and the schemes that they run therefore impinge on the bishop's story at every point, especially when one bishop leaves and a new bishop is appointed.

In truth, bishops within the Church of England have very much less freedom than their counterparts in other areas of the Anglican Communion for the way in which ministry can develop within their dioceses. Although each diocesan bishop retains a measure of executive power in his area, the House of Bishops have continued to have a key role in the selection and training of accredited ministry through the group which has been variously known in the last few years as ACCM (Advisory Council for Church Ministry), ABM (Advisory Board for Ministry) and, now, The Ministry Division of the Archbishop's Council. To understand the way in which the story of various bishops has enabled the development of ordained local ministry in the Church of England it is necessary to know something of the developing role of those who advise them.

The Ministry Division and its immediate predecessors have played three key roles in the development of ordained local ministry. They have attempted to define OLM and establish good practice in selection and training through three key reports: ABM Paper 1 published in 1991, ABM Paper 4 published in 1994, and *Stranger in the Wings* published in 1999. These have clearly helped to share and promote acceptable practice while recognizing the wide variety of expressions of OLM across the Church of England.

The Ministry Division advises the bishops on the selection of candidates for ministry by supporting residential selection conferences. They have long advised the bishops on candidates for stipendiary ministry and, in more recent times, have also advised on the suitability of candidates for non-stipendiary ministry (NSM). Although some early OLM schemes did not use selection conferences, it is now common practice within the Church of England for those testing a vocation to ordained local ministry also to attend residential conferences supported by the Ministry Division.

The third way in which the Ministry Division influences the development of ordained ministry in the Church of England is through the validation and inspection of the theological and ministerial training offered to stipendiary and non-stipendiary clergy in theological colleges and regional courses, and to OLMs in diocesan schemes. Although many of the first OLM schemes began life as 'experiments' or 'pilot schemes' in dioceses, with the increase in the experience, knowledge and understanding of selection and training for ordained local ministry, schemes that are starting today have much more clearly defined parameters in which they are expected to operate. Through the validation and inspection of schemes, the Ministry Division operates a process of quality control to ensure appropriate standards across the Church of England. Although committed to appropriate variations in training from college to college, course to course and scheme to scheme, the ministry Division is nevertheless committed to promoting appropriate common learning outcomes for ordained ministry and promoting the highest possible standards of training.

ACCM, ABM and the Ministry Division have therefore helped to shape the way in which ordained local ministry operates within the Church of England, promoting good practice and providing quality control in the area of selection and training. This gives dioceses less room for experimentation within these areas but provides a stronger, more rigorous and consistent training process for ordained local ministry across the Church of England.

In 1986, responsibility for the training of readers passed from the Central Readers' Conference to ACCM. Since then, ACCM, ABM and the Ministry Division have worked with the Central Readers' Conference to undertake a similar process with regard to reader selection and training. Through reports and 'occasional papers', through the national accreditation of training schemes and through the award of the General Readers' Certificate, national standards have been raised and made gradually more consistent. Diocesan bishops retain a responsibility for the selection and training of readers in their diocese but, as with ordained ministry, they are by and large keen to work with the advice given by the national church.

National structures that are accountable to the House of Bishops put the story of individual bishops in the Church of England into a context not experienced by those in Anglican dioceses abroad. There will always be bishops who choose to ignore the advice of the centre and to promote more individualistic strategies in their dioceses but this is slowly becoming less common in ministerial selection and training as the need for collaboration in the development and maintenance of consistent standards across the Church of England becomes clearer.

Beginning Local Ministry

BISHOP JOHN'S STORY

As has been noted before, some dioceses in the Church of England have developed strategies for local ministry that have included ordained local ministry and some have not. For Bishop John, ordained local ministry was not an initial priority. He was made suffragan bishop in a mainly rural diocese and given a ministry brief. As 'Warden of Readers' in the diocese, his initial concern was to improve reader training and to give this ministry a higher profile in the diocese. As this developed, the attention of the diocese increasingly centred on the parochial unit and how parochial-centred local ministry could be supervised and rooted. In the early 1990s, the Diocesan Synod responded to a call for 'a priest in every parish' through the adoption of a scheme for ordained local ministry, an initiative that was supported by the new diocesan bishop. Although a rallying cry of considerable force, there was concern among those who were working to develop local ministry in the diocese that this was not a practical possibility within the near future. There was also concern that ordained local ministers would need to emerge from parishes committed to collaborative ministry and the development of local ministry teams. Therefore, work continued to develop ministry teams in parishes with a recognition that these might or might not produce ordinands for ordained local ministry. Nevertheless, Bishop John, as chairman of the Board of Ministry, helped steer the scheme through the process of accreditation by the House of Bishops as an OLM scheme.

For Bishop John, these were exciting times but they were not without their problems. When a 'local ministry parish' became vacant it was not always easy to make an appointment. Few clergy had experience of working with ministry teams and it was not always clear from conversations with applicants whether the enthusiastic words spoken at interview would be transferred into appropriate action once they were appointed. And, of course, Bishop John had to balance a number of issues when appointing a new incumbent to a benefice. In this area he often had little room for manoeuvre. There were not always a large number of applicants, the bishop was not always the patron and the whole staffing exercise was rather like working on a large and complex jigsaw puzzle. It was, however, important to find ways in which the local ministry team could be involved in the appointment of a new incumbent. They were not and could not be part of the official procedure but they *could* meet with prospective candidates and be part of the general consultation process.

Pastoral reorganization also proved problematic. It has often proved necessary in a diocese to link parishes together into benefices so that they can share in the ministry of one parish priest. In the early days of the scheme it was occasionally necessary to link local ministry parishes with those who had not embraced this way of working and whose parish priests were not sympathetic. This had led to the demise of the occasional embryonic team. Bishop John was also aware that, even though many parishes and benefices embraced the local ministry scheme, there was a degree of local ministry in the diocese that was not expressed in this way and needed to be affirmed and supported. This also raised issues about the status of ministers who were already operating in parishes that did embrace the scheme. Urgent attention needed to be given to the reader who had served the parish for many years when the new team came into existence.

Bishop John was certainly aware that much practical opposition to the local ministry scheme was formed around issues such as these and was therefore keen to make it clear that these difficulties were not insuperable and could be managed creatively.

For Bishop John, the early stages of this enterprise involved himself and the diocesan officers in the nurturing and cherishing of newly formed local ministry teams. However, it was clear, even at the beginning, that the diocese would need to commit itself to the ongoing maintenance of this ministry and to develop strategies whereby new people could join existing teams and be helped to grow and develop. This would ultimately be a huge exercise and would raise questions about the appropriate way in which it might be done. In the early stages of the schemes, readers and OLMs were not trained within the local team but by the regional course. The relationship of reader and OLM training to the scheme would further need to be clarified as it developed in the future.

The Story of One Diocese and Two Bishops

BISHOP ANDREW'S STORY

Those that have developed OLM schemes have often needed to pioneer processes of selection and training, and to work through the implications that OLM has for the way that other ordained and local ministries operate in the diocese. The story of Bishop Andrew, and his successor, Bishop Thomas, will both help to illustrate the way in which ordained local ministry has developed in the last few years and bring the issues that face it today into sharp focus.

Bishop Andrew took up his appointment as diocesan bishop in a rural diocese in the mid-eighties. He had been a suffragan bishop in a diocese that had been discussing ordained local ministry for some time and was pleased to lead a diocese that had made a decision in principle to pursue the matter further. He had been a parish priest in a large urban diocese and had learned through the years to support local initiatives, to work with individuals in support of their ministry and to give the Holy Spirit room to work within the Church. Had he been a gardener, he would have preferred informal to formal borders and would have experienced endless joy in the discovery of a flower that had grown rather unexpectedly in a slightly unusual spot. In common with many dioceses at that time, his rural patch was to experience a financial crisis and a severe reduction in stipendiary ministry during the years that he was its bishop. The scheme for the selection and training of ordained local ministry that he left the diocese on retirement was, he felt, all the more important in the light of this.

Before the publication of ABM Paper 1 there were no guidelines for OLM schemes and very little experience of them in other dioceses. The pilot scheme that Bishop Andrew set in motion therefore had to construct a scheme that could support the selection and training of OLMs. The person chosen to do this had only 25 per cent of his time allocated to this task, but this was deemed to be adequate at the time. The officer was skilled in adult education and provided a good basic course for groups of people from parishes and benefices who came together for a three-year period to explore their faith and learn the skills of ministry. Selection for ordained local ministry and readership took place at the end of the first year with ordination and licensing at the end of the third year. The group remained together for that period of training, with those not called to accredited ministry working with and supporting those who were. Selection for OLM began with the identification of candidates in the parish and was completed by the bishop's selectors who interviewed candidates in their own homes. The bishop was an active supporter of this process and rejoiced in the new vocations that emerged and the effect that the scheme was having on those parishes that initially engaged with it.

It is important to describe the shape of the pilot scheme and the decisions that were taken at that time because they had an important influence on what was to occur subsequently. A great deal of responsibility for selection and training was given to the local church at the beginning of the process. The parish priest had a pivotal role in the training process and the church was encouraged to identify potential candidates with an expectation that, unless the selectors found good reason not to recommend them to the bishop, they would go forward to ordination. Local churches rejoiced in this responsibility but many other clergy in the diocese muttered darkly about low standards and poor quality. Andrew also gave permission for readers to be trained on the new scheme when they emerged from parishes that were undertaking the pilot scheme. It seemed sensible for the new ministers to train together, under their incumbent, with the material provided by the diocese. However, a new readers' course was being completed at that time and there was every reason to believe that it was going to offer high-quality reader training. Not surprisingly, the news that readers could also be trained on the local ministry course did not meet with universal approval, especially as many people judged the new readers' course to be of higher quality. Certainly it provided training that was more complete and sys-tematic at that time.

There was also a concern from a sizeable constituency in the diocese that the development of local ministry was being hijacked. Those who were committed to collaborative ministry and wanted to develop various expressions of lay ministry but felt that a three-year training programme was inappropriate for them, objected that the diocese had little to offer them. There was debate, even at that time, as to whether the diocese should have begun with a scheme designed to train ordained local ministers or whether it should have begun by encouraging the development of local ministry teams on to which training for ordained local ministry could have been subsequently added. The vision for ordained local ministry had begun with a working party chaired by the suffragan bishop several years before and had been debated and passed by diocesan synod. An officer had been appointed and a group to support his work had been established. The pilot scheme had appealed to many in the diocese who had embraced it willingly. Yet there was still significant opposition to its development among readers, parish clergy and diocesan officers who felt that too many resources were being allocated to the scheme at the expense of other work. There were, therefore, voices of dissent that would seek a hearing in the future.

When Andrew retired, the pilot scheme had run for a considerable period and the scheme had just gained accreditation with the House of Bishops. A full-time principal had been appointed and many in the diocese were keen to inform the officials from the Crown Appointments Committee that they wanted a new bishop who was sympathetic to ordained local ministry and was prepared to develop this work further.

APPOINTMENTS ARE KEY

Much in the development of local ministry turns around appointments. Clergy unsympathetic to its development can consciously or unconsciously undo the work of years in a frighteningly short period of time. The same fear invades dioceses when bishops change. It is probably true to say that PCCs and churchwardens are not entirely convinced that their archdeacons and bishops actually hear what they are saying during the process of consultation, and there is little evidence to suggest that the process is different when it comes to the appointment of bishops. However, there are clearly problems on both sides. Matching people that are available with jobs that are vacant is not always easy, added to which it is not unusual for people with responsibility for appointments to take a view about what a parish or diocese needs rather than what it claims it wants. It has been known for bishops who have been clear in their opposition to ordained local ministry to take a different view when appointed to a diocese in which a scheme is flourishing, pointing out to the more sceptical hearers that although in general his view hadn't changed, this particular scheme was clearly right for his new diocese at that time. Many would see this as a laudable attempt to value the history and experience of the diocese that he has joined and agree that it is infinitely preferable to the bishop who might systematically undermine a scheme that his predecessor had introduced. Any stipendiary priest will witness to the difficulty of joining a new benefice and to the time that it takes to learn its history, engage in its experience, sort out the way things work and identify those things in need of nurture and those in need of challenge. This is clearly also true of bishops. It is inevitably the role of the person who comes in from the outside to bring a broader perspective and to engage critically with the local and its values.

BISHOP THOMAS'S STORY

When Bishop Thomas succeeded Bishop Andrew he must have experienced some misgivings about what he saw in the diocese. Had he been a gardener he may well have found a certain amount of disorder and free expression agreeable, so long as there was a plan which was clear and manageable. However, there was obviously one enormous plant in this patch that seemed to be dominating the entire environment. The local ministry scheme was clearly a productive plant and, although he had not had close contact with this particular variety before, it was not obviously diseased or of poor stock. The questions rather were: (1) Was it an appropriate specimen? (2) Was it stopping other things from growing and flowering? and (3) Was it growing out of control? There were clearly some questions about the nature of ministry that needed to be addressed again and some questions about the way in which different ministries related to each other and to the missionary work of the Church. There was a need to look at the diocese as a whole and to review its vision and strategy.

It was at this point that those questions that had emerged through the pilot scheme needed to be addressed. The Diocesan Synod had requested the pilot scheme and had enthusiastically endorsed the local ministry scheme so it was possible to argue that the vision for local ministry could be located within the diocese with bishop and synod and entrusted for its delivery to those who ran the scheme. Yet it was clear that there were voices of protest that had been muted and people in the diocese who felt excluded from what was happening. How might it be possible to hear again from a wider constituency and respond again to their needs? Since the pilot scheme had received accreditation by the House of Bishops it had gained in educational strength and rigour but this had led to a much more significant role for diocesan staff and tutors, and an inevitable weakening of the role of the parish priest in the educational process. Since the scheme was now using residential selection conferences, many felt that the voice of the local church had been reduced in strength and significance. This led to the question that was never openly articulated but was of great significance: What kind of relationship between the bishop and the local church was the scheme to reflect and model?

The Readers' Council had been faced with a new environment in which collaborative ministerial practice was valued and in which the needs of the local community were increasingly key to the development of ministry. It therefore promoted a selection and training process which required readers to be earthed in local ministry teams and to have clear expectations of the job that they would be required to do in that place. It also defined reader ministry as primarily a lay order for teaching and preaching in the face of many who wanted to become readers so as to develop a ministry that was primarily focused in pastoral care. However, the diocese now had two courses for reader training? What should it do about this and what implications would that hold for the future?

A DIOCESAN REVIEW

The review was chaired by the suffragan bishop and attempted to deal with the way in which the role of stipendiary clergy,

NSMs and OLMs could be viewed as complementary within a broader ministerial provision. Since the development of ordained local ministry, the role of the NSM had been under scrutiny. A very few NSMs focused their ministry in the workplace. A few had been deployed in parishes where they were not resident to support the ministry in that place. However, the majority were working in their home parishes and operating to all intents and purposes as OLMs. If this were to continue it would be almost impossible to decide whether an individual should be selected and trained as an NSM or an OLM. Some had thought that the difference might lie in the quality of the training. The 'better' or 'more academic' candidates should train on the regional course as NSMs, the 'less academic' on the diocesan course, a kind of grammar and secondary modern school approach, but this was deemed entirely unacceptable. Others had given a great deal of weight to the concept of 'deployability'. If NSMs were deployable by the bishop rather than wedded to their home parish then that might provide a key defining feature. However, deployability is, in practice, extremely difficult for those who are not paid and employed by the Church, and to use it as the defining feature for a particular type of ministry risks giving it a weight that it does not warrant. In the event, the review suggested to Bishop Thomas that the grounds for the distinction between the different expressions of priesthood might best be sought in the concept of the 'benefice' and the 'non-benefice' priest. The benefice priest, stipendiary or non-stipendiary would have responsibility for a parish or benefice and be given the 'cure of souls' for that place. The non-benefice priest would be an 'assistant priest' called to a priestly ministry but not to the leadership of a benefice. A person who felt called to be a priest in their own benefice would always go forward as an OLM. A person called to stipendiary ministry would go forward in that capacity but a person who felt called, now or in the future, to exercise a ministry that might involve the leadership of a benefice or one who would wish to fulfil a ministry outside the local congregation would go forward as an NSM.

BALKANIZATION

This kind of diocesan thinking becomes necessary in an environment in which the national church supports three types of ordained ministry which each have mutually exclusive systems of selection and training and yet are not mutually exclusive in the way that they are expressed at parish level. Bishop Thomas wanted his DDO to have a clear set of criteria to work with when confronted with those who felt called to ordained ministry, especially as the Church demands that the decision is made as to whether a person should correctly go forward for stipendiary, NSM or OLM training before selection and training. This is made even more confusing because there is a selection category entitled 'Permanent NSM'. This is precisely for candidates who want to go forward as NSMs but want to stay within their own parishes.

This category gives dioceses that do not have OLM schemes the capacity to have ordained priests that emerge from their local church to minister there but is clearly a category that could not reasonably be used in dioceses that have schemes. Those who may be inclined to defend this system will admit that it suffers from the classic Anglican 'add on' syndrome. A new form of ministry is merely 'added on' to the provision that already exists without any attempt to integrate it with what is there already. OLM has been 'added on' to NSM without any systematic attempt to relate them to each other. Defenders will also admit that the systems are 'balkanized'; each has its own system of selection and its own scheme for training. Colleges and regional courses can train stipendiaries and NSMs but they cannot train OLMs. Diocesan schemes can train OLMs but not NSMs and stipendiaries. It is possible to see how it has happened and why it is so but it is less easy to see how it might develop in the future. Indeed many bishops were against the development of OLM precisely because it was not integrated with NSM and stipendiary ministry. However, the defender will point to the fact that the church now has a variety of options to offer to dioceses. Those uncomfortable with ordained local ministry can access both permanent and deployable non-stipendiary ministry, and those who have OLM schemes must do as Bishop Thomas's diocese has done and look for credible ways of integrating these different expressions of priesthood.

READER MINISTRY

Bishop Thomas also recognized that a hard decision would need to be taken concerning reader training. Reader ministry had flourished in the diocese over past years and the new course had promoted good practice in selection and training. However, in common with a lot of the Church of England, reader ministry had reached something of a crisis. It had grown in an environment in which public ministry was viewed individualistically and hierarchically. Readers were vulnerable to the way in which successive incumbents might value or use their ministry and many had developed a preaching ministry across a wide geographical area. Also, as the number of stipendiary clergy decreased in the rural areas, many readers took on the role traditionally associated with the parish priest of pastor and teacher within a particular village community. This was further supported by the growing practice of 'extended communion' which allowed readers to lead the service of Holy Communion with bread and wine consecrated at a previous service in the benefice. Some readers had also been asked to take baptisms on a regular basis and had grown to see this as an integral part of their ministry. These two activities had become part of a developing new identity for readers that had extended their traditional role of teachers, preachers and leaders of liturgy into a quasi-sacramental area.

However, the introduction of ordained local ministry challenged the identity of readers. Some of those roles which were being exercised by readers in multi-parish benefices clearly overlapped with those of the OLM. And, although nobody had suggested that individuals and benefices should immediately change the way that they operated, Bishop Thomas was forced to ban the practice of readers undertaking baptism. The practice had never been authorized at national level, had never been officially sanctioned at diocesan level and had never been part of the reader's remit. The bishop also required the practice of extended Communion to be controlled through being subject to his authorization in each case. These measures, reasonable and understandable in their own right, nevertheless made readers feel that their ministry was being in some way reduced and seen to be of less value in the diocese.

The review recommended that the local ministry course be

renamed the Diocesan Ministry Course and be developed to accommodate the training of all readers in the diocese and Bishop Thomas accepted this. There was inevitably a strong sense of bereavement among those who had been trained on the course, those who had staffed it and those who had valued its contribution to the ministry of readers in the diocese. There was also suspicion that the newly revised local ministry course might not prove an appropriate way to train readers for their distinctive ministry. However, the bishop opted to support a scheme that was committed to training OLMs and readers in ways that modelled the collaborative environment in which they would be expected to work, which related theology to context and promoted reflective ministerial practice – key values and concerns in the majority of training schemes for ordained local ministry.

This story of one diocese and two bishops tells the story of an experiment which flourished yet needed ultimately to be integrated into the broader provision that the diocese offers. It raised issues about the role the bishop in the diocese which echoed the conversations held in San Francisco. Where is the vision of the diocese located? Is it primarily expressed through the diocesan synod, the bishop and/or his staff? How can the views and experience of a broader constituency be included? What is the role of the one who comes in from the outside to take up a ministry in a new place? How does he relate to the history of that place and yet be accountable for its life? Local ministry has given greater responsibility to the local church for its mission and ministry and to the individual diocese for the way that it structures its ministerial provision within the parameters set out by the broader church. If Stewart Zabriskie is right in his assertion that the new collaborative working environment will require bishops to promote a new language of episcopal ministry and investigate new, more inclusive working practices, then dioceses will need time to discover and live a vision of Church that is appropriate to their environment. The hierarchical, individualistic culture which has set people apart for episcopacy and has driven them with an unrealistic workload to be chief pastor of their church and the focus of its missionary activity in the world needs urgent attention. Key to the success of any collaborative venture will be the relationship that exists between the local church and the bishop. Bishops in local ministry dioceses abroad have far fewer churches even if they have far larger geographical areas. Even in this environment, they find the need to extend episcopacy to stipendiary priest colleagues. The Church of England is generally recognized to have too much structure. The parish, the benefice, the deanery, the archdeaconry, the diocese and the national church all demand attention, all have committees and all confound the attempts of the Church to share a common life. For local ministry to flourish, the structures must be managed in such a way that local people can be energized rather than disabled and given a creative and stimulating part in the way that the Church is developing into the future. The vision, or visions, must come from a broad constituency so that they can be reflected and focused by the bishop and those who represent him in the diocese. Wild gardens allow only the fittest plants to survive but carefully integrated borders place control firmly with the gardener. It should, therefore, be a matter of critical concern if parishes feel that they are not being as creative as they might be in the development of their ministry in support of their mission.

Bishop Thomas was keen for all parishes to undergo a thorough, regular and systematic review of their life and work together and provision was built into the ministry review to support this. Such a review would help parishes to identify opportunities for mission and to explore the shape of ministry that could enable and support them. Parishes could then call upon the Adult Education Officer, the Youth and Children's Officer or the Diocesan Ministry Course to support the way forward that they thought appropriate. Such a process is common to many dioceses. Most have allocated resources to support the way in which the diocese has chosen to explore and promote local ministry.

There are many other stories that could be told about the development of local ministry courses that include the provision of ordained local ministry. The story would in each case be different but would identify similar sets of issues. Those dioceses that have developed local ministry schemes without OLM have largely done so because there are theological misgivings among the bishops, their staff and senior figures in the diocese.

Local Ministry Without Ordained Local Ministry

BISHOP ALAN'S STORY

Bishop Alan's diocese and the story that he tells will illustrate this point. He has reflected on the need to develop the ministry of all baptized Christians in the diocese in the service of Christ and the mission of the Church. He has rejoiced in the way in which theology has rediscovered the Trinity and helped the Church to explore a God who exists in loving relationship, a communion of three persons whose love nevertheless flows out to create and redeem the world. He has further rejoiced in a Church that dares to imitate its God in the development of mutual relationships in a community that supports, nurtures and encourages a love that similarly flows out to the world in Christ's name. He acknowledges that such a vision of God and Church requires that the diocese works at new ways of being related in community that is mutually enhancing but not hierarchical.

However, in Bishop Alan's diocese, priesthood is, by definition, deployable. Both he and the majority of his senior staff have severe theological and ecclesiastical objections to the development of ordained local ministry. They feel that the development of a new expression of priesthood is inappropriate at this time and should not have been supported by the House of Bishops. They remain concerned that this new ministry, with its own discrete and separate processes of selection and training, materially affects the ministry of stipendiaries, NSMs and readers, and has been developed in relative haste and without the full implications of its effect on the life of the Church being properly debated. For them, the debate revolves around the way in which priesthood itself can be understood and described. And for Bishop Alan, the doctrine of any foundation of the Church and of ministry has to be built on Christ himself.

The life and work of Christ is characterized by sacrificial love, obedience and self-offering and there is an expectation that all those who are called, through baptism, to be 'in Christ' should share in those characteristics. The Church's vocation 'in Christ' is to be priestly, sacrificial and obedient, and those called to celebrate the eucharist and offer the spiritual sacrifices of the

Church on behalf of the people became known as priests. Although developed after the New Testament period had ended, priesthood is part of the historic threefold ministry of the Church and is consistent with New Testament understandings of the church community. Priests were seen to be representatives of both the priestly people of God and Christ, the great high priest.

Throughout the history of the Christian Church the role of priest has been defined in different ways within different constituencies of the Church. Some have understood the priest to be a functionary of the church community, called out to do certain jobs on its behalf. Others have pointed to an ontological understanding in which the nature of a person's very being is changed through ordination, joining them to an order that is in special relationship to Christ. Bishop Alan sees the dangers in both traditions. For him the priest cannot be in an order that is superior to the church community that he or she represents, nor can (s)he merely be its functionary, deputed to undertake certain tasks on its behalf. Perhaps it is better to think of priesthood as existing in a set of key relationships. Clearly the priest is related to the church community that he or she represents. Equally, the priest exists in relationship to Christ and with a special authority that comes from Christ, via the apostles and their successors, through ordination. (S)he would agree with the joint Anglican/Roman Catholic (ARCIC) statement on Ministry and Ordination, that priesthood 'belongs to another realm of the gifts of the Spirit'. The priest has a particular sacramental relationship with Christ that is different, but in no way superior, to the relationship that all the baptized have with Christ. Indeed, the ordained priesthood is given to the Church as a sign of Christ's priestly ministry and of the priestly calling of all baptized Christians to enable the whole Church to become more priestly and to grow in obedience and sacrificial love.

Bishop Alan's understanding of Church and ministry makes him suspicious of ordained local ministry and of the views of many who support it. He is concerned that many understand the ordained local minister as nothing more than the local church's representative, authorized to function as a priest on its behalf but not authorized to be priest outside that community. For Bishop Alan this denies the catholic and universal nature of priesthood which cannot be restricted to a particular community or locality.

In his or her ministry, the priest represents the historic catholic and apostolic Church and not just the community in which she or he works. It is, therefore, inappropriate to have a selection conference, as with ordained local ministry, that asks whether the person is called to be a priest *in a particular locality*. For Bishop Alan, the question is problematic. Either a person is called to be a priest or they are not, and if called to be a priest then he or she should work where their ministry is most valuable to Christ's work in the diocese.

He does accept that some who are called to be non-stipendiary priests will serve within the parishes from which they have emerged but he is comfortable that the present arrangements to select and train them are adequate. For Bishop Alan, it is more important for his diocese to find ways in which the Church can support and enable the ministry of all the baptized through parish development and education programmes. This does not mean that each benefice or parish will be encouraged to develop ministry teams, although many have opted to grow in that way, but that they will all be encouraged to express ministry in a variety of appropriate ways in support of the mission of the Church. The diocese has therefore invested heavily in staff and resources to develop lay education and reader ministry to support the work of the local church and the ministry of all God's people in his world. Bishop Alan rejoices in the developing sense of collaboration in the diocese between those called to a variety of ministries in Church and world and the key ways in which the clergy have enabled and supported this.

BISHOP DAVID'S STORY

Bishop David could understand Alan's feelings on the subject of ordained local ministry. He had also been concerned that the movement towards ordained local ministry had been driven by laudable attempts to develop a truly local and indigenous ministry for the Church but without a thorough theological debate. OLM schemes should be applauded in his view for finding and nurturing priestly vocation among those that the Church had traditionally overlooked and for applying good educational principles to the work of training people for ministry. He had been a suffragan bishop in a diocese that had undertaken an OLM scheme and he had taken up the post of diocesan bishop in another part of the country with some concern about the standard of selection and training that was prevalent at that time. He was certainly happier now that MINDAC (Ministry Division of Archbishop's Council) had worked with dioceses to promote better practice and higher standards of selection and training for OLM but was still concerned about the standard of theological debate.

Bishop David would agree with much that Bishop Alan believes. However, for him there is a key issue about the way that the catholic nature of the Church is expressed in the local. For Bishop David the way that priesthood emerged in the Church is of key significance. The bishop had emerged as the leader of the Church in each locality, to promote teaching that was true to the apostolic tradition and to administer the sacraments. As the Church grew in each locality and new churches were established, the bishop could no longer manage the Church personally. The bishops therefore ordained men to be their representatives in the local church, to lead that community, to administer communion and to be teacher and pastor on their behalf. The priest therefore emerged as the local representative of the bishop and had, from the beginning, a dual role. He shared in the bishop's episcopacy, which represented the catholic ministry of the Church and the authority of the apostles, while representing the local community in which he was set. For many centuries, the priest would be chosen from the local community to work there because there was no organized professional peripatetic priesthood but he carried the mark of the universal Church through ordination and through having what later generations would call the 'cure of souls' in that place.

Bishop David agreed with Bishop Alan that priesthood was more than a function undertaken on behalf of the local community but believed that it always contained within it marks of the universal and marks of the local, a sign of Christ's priestly ministry and a sign of his incarnation in each particular context. Bishop David recognized that in the Church of England today it is the stipendiary priest, the vicar or rector, who is given the cure of souls by the bishop, who says to him or her, 'Receive the cure of souls which is both mine and yours.' The stipendiary priest has an increasingly episcopal role in the benefice, enabling and supporting the ministry of others, exercising oversight and bringing a wider experience to inform and often challenge the local. It does, however, take time for the stipendiary to become sufficiently 'local' to be able to effectively offer up the experience of the community in which (s)he works. For Bishop David, priesthood is not weakened by the complementary ministry of those who may be called in a local situation to be ordained priest, to share priesthood with the stipendiary and to assist her or him in the exercise of priesthood. Their priesthood will still bear the marks of the universal but will be more able to focus and offer up the local. In partnership, stipendiary priests and priests who emerge from the local church to minister in the local community will offer a richness in priestly ministry that will do justice to both the universal and the local.

However, Bishop David opted to begin the development of local ministry in his new diocese by resourcing the development of a local ministry scheme that in the first phase would not involve ordained local ministry. He felt that the diocese needed to work, initially, with the development of lay ministry and to provide opportunities for lay people to engage with theology and grow in faith. He was concerned that if the diocese introduced ordained local ministry too early, he would send out the message that the only local ministry that was of any real value was that which led to ordination. He was, however, committed to the principle of OLM and ready to provide that option in the diocese when the development of local ministry had reached an appropriate stage.

Collaborative Episcopacy?

At a recent consecration, one bishop was heard to welcome his new colleague with the words, 'welcome to the club'. It was a rather sardonic comment but was said with some feeling. The preacher had warned the new bishops of the lonely road that lay ahead of them and of the way that the Church isolates individuals called to episcopacy. She warned of the temptations to use the power and authority that had been given to them in ways that were inappropriate for today's Church. It is difficult to know what qualities attract those charged with the duty to select men for episcopacy but, until recently, they have inevitably identified those who have been successful exponents of traditional ministry.

To model an episcopal ministry in the Church of England which will truly reflect the collaborative ministerial practice that is developing in local ministry parishes is not an easy task. Many bishops remain uneasy about the way in which individual parishes and benefice units want to express their individuality and independence. They are frustrated when faced with a workforce that is increasingly difficult to deploy. Vacancies are harder to fill because both clergy and parishes are more demanding about their requirements, and the growing number of OLMs and NSMs create a volunteer workforce with a large degree of independence. The Church of England has been living within a society which has witnessed the demise of all forms of national institutional life and the breakdown of any authority which is based on status and position. In a participatory society which individuals expect to be actively involved in and personally responsible for their lifestyle choices and leisure activities, bishops are facing congregations that are energized by the ministry of the local church but suspicious of the role of the broader institution. In a society where those in authority are judged both by their own personal effectiveness and their ability to enable the work and personal fulfilment of others, bishops are being asked to create systems in which a common diocesan vision for mission and ministry can be owned and developed by each individual parish or benefice.

The story that bishops tell in local ministry dioceses in other parts of the Anglican Communion should alert us to the need for bishops to engage in the continuing quest to employ a language and engage structures that share or extend episcopacy in ways that enable and support the life and work of the whole Church. In England, the bishops' story is also owned in part by those who advise the bishops on selection and training on behalf of the national church, and those officers within the dioceses who are charged with the endeavour of creating and managing schemes of education, training and parish development. The story of each bishop is, therefore, to some extent both the story of the Church of England at this time and the story of each individual diocese as it struggles to develop strategies for mission and ministry that are acceptable to the broader church and appropriate to the local context.

7

⏤⏤⏤

Local Ministry Around the World

Local ministry is not just an English phenomenon. In this chapter we see how 'Total Ministry' emerged in the Americas and we look at some key features of how it works in the dioceses of Nevada and North Michigan. Australasia has been influenced by the pioneer work of the Americans but this has naturally been adapted to suit the local context. We look in some detail at what it is like to be a member of a 'Total Ministry' parish in New Zealand and we conclude that this is an exciting experiment which is beginning to revitalize many small churches which seemed on the point of closure.

The USA – the Story So Far

Local ministry, or 'Total Ministry' as they call it in the USA and Canada, has emerged as a result of the problems of the 'small church'. Because of the way churches are organized there, 'small church' means small congregation, whether it be in the town or the countryside. The reason the small church is a 'problem' is because the congregation cannot raise the money to pay for a minister themselves and therefore rely on the generosity of large 'successful' congregations; in other words, they have to be subsidized. To an English person, brought up in a broad-based national church, it can seem extraordinary that Episcopalians want to keep these tiny congregations going when there are so many alternative denominations to choose from. Even in deep rural areas, the Episcopal congregation is rarely the only church in a settlement, and it is difficult to understand why Christians cannot see the glaringly obvious 'solution' and go for grassroots ecumenical mergers. However, Jesus gave some telling advice about 'motes' and 'beams' in the eye of the beholder, and we simply have to accept the fact that for most Christians in other parts of the English-speaking world denominational loyalty is very important indeed. Except in isolated cases, they are not, therefore, prepared to contemplate amalgamation as a solution to the 'problem' of the small subsidized church.

We also need to remember that their context is very different from ours. The USA and Canada are enormous countries, and many Episcopal dioceses cover an area larger than the British Isles. The settlement pattern is different, in that almost everyone lives in cities or townships, except in deep rural areas where there are isolated homesteads. There are virtually no English-style villages. Further, the Episcopal Church is very small in comparison with the Roman Catholics or Methodists and is in no sense an 'established' church. This means that while bishops have a much smaller staff than is normal in the UK they have a much greater power to make radical changes if the will is there.

ENCOURAGING SMALL CHURCHES

It was initially believed that the key to helping a small church to become financially viable was to rebuild the confidence of the congregation. This could, of course, be achieved by members catching fire with the Holy Spirit but, as rural sociologists realized, this was extremely unlikely to happen, particularly in stable rural farming areas where the congregation was largely made up of families who had been worshipping there for generations. The social dynamics of a rural area militate against pentecostal evangelism.

Out of this realization that things had to be done some other way grew an important literature which aimed to restore the confidence of small congregations by getting them to count their blessings and recognize their real achievements. Far from being a failure, the small church exemplifies Christian values which tend to become lost in the large congregation. The key text for this movement was provided by Carl S. Dudley in his book *Making the Small Church Effective* (Abingdon, 1978).

In a big world, the small church has remained intimate.
In a fast world, the small church has been steady.
In an expensive world, the small church has remained plain.
In a complex world, the small church has remained simple.
In a rational world, the small church has kept feeling.
In a mobile world, the small church has been an anchor.
In an anonymous world, the small church calls us by name.

Other books followed. *The Small Rural Parish* (1980) by Bernard Quinn for the Roman Catholics, *Small Churches are the Right Size* (1982) by David Roy, a Congregationalist and, in 1997, (designated 'The Year of the Small Church') *Vision Fulfilling* by Leo Brown, William Davidson and Allen Brown, which brings together, under one cover, a record of the many achievements and manifestations of the movement.

As John Clark, the former director of the Arthur Rank Centre in England so memorably put it, 'A small church is not a failed large church – it is a different sort of animal', and the recognition of this truth has gone a long way to restore the confidence of small congregations in the validity of their vocation to be God's people in their own local place. It is all too easy for them to feel inferior and inadequate in comparison with their busy urban counterparts; and the ever-increasing demands on them to adopt worthy projects, to be involved in diocesan programmes and to burst into technicolour forms of worship (which supposedly reflect contemporary culture) just pile on the guilt.

This is a point taken up in Bishop Zabriskie's book *Total Ministry*. He suggests that small churches need to be told not to worry about pleasing diocesan bureaucracy but to concentrate on ministry in their local setting.

> In areas where the church is small and even remotely located, we ask each local parish to pray about and consider what its vocation is in the community where the parish is called to be unique. For instance, consider a parish in one sparsely populated area of the state that has somewhere between ten and twenty-five members. They have two local priests, who call themselves the 'white-haired ladies'. (A tourist passing through asked the husband of one of them, 'Is that the church where the white-haired ladies are?' It stuck and continues to be a source of local merriment.) Most in the congregation tithe; they are mindful of the needs of strangers travelling through or getting lost; they have some wonderful stories to tell about wayfaring strangers.

They are very much in the community as church people, and they are recognised as that by other residents. The church even provides some leadership in community events. They have no evangelism, stewardship, Christian social relations, or mission committees, but they are doing those expressions of ministry where they are as who they are. They do not spend a lot of time in church maintaining functions. They *are* church where they live, and I would commend that as a form of mission where it is often most difficult: at home. (p. 43)

FROM COMMUNITIES GATHERED ROUND A MINISTER TO MINISTERING COMMUNITIES

Thanks to the intelligent encouragement of a generation of bishops and diocesan trainers nurtured in these ideas, many small congregations in USA and Canada have taken new heart and have forged ahead. But, early on in the process, it became clear to a number of reflective practitioners that, however hard they studied and however enthusiastic they became, many small congregations would never be able to pay their minister an adequate salary. They would always be exhaustedly struggling to carry a gigantic financial burden or be disillusioned and guilty because they could not raise the cash needed. The fundamental problem was that they were hooked on the idea that a church is not a church unless it has a paid minister, who has come from outside and who has been seminary trained. The Diocese of Northern Michigan (1996, p. 2) puts it this way:

Our problem is consumerism: ministry is seen to be purchased from the professional provider. This creates dependency on the dollar subsidy and imported clergy. The church is thus limited by the quality and availability of the professional priest; while most gifts in the community go unused or unrecognised.

But this is *not* the only model of 'church' available.

Our goal is to transform our congregations from being communities gathered around a minister into ministering communities. Our slogan – stop attending church, start being the church. (*idem*)

In 1973, Baldwin Lloyd shared his thoughts on new forms of ministry with other members of APSO (The Appalachian Peoples

Service Organization). He quotes an example of a parish where a new form of ministry is needed:

> Pearisburg, Virginia, had like so many small missions, about 50 communicants; not growing; mostly middle-class, white-collar professional-type families; they do not have enough money to finance their own priest but do have and use lay readers; yet they have very able people in the community, quite able to have adequate local leadership if trained. Biggest problem: being freed from old traditional ways as the only way, and lack of confidence in themselves.

> Too often small parishes and missions of towns and rural areas are in relationship to a diocese or another parish as a cripple is to those from whom he begs. They have to be carried as a crippled person, they have to beg for crumbs. They are dependant on the whims of circumstance as to whether they will receive adequate leadership, if any at all, or sufficient financial assistance to operate; and they remain a cripple.

> The only important gift we can give is the sharing of the power of life – in the Reality of the Presence of Jesus Christ. Then for a struggling parish or mission, what is important is to discover the strength and skills within themselves to stand on their own feet – and discovering the ability to stand and to walk on their own, to jump and leap for joy!

> This may mean to provide the necessary training to develop their own strengths and skills of leadership. It is to enable them to have their own leadership to carry on the healing/life-giving ministry in their own community – to find through Christ wholeness in themselves which they can share in their ministry with others. (cited in Brown *et al.* (1997), p. 194)

THE INFLUENCE OF ROLAND ALLEN

As in the United Kingdom, the catalyst for this kind of thinking was the rediscovery of the writings of Roland Allen and, through them, a return to the study of the Church in the pages of the New Testament. In 1982, the authors of the report *Against All Odds* identified Allen's philosophy of mission and ministry as the inspiration behind many of the radical things that were happening in small congregations.

> A new vision of ministry has been making its way around the Episcopal Church for some time now. It has to do with the idea that

every member of the church is a minister and that the total sacrament of the church should be present in every congregation regardless of size and location. (Wilson and Davenport, 1982, cited in Brown *et al.*, 1997, pp. 234–5)

The authors instance one manifestation of this as the ordination in 1970 of indigenous priests to serve in a number of villages in Alaska which were only accessible by sledge. Bishop Gordon who carried out the ordinations spoke widely about Roland Allen's theories and his own experiences, and convinced Bishop Frensdorff of Nevada that it could be the way forward for the small isolated congregations of that area.

Another example of Roland Allen's influence was the start of a programme in the Haggerstown area of the Diocese of Maryland in 1974 which led to the setting up of what we would now call local ministry teams in three congregations. The three-year programme involved appointing a stipendiary priest as trainer or facilitator to work with the congregations. His job was to discern gifts and to call out and train teams. The idea was that, like the apostles sent out by Jesus, they should work in pairs – two for children's work, two for administration, two for pastoral care of the elderly and so on. The facilitator helped the teams to begin working together and everyone involved seemed to grow in confidence and spiritual stature. At least in the early stages, they managed to activate others in the congregation to work with them rather than themselves becoming an immovable elite. The two priests at Clearsprings were a wonderfully complementary pair. Hiram was a high-flying Washington lawyer who represented the growing band of commuters in the area, while Jim, a tall, silver-haired retired farmer born and bred in the settlement, was the natural and highly respected elder statesman who represented the congregations' roots in the past. A 1970s visitor to their Sunday morning worship was amazed by the number of people involved in the service and by the unobtrusive yet presidential role played by the priests. Moira Mathiesan wrote about the project in *Delectable Mountains* and, if the diocesan involvement was a trifle heavy-handed it certainly showed that implementing a New Testament model of ministry could transform small congregations.

NEW DIRECTIONS IN MINISTRY

In 1972, 'New Directions for Churches in Small Communities' (ND) was formed, the brainchild of Boone Porter, director of Roanridge National Town and Country Institute. Recognizing that, in the long term, small churches needed to adopt 'new directions' in ministry if they were to survive, Porter and his allies determined to put together a training programme which would prepare congregations for a DIY future in which they would be able to provide priests, deacons and other authorized ministers from their own ranks and no longer rely on seminarians parachuted in from outside. The course lasted for two weeks and was a major 'conversion experience' for those who went on it. It was, in large part, LAND (Leadership Academy for New Directions) which trained the leaders who have today begun to bring about the cultural revolution which is 'Total Ministry'.

Wesley Frensdorff, one of the key figures in this development, put the vision this way:

> Let us dream of a Church
> > with a radically renewed concept and practice of ministry,
> > and a primitive understanding of the ordained offices;
> Where there is no clerical status and there are no classes of Christians, but all together know themselves to be part of the laos, the holy people of God;
> That is a ministering community rather than a community gathered around a minister;
> Where ordained people, professional or not, employed or not, are present for the sake of ordering and signing the Church's life and mission, not as signs of authority or dependency, nor of spiritual or intellectual superiority. (Brown *et al.*, 1997, p. 345)

By 1987, there was enough experience to hold a three-day conference at Rosemont, Illinois. Perhaps the most important aspect of the conference was the sharing of the many diverse ways in which local ministry was being lived out. From a somewhat traditional 'mission field', with one priest serving a number of widely scattered congregations, to a cluster of clergy serving clusters of widely scattered congregations, to Church agencies; no particular model was seen as best, and no 'party line method' was promulgated. Rather, the discovery of common principles and themes along with their elucidation in various methods of praxis was affirmed, as participants shared in small groups their hopes and hurts and visions. At the conference, Jim Kelsey talked about 'Shared Servant Leadership'.

> Total Ministry can answer the question. 'How can we work together?' Clericalism, the predominant model in the Church, sees the priest as the minister, with all others as passive consumers. Moving into 'team ministry' the priest and some lay leaders become 'the ministers' but all others still remain as passive recipients. Total Ministry begins with the knowledge and assent that all ministry is Christ's . . . All persons baptised into His Body minister, each according to gifts. The priest and others ordained are ordained to 'office', in order that all baptised may be enabled to minister together, becoming a 'Community of Faith and Life', manifesting 'Shared Servant Leadership'. (Brown *et al.*, 1997, p. 275)

The authors of *Vision Fulfilling* continue:

> Shared Servant Leadership as a part of Total Ministry was characterised at the 1986 Sindicators Conference as leadership that

1. is always consultative
2. opens up the system
3. takes more time
4. considers the context in which we minister and live out our life as Church
5. builds ownership of decision
6. uses and integrates the gifts of the whole community
7. has to begin somewhere
8. allows the possibility of calling any baptised person to any office
9. involves discernment and election by the community.

NEVADA AND NORTHERN MICHIGAN

The classic examples of Total Ministry in action are the Diocese of Nevada, where Stewart Zabriskie was the bishop, and the Diocese of Northern Michigan where the key players are Bishop Thomas Ray and Jim Kelsey. Michigan has become a 'pilgrimage centre' for those interested in the movement, and visitors' weekends have been established twice a year to cope with this influx. After an introductory talk at Marquette, the cathedral city of the diocese, participants travel to regional points where they meet participants, listen to stories and ask questions. On Sunday they worship in Total Ministry parishes, and this is followed by a debriefing in Marquette where emphasis is given to relating the experience to the participants' home setting.

Different dioceses do things in slightly different ways, but the North Michigan paper on 'Process' is so clear that it is worth printing in full as an example of the sort of principles which seem important to the American church.

Understanding the Plan

The following section is taken from *A Plan for Mutual Ministry Development in the Diocese of North Michigan*: (pp. 2–4)

Q. What is the mission of the Church?

A. The MISSION of the Church is to restore all people to unity with God and each other in Christ.

Our Problem	is consumerism: ministry is seen to be purchased from the professional provider.
	This creates dependency on $ subsidy and imported clergy; the church is thus limited by the quality and availability of the professional priest; most gifts in the community go unused or unrecognised.
Our Goal	is to transform our congregations from being communities gathered around a minister into MINISTERING COMMUNITIES.
	A slogan 'stop attending church; start being the church'.
Our Strategy	is Mutual Ministry Development.
Our Tactics	developing local Ministry Support Teams to engage the ministry of all the baptised.

The Covenant Group Process

Invitation   The Bishop (or a representative) meets with the local Bishop's Committee or Vestry for a two-hour session to present the possibility of refocusing the daily life and mission of that congregation.

Presentation to Congregation   If the local leadership desires to proceed, the Bishop (or a representative) visits on a Sunday morning to preach and then leads a full presentation of the possibilities to the full congregation. Members of the Bishop's Committee or Vestry share in the presentation.

Consultant   If the consensus is to proceed, a Consultant is selected who will be with the congregation throughout the process.

Discovery Process   The Consultant leads a series of four meetings attended by members of the Bishop's Committee or Vestry and any other leaders identified by them. The full membership list of the congregation is reviewed in light of the need to support all the baptised in daily ministry, and persons are identified for various roles on the Ministry Support Team. No individual is identified for more than two positions.

Covenant Group   Those identified for these roles are invited to covenant for a period of preparation. All members of the congregation are invited to join this Covenant Group as members-at-large. The Covenant Group meets twice a month for 3–4 hour sessions with the Consultant attending at least every other session. These meetings are shaped by the curriculum which has been prepared by the diocesan team of Consultants. It is anticipated that it will take 18–24 months for the curriculum to be completed. In addition to these fortnightly sessions there are periodic diocesan-wide workshops for persons preparing for various roles in their Ministry Support Team. Upon completion of the curriculum, the members of the Covenant Group are examined together as a team by the Commission on Ministry.

Ministry Support Team   Following this preparation, and all necessary approvals by the Bishop, the Standing Committee, and the Commission on Ministry, the Ministry Support Team is commissioned at a liturgy during which the ministry of all the baptised is affirmed, and those who will serve on the Team are duly ordained and licensed.

Who Makes up a Congregational Ministry Support Team?

Diaconal

Deacons

Helping those gifted for serving/caring ministry to be discovered and affirmed by congregations and themselves. Co-ordinating efforts to sensitise fellow members to issues of peace and justice, and to local and international social concerns and responsibilities. Sharing in co-ordination of education/training of diaconal ministers. Sharing in identifying need for pastoral care among members and in the local community.

Diaconal Ministry Co-ordinators

Scheduling those providing local serving/caring ministry among members and in the community. Sharing in co-ordination of education/training of diaconal ministries. Sharing in identifying need for pastoral care among members and in the local community.

Apostolic

Stewardship Co-ordinators

Sharing in discovering and deploying the talent and money necessary to support the daily ministry of the congregation.

Education Co-ordinators

Overseeing and encouraging fellow members gifted for: (a) cathechetic preparation; (b) aiding adult theological reflection for Christian responsibility; (c) assisting children/youth in growth in Christian responsibility. Sharing in co-ordination of education/training of these persons. Encouraging and enabling youth and adult preparation for sharing the Good News with those they encounter in daily situations. Scheduling and monitoring the congregation's educational activities.

Ecumenical Co-ordinators

Being in touch with representatives of other denominations and religious groups in the local community. Identifying local and regional opportunities for co-operative Christian action in support of our common mission. Encouraging member's participation in such actions.

Missioners/ Rectors, etc.	Providing consulting, supervising, and mentoring services to congregations and regions as mutually agreed to by Bishop's Committees, Vestries, Regional Boards, Bishop, Council and themselves.

Priestly

Presbyters/ Priests	Presiding at and administering sacramental worship invitingly and with care. Helping the smooth interaction of various worship participants. Sharing in the planning and rehearsal of worship.
Preachers	Focusing the congregation's attention on God's loving initiative in history, in Christ, in sacramental presence, and in relationships, making possible harmony with God and humanity.
Priestly Ministry Co-ordinators	Sharing in planning and rehearsal of liturgy; planning the worship calendar. Scheduling worship leadership. Encouraging and co-ordinating education/training or worship leadership.

Some Key Features of Total Ministry

THE GIFTING EXERCISE

A number of features about Total Ministry deserve to be highlighted. As we have seen, the fundamental challenge is for lay people to accept their baptismal calling to ministry and mission – 'to stop attending church and start being the church'. Total Ministry is not just about creating leadership teams, let alone just about ordaining indigenous priests; it is about energizing baptized Christians.

For this reason a 'gifting day' plays a big part in the process. At St Stephen's, two stipendiary priests left in quick succession. The demoralized congregation invited a priest with professional skills as a facilitator to help them through the process of healing.

They began in the right place. Instead of rushing to call clergy, they looked at themselves and asked, 'What gifts do we have for ministry as this parish?' They put up big signs around the parish hall representing different areas of ministry gifts. Some appropriate education prefaced the congregation's exposure to those open lists and then people were invited to identify where their gifts might be best used.

The symbolism of the process was good, since it all happened in one room. There was no mistaking that these gifts were to be co-ordinated in one ministry. (Zabriskie, 1995, p. 56)

TRAINING PROGRAMMES

The churches in the USA and Canada make a big thing of 'training programs' which tend to strike the English as desperately earnest and slightly over the top. But there is no avoiding the fact that the success of Total Ministry is in large part due to this transatlantic emphasis on the need for Christian education and spiritual training.

St Christopher's had a bumpy history. The building was taken over by a splinter group who declared UDI from the diocese – until the church building was burned down. Even after a restart, the diocese had to inhibit (take away his licence) a visiting retired priest and withdraw the licence from a local lay reader. The response of the congregation to this electric situation was to decide to embark on two years of concentrated study of the New Testament Church. As a result, when the bishop next visited the church, the entire parish came, one by one, for the re-affirmation of the baptismal covenant. They came singly to acknowledge obedience to the promises made in baptism, to receive support from others and to offer the same to one another as a ministering community.

A Christian education programme, this time an Alpha course, was the basis for revival in a South African parish pastored by an American minister. The congregation was depressed because they could not find the money to attract a minister to stay for long. Bob agreed to a two-year contract on the understanding that members got down to some serious study. Sophie described what followed as being like a successful cataract operation: the skin was peeled away and the congregation suddenly realized that, with God, they could minister to each other. Three years later, with a church plant and two mission projects in Mozambique under their belt, they have just agreed to begin a full-scale EFM (Education for Ministry) course.

EFM is itself an American training programme, marketed by the University of the South at Sewanee, Tennessee, which gives lay people the opportunity to advance their theological understanding so that they can minister effectively in their local place. The 'learning in community' model is used with a seminar group of six to ten students. The 'mentors' (facilitators, tutors) are vetted and trained by Sewanee before they are allowed to lead the course. The course has been widely used all over the world and has proved an excellent springboard for the forming of local ministry teams. In the Cromhall benefice in Gloucestershire, four of the six members of the team are EFM trained and this has meant that the job of the tutor has been to encourage mutual education rather than to 'impart knowledge'.

Zabriskie outlines the style of education used in Nevada, and underlines its value.

> Eric, one of our regional vicars, brought our diocese a fresh understanding of educational principles, and he has retrained us to appreciate a participatory education and deeper learning experience. One of the vicars uses paper midrash as a right-brain activity that evokes excellent theological reflection. For paper midrash you need paper of various colours and textures and glue sticks – that's all. Ask participants to use these resources to express non-verbal theological responses to a text and then to share them with one another.
>
> There are so many possibilities for living theological education, in which learning ceases to be 'ought to know'; it becomes 'want to know'. I see that as a healthy transition from duty to desire, from 'we must' to 'we enjoy this'. (Zabriski, 1995, pp. 63–5)

He also emphasizes how a parish needs to go on studying rather than give it up after the initial training period. For continuing study helps to keep a perspective not only on who we are but whose we are; not only on what we do but on why and for whom we are doing it.

SOCIAL OUTREACH

One of the most striking things about Total Ministry on the other side of the pond is the emphasis it puts on social outreach. St Christopher's was the driving force behind an ecumenical respite-care scheme in its area. The deacon worked with an experienced social worker to provide training for volunteers and the scheme soon acquired a high-profile place in the community. The bishop was having a meal at a local restaurant on one occasion and the waiter asked him what church he 'worked at'. When he mentioned St Stephen's the waiter said, 'Oh, that's the church that cares about shut-in people and their families.'

Saint Mary's church is in a small city on Interstate 80. The parish has no building of its own, the old church having been sold a number of years ago and now serving as a local museum. The church as people is hardly a museum, however. They meet in a Missouri Synod Lutheran building. Worship is central for the people of Saint Mary's; visiting clergy come over once or twice a month for eucharist, and lay leaders provide morning prayer on the other Sundays. But their worship has body to it in that it moves out into the community. Members of the parish are active in community service in any number of ways. The parish is recognized as Saint Mary's Episcopal Church because of how members minister in the community and not because of what their building looks like.

The magazine of the Rural Chaplains' Association carries a number of stories of small congregations who have become involved in social outreach. For instance, Upper Sand Mountain parish, Alabama are helping rural communities in Russia and Casa Betal parish supports a local orphanage.

THE OFFICE OF DEACON

A key feature of social outreach in some Episcopal churches has been the revival of the ministry of deacons, who are seen as organizers of service to the community.

It is important to stress that the office of deacon is not primarily a liturgical role. Whatever liturgical functions remain for the deacon (reading the Gospel at the Eucharist, setting the table, and announcing the dismissal) have integrity only as they express what the deacon is doing outside the liturgical life of the congregation. It has been our experience that those called locally for diaconate are people who have been exercising diaconal ministry in numbers of ways for some time, and we have come to expect that prior activity in parish callings. Their commendation by, and subsequent training with, the congregation adds the dimension of communicator to the role they have already been carrying out. As ordained deacons they are interpreting the 'needs, hopes and concerns of the world' to the church, and they are learning to help marshal and train parishioners who have good intentions for active ministry in the community. Neither the deacon nor the priest is offered a solitary role. (Zabriskie, 1995, pp. 29–30)

Carolyn, Lionel and Jim all serve as deacons in one small parish. One works with handicapped children, another in health services to people with HIV/AIDS, and the other as a corrections officer. That's what they call 'work'. In addition, they work to stimulate the parish's commitment to reach out to the hungry by stocking a parish pantry for distribution, they support particular ministries among at-risk youth, and they continue to encourage visions of where the church can offer specific service to its community. It is a slow process but they are persistent people.

At Christ Church the deacons are the key to ministry outreach. When the homeless population began to swell in the city, one of the deacons worked with lay people and other clergy to begin an emergency shelter in one of the smallest local parishes. A food bank, somewhat like a mini-mart for the hungry, was opened in a former classroom that faced out on to the parking lot. It attracts queues of people five days a week. Everyone is treated with dignity and respect as volunteers try to meet their needs and those of their families. One of the deacons was responsible for getting this ministry going, but it is entirely staffed by lay-people from Christ Church and another city parish, while still other parishes contribute food for distribution.

Both deacons at Christ Church are also actively involved in a new venture, remodelling an old motel into single-residence occupancy for people who are homeless and re-entering the workforce. A member of the diocesan staff serves on the board, which is now ecumenical and community-based in representation. The parish does not need to work alone in meeting needs in the city.

One of the deacons has extensive experience in the banking field, and she is among several people exploring new ways of using money loaned by the church to help the poor.

LOCAL PRIESTS

Carl Dudley suggests that small churches want their pastors to be 'lovers' rather than professionals or specialists (*Making the Small Church Effective*, p. 71). David Ray in *Small Churches are the*

Right Size (p. 151) says, 'They want leaders who are human, approachable, and responsive. Thus, what is needed in small churches are "homemakers" rather than "housekeepers".' It is a good metaphor which excellently expresses the sort of qualities generally found in those called to local priesthood.

Dale had been the pharmacist in his community for many years when he was called to study for priesthood with his congregation. In the local drug-store, near the town's junior and senior high schools and complete with soda fountain, Dale had been a community-gatherer in a very real sense. And so he has continued to be since his ordination as priest, gathering the community for sacramental worship and the sharing of the Word.

Madge and Estelle had been long-time residents of their community when they were both commended for priesthood. Madge ran the local hardware-plus-a-lot-of-other-goods store, where people gathered not only to buy but also to chat and share bits of their lives with one another. Estelle was equally active in the small community, a former mining town on the side of a mountain. Both women were known for their unpretentious but strong faith.

Burt is a paediatrician who is also a gifted musician. He has revolutionized the music in his local church and has also helped the congregation to understand the rhythm of liturgy.

Ken works in a rural hospital and also runs a mail route in a remote rural area. He has a great gift for bringing people together and, when he was ordained, people on the mail route decided to club together and organize a barbecue for everyone after the service.

Kay works for the National Park and helps the congregation to take their responsibilities for the rest of creation seriously.

All local priests have something special to offer and they are all recognized by the congregation as being appropriate people to preside at the eucharist for them. But not all of them are expected to be a 'Jack-of-all-trades'.

In the Diocese of Nevada we tend to oversimplify the roles of ordained ministry to some degree, for the sake of a basic clarity. We say that the priest is the community gatherer, responsible for the sacramental worship of the local community. The priest may have other gifts as well, but with our locally called and trained clergy we are careful to ensure that every gift is not offered simultaneously. Real or imagined omnicompetence is a method of control and does not allow a congregation to express its shared ministry. We ask that the call to priesthood be supplemented by an intentional offering of one other gift besides the ministry of the Sacraments. For some that may be as preacher, for which the candidate will be trained and licensed. But not all priests are called to preaching. Some may be gifted as hospital visitors or as school board members or for any number of commitments in the community. We need also to remember that many of our local clergy are employed in full-time jobs in their communities, and they are not paid for their exercise as priest or deacon in the local parish. (Zabriskie, 1995, p. 27)

EUCHARISTIC MINISTERS

The Use of Eucharistic ministers is commonplace in the Roman Catholic Church (as in the UK), but in other denominations it is something of an innovation and it has clearly helped some ministers and congregations to jump the cultural divide between the traditional ministry and 'new directions'.

In his pamphlet *Small Parishes and Ministry*, Raymond Bierlein refers to this.

The use of Lay Eucharistic Ministers (LEMs) was an enlightening experience. This action of the LEMs, taking the Sacrament from the altar on a Sunday to the sick and shut-ins of the parish family, became a strong parish act of prayer. In church the LEMs prayed for those to whom the sacrament was to be taken, saying their names aloud during the Prayers of the People. After the worship service the LEMs made their visits, sometimes accompanied by other members of the congregation. Each LEM took the Sacrament to one person each week, and was expected to contact that person during the following week for a more social visit.

I saw so many excellent results of this ministry. The sick and shut-in really felt themselves a part of the congregation and of its Sunday worship; the congregation was kept vividly aware of their sick and shut-in members; the people participated regularly in significant acts of love towards their incapacitated fellow Christians; and not least, the people realised that all the people of God, not just the clergy, were involved in the holy things of God. (Brown *et al.*, 1997, p. 306)

THE SEMINARY-TRAINED PRIEST

Is there any job left for the seminary-trained stipendiary priest in this brave new church? The answer seems to be yes, but it will be a different job.

Zabriskie is clear that clergy (and laity) who come from another diocese need an induction course if they are to understand and work with the new culture. 'The question I now know I must ask is – "Are you trainable?" Some are and some are not; some know it and some do not'. (Zabriskie, 1995, p. 31)

There is also an issue about whether seminaries prepare students for Total Ministry and about whether dioceses realize how necessary it is to induct new ministers into the local context. There may be a 'national' church but there is no such thing as a national model for ministry; each context is unique.

But, undoubtedly, there is a leadership job for the stipendiary, just as there was for the 'overseers' and 'apostles' of biblical times. The first thing is that, as resident ministers, they are needed to keep the parish 'centred'. They are the 'keepers of the vision' and they need to ask hard questions so that the vision may be 'centred' or 'focused' on the Lord. The second is that they may, as 'visitors' (or apostles), facilitate the development of a parish towards Total Ministry. They are needed in a consultancy role.

When St Stephens had decided not to call a stipendiary minister, they recognized that they still needed someone to help them to choose and train a team. Later in the process, tension arose between the vestry, the team and the rest of the congregation: not enough consultation, elite group, questions like 'who do they think the are?' etc. Once again they needed the visitor from outside to help them to admit their inadequacies and to help to heal the wounds. As we saw above, North Michigan Diocese attach a stipendiary 'consultant' to each team. This facilitator plays a vital (and fascinating) role as 'midwife'.

THE ROLE OF THE BISHOP

Naturally the role of the bishop also needs to change. Zabriskie (1995, p. 36) writes perceptively about his experience in *Total Ministry*, chapter 3.

More and more I have seen myself, not as a leader who charges out in front of his flock, always admonishing them to 'do more' or 'be more', but as the cornerstone of ministry support and development in the diocese.

It is the function of the bishop to listen to and hold up the vision of the diocese's mission. The listening part is essential. It is not unlike the role of a spiritual director, who assists and nurtures growth by listening to those with whom he is working. The bishop listens to and watches for where the Lord is working, where the Spirit may be co-ordinating or reforming the balance of gifts; then the bishop helps to articulate the vision so that it may be truly owned by the ministering communities.

An interesting development which is mirrored in other dioceses is the use of 'regional vicars', who are perhaps more 'bishops-in-little' than assistant bishops, to share the burden of oversight with the diocesan.

At present I work with three regional vicars who are seminary-trained priests, and we are planning to add one more for one of our most remote areas. We understand that they are extended episcopate, in that they provide consistent teaching, training and pastoral care; they articulate the bishop's role as leaven in the areas of their responsibility. The four of us form a collegium that shares and expresses the call to ministry support and ministry development. We meet regularly to share the total picture of the diocese, to listen to what people are telling or showing us about their parish developments, and to offer insight and support to one another in our listening and responding to those with whom we work. One healthy spin-off of this understanding of leadership is that the old saw about life being 'lonely at the top' needn't be true any more. (*Ibid.*, p. 34)

In an interesting section on exercising discipline he points out that local priests are likely to be 'safe' priests.

When a diocese is using the proper process for calling local clergy, if that process is grounded in study and prayer, those called are generally not prone to canonical offences the likes of which are consuming so much of the church's time today. When the Spirit moves in a small, rural town, the Spirit is moving in a place where no secrets are hid. (p. 36)

TOTAL MINISTRY AND EVANGELISM

We have seen how Total Ministry can re-activate depressed congregations and help them to begin imaginative social outreach in their communities. It can also help them to think intelligently and imaginatively about evangelism – though it is more likely to be transformation-by-example than battery-by-Bible!

The churchwarden of one parish had great expertise in a form of martial arts. He began to develop a class for this, using its discipline as an attraction for local youth of any or no religious persuasion. Each session was framed in a form of prayer and continued with the development of respect for oneself and for others. Commandment becomes discipline and lifestyle. Out of this programme came Saint Luke's karate team, which travels and wins awards. The team is the first imaginative programmatic step towards a 'centre for community' to be built on the church grounds.

TOTAL MINISTRY AND ECUMENISM

As we have already seen, Total Ministry can lead beyond denominationalism to sharing programmes with other churches. It can also pave the way for real integration.

St Francis had been sharing worship with the local Methodist Church for twenty years. Eventually the decision was taken to close the Anglican church and to share the Methodist building for worship. Obviously there was grieving, but thanks to the ability of the congregation to share and to collaborate, the 'loss' was seen as an 'opportunity' for establishing a much-needed community facility, and now the former Anglican church building is in constant use again, not as a place of worship but as a base for gospel outreach.

The Anglican experience has been that, even as a minority denomination, congregations who initiate a programme for the poor, the hungry, the homeless or those in prison, or all of the above, find that help comes from many directions. The homeless shelter for women and children started out in an Episcopal church basement, and immediate help came from some Roman Catholic Franciscans. Now in its own building, the shelter has workers and supporters from a wide variety of faith expressions. Another effort to help the homeless began with a deacon's vision and now has a board that includes civic representatives, other denominations and a Muslim leader.

TOTAL MINISTRY AND THE INDIGENOUS PEOPLES

When Bishop Wesley Frensdorff retired from Nevada he became assistant bishop of Navajoland. There had been an Episcopal mission to the Navajo Indians for a century. The legacy was a number of medical centres, boarding schools and mission compounds with numerous decaying buildings. Frensdorff believed that indigenous ministry must be encouraged and he set about achieving this with determination and sensitivity. As a result the Episcopal Church in Navajoland now has about 1500 members, ten congregations and four house churches. There are four Navajo priests of whom one was consecrated in 1988.

Interestingly, while indigenous ministry has thrived, Total Ministry did not mesh well with the Navajo culture. It was found that the role of the 'holy man', the 'sacral person', set apart from and supported by the community is in fact highly indigenous to Navajo culture. Commenting on this in *Reshaping Ministry*, George Sumner suggests that what 'the total ministry camp bemoans is professionalism: what the Navajo values is sacrality'. Interestingly the Pakeha in New Zealand have had much the same experience in trying to 'export' total ministry to the Maori church.

Bishop Frensdorff was also responsible for the spread of Roland Allen's ideas in the Spanish-speaking Episcopal Church of Honduras. Bishop Leo Frade chronicles the results in *Reshaping Ministry*, chapter 6.

Church growth in Honduras has been extraordinary and exciting. The church is strong, dynamic and growing by leaps and bounds. In 1980 it consisted of nine congregations with about 1000 members. Today we have 45 congregations with over 10,000 members. The challenge is keeping up with ministry training to serve the needs of our members.

He also notes that it is not just a matter of training indigenous clergy; the laity are thirsty for Christian education and are fully involved in ministry.

INTERNATIONAL LINKS

Another exciting spin-off of the development of Total Ministry in Canada and USA has been the way it has inspired churches in Australia and New Zealand. Zabriskie visited New Zealand in 1990 and 1993 and, as we shall see in the second part of this chapter, he had a great influence on developments there. Three New Zealanders showed up at the LAND conference in 1996 and, at the Living Stones conference, there were a New Zealander and a South African. In 1999, a major international conference on Collaborative Ministry took place in San Francisco attended by over a hundred delegates worldwide, including twelve from the UK.

LOCAL MINISTRY AND THE DIOCESE

Total Ministry affirms the localness of the local congregation. But ironically it can be the catalyst for a new recognition of the importance of the diocese.

> One of the most interesting and helpful developments to date has been the gradual release from a kind of congregationalism that has long been a part of the Episcopal Church's unwritten tradition and which had nurtured a kind of adversarial stance of local parish to diocese: 'us' and 'them'. It still surfaces now and then, but now it is a surprise rather than a given. The old categorical systems and the structures that grew out of them were far more conducive to that particular kind of insular congregationalism. Total-ministry development moves people and parishes into relationships that extend beyond the local scene. (Zabriskie, 1995, p. 73)

From Ancaster in Ontario we have the same story.

> Most importantly, we are developing a sense of common mission. There is talk of unifying a couple of parishes to better serve the community. There are people being trained by the Diocese to provide leadership in revitalisation. Fifteen of our young people went on the diocesan youth camp last year, and we sent four youth representatives on the Diocesan Convention. There is a new awareness that our relationship with the Diocese is not adversarial but a realisation that 'we' are the Diocese. There is trust developing within the Deanery. Trust that the Holy Spirit is with us. Trust that, having eaten at our

> Lord's table, we should now work in His fields. Trust that, having turned to Christ, He is there. (Brown *et al.*, p. 333)

As was pointed out earlier, the American bishop is very well placed to take a strong leadership role and to adopt radical measures. Numbers of clergy are small and they do not have a freehold tenure. If the bishop has the charisma to 'sell' a vision and enjoys the respect of the members of the Convention, a new strategy for ministry can be worked out and put in place in a relatively short time. The Diocesan Office in North Michigan sends tapes of addresses by the bishop to enquirers about Total Ministry which show exactly how this can be done. Radical English bishops might find life more difficult!

A SUCCESS STORY

Finally, an exciting report on the effect of Total Ministry in Calumet in the Diocese of Northern Indiana.

> Imagine two pictures. The first is a region, a deanery of seven parishes that have only four priests. A region that is racked with financial difficulties in just keeping the doors open. A region weary of rummage sales just to keep the light-bills paid, weary of hearing of one crisis after another. A region that could easily fall head down into maintenance mode until the last person out of the doors turns off the lights.
>
> The second picture is of a region that has developed a new sense of mission, a fresh purpose. This region has a revitalised laity. A laity that has decided that the reason we show up every Sunday morning is to 'celebrate', not just congregate. The reason they are Episcopalians is that they are Christians, not just descendants of founding fathers. A region that is experiencing a revitalisation of the Holy Spirit in its approach to 'being' Church.
>
> These two pictures are of the same place: the Calumet Deanery. In the shadow of the once mighty steel mills, the Calumet (as it is known locally) stands in tatters. We have a dearth of clergy. Two of the remaining four priests are essentially non-stipendiary out of necessity. And one of the remaining priests has announced his retirement in September.
>
> There have been tremendous upheavals in the past two years. Yet, something glorious is happening. An enlivened and aware laity has emerged with a vision of mission for the church. (Brown *et al.*, p. 332)

New Zealand

A recent visitor to a number of Total Ministry parishes in New Zealand began his report as follows.

> 'You English, you have your roots in the past; but for us Kiwis, our roots are in the future.' What the Bishop of Waiapu intended as a pithy debating point exactly highlights what seems to me to be the chief characteristic of the New Zealand Anglican Church – a readiness to take risks. Moving within weeks from the General Synod Debate on 'Stranger in the Wings' to a church where local people are ordained after a dozen 'training' evenings was a 'Fidelio' experience.
>
> The Kiwis are practical people, and the bottom line is not what do the rules say but does it work. 'We believe God wants less red tape and more pink elastic', and they certainly leave plenty of room for the Holy Spirit to spread his wings.
>
> Total/Mutual Ministry is part of the risk-taking process. In a church which has no provincial advisory board for ministry, each diocese does it differently, and teams are very local indeed. One gets the impression that they make up the rules as they go along, while the diocesan authorities breathlessly try to catch up with them. It's all very New Testament and free and, by contrast, I cannot help feeling we are indeed in chains.

A first visit to New Zealand can be a heady experience but, of course, their context is not our context. Distances are much the same but the population is only four million, of whom one million live in Auckland. Rural areas can be very sparsely populated indeed. They are also tucked away on the edge of the world and are very conscious that what they do not do for themselves no one else will do for them.

The Anglican Church is in no sense established but, historically, it has had and still does have a significant place in Pakeha (white) culture. There is also an Anglican Maori church which now has its own parallel organization. In contrast, therefore, to North America, the first peoples already have their own well-established church with its own hierarchy and synodical government.

WHAT DRIVES TOTAL MINISTRY?

No one likes change and few are willing to accept it unless they are uncomfortable where they are. Invariably what has driven Total Ministry in New Zealand has been lack of money.

Half of the parishes in one diocese cannot pay their way and many have been receiving a subsidy from 'the centre' for generations. For as long as anyone could remember, the congregation at Kateora had devoted most of their energy to raising money to pay for a minister. Their failure, despite all their efforts, inevitably had a debilitating effect on the congregation and, as numbers dwindled, the church building fell into disrepair. Determined that their church should stay open, they agreed to try the Total Ministry option. Becoming a Total Ministry parish meant that they no longer had to contribute to the stipends fund and, as a result, they have been able to reorder their church, refurbish their parish rooms (which are now heavily used by the local community) and fund an imaginative social welfare scheme in the area.

The parish of Merridon could no longer afford a minister, so it decided to share one with a neighbouring congregation. Even that proved too much of a financial challenge, and, eventually, all they could afford was a quarter of the stipend of a minister who was expected to serve four congregations scattered over 150 square miles. Unsurprisingly, this proved pretty unsatisfactory. The minister could not possibly visit more than two churches on a Sunday and pastoral visiting was extremely difficult because of the distances involved. Nevertheless, each congregation expected 95 per cent of the minister for themselves and, because they still officially had 'their own minister', (s)he was expected to fill the familiar autocratic leadership role model and to chair every committee. For them, Total Ministry has cut the Gordian knot. They are now happy to accept a shared responsibility for the success or failure of 'their' church, and numbers are growing again.

Like most rural parishes, the congregations in the area of Naronga were determined that the doors of their beloved churches should not close but, like the others, they could no longer afford the stipend of a minister. Their three church buildings are all within ten miles of what, by New Zealand standards, is a large town with its own self-supporting Anglican church. They were offered the option of linking with big sister in the town but, like so many rural congregations in the UK, they did not take kindly to the idea. The diocese encouraged them to visit a Total Ministry parish on the other side of the mountains and they were so impressed that they decided to have a go at 'do it yourself' ministry themselves. Four years later, two of the three congregations are growing, one in a Maori area has a youth ministry explosion on its hands and they have no less then five (FIVE!) priests with local licence. The churches and church halls are now in excellent repair and they are about to undertake a major old-peoples' social housing project on some land they have discovered they own.

Jenny who was preparing the parish for total ministry put it this way:

> *I kept saying, 'Your future is in your own hands.' That started to mean something when they realized that it could mean freedom from having to find a whole stipend. 'It will mean that no one can close you down.' I talked about us becoming an anarchist collective and exercising direct democracy as opposed to representative democracy.*

There are examples of parishes which had gone 'Total', experienced revival and have now raised the money to pay for a minister of their own again, but most are adamant that they do not want to return to the old model of 'paid minister rules, OK'.

An unexpected, and perhaps unhelpful, corollary of the 'money' factor is that, to date, virtually no Total Ministry parish has a stipendiary priest; Total Ministry is not seen as appropriate for large successful parishes. The dioceses recognize the theological inconsistency of this but also recognize the difficulties of a stipendiary in the team.

WHERE DID IT COME FROM?

Lack of money may be what sets the ball rolling but it is the theological vision of Total Ministry which has fired peoples' resolve to give it a try. The visit of Bishop Zabriskie from the Diocese of Nevada, USA, was clearly enormously influential and, to a large extent, his vision is their vision. It has about it a simple coherence which wins converts.

In May 1994, Canterbury Diocese produced a handbook on how to initiate Total Ministry, with accompanying guidelines for the training of licensed lay ministers. Dunedin Diocese now has a large number of 'total' parishes and, in the North Island, it is very much flavour of the month. The Trans-Tasman Conference on Rural Ministry and the Canterbury Rural Ministry Unit have also had a major influence in spreading Roland Allen's ideas both in New Zealand and Australia, as their reports show. A recent book by John Mavor from Australia, *Calling Us by Name*, comes from the same stable.

GIFTING AND CHOOSING

Like our own Canon Tiller, Total Ministry Dioceses in New Zealand begin by emphasizing the importance of baptism as a sacrament implying 'ordination to ministry'. Ministry should be the vocation of the whole congregation, not of a single individual. As the members of the Merridon team talked about the origins of Total Ministry in their parish, they agreed that the seed had been sown long before. In retrospect, they could see that ministers had been preaching the gospel of 'collaborative ministry' for at least twenty years. What struck most of them as new was a diocesan-inspired 'gifting day' exercise when, after teaching based on 1 Corinthians 12, each member of the congregation was encouraged to offer what they perceived to be their gifts and people were allowed to name the gifts that they perceived in others. The fact that this gifting exercise was not limited to church activities but included 'secular' life as well was delightfully illustrated by a six-year-old who said that her ministry was to look after the cat! Weston is not a Total Ministry parish but each year they have a special service which recognizes and gives thanks for the varied gifts of those who serve the church: the priests, the musicians, the children, the cleaners. The organist's contribution one year was a delightful little composition which wound together thirty well-known hymn tunes within four minutes!

The gifting exercise is linked with the identification of parish needs. The Canterbury Diocese booklet referred to, suggests the following: preachers, worship leaders, catechists, pastoral ministers, Eucharistic ministers, evangelists, administrators and healers, besides local priests and deacons. In Chiltern parish, the congregation identified their areas of need as pastoral, worship, young people, social ministry, evangelism, administration; and the gifting exercise aimed to match names to needs with (hopefully) a committee for each area identified. (No prizes for guessing which committees have not yet been formed!) Significantly, the areas of need which are rarely identified are 'leadership' and 'co-ordination'. In some parishes there is an ad hoc leadership team which includes the authorized ministers and the leaders of the various committees; in others, leadership is exercised through the vestry (PCC). Putting 'gifting' first and 'leadership' last gives their Total Ministry a very different flavour from some of the UK local ministry models.

As in Nevada, USA, the local congregation must 'approve' those who will minister to them and in their name. But, since the gifting exercise comes first and no one wants to undermine a neighbour's perceptions of their own gifts, different parishes seem to have different ways of doing things. In Chiltern parish, members of the committees are volunteers but the conveners (leaders) are 'chosen'. In Wanata parish, all those on all committees are 'chosen'; and, in both cases, all those on committees are presented to the congregation and to the bishop, and in some sense authorized by him.

In all dioceses the 'gifting day' is later followed by a 'choosing day'. In one diocese this relates to choosing the conveners of committees and those to be presented for ordination; in another the 'choosing' day is exclusively about identifying those who might be recommended for ordination. In either case, the importance of the day is recognized by everyone, as the following example shows.

The parish of Merridon have been in and out of something like Total Ministry for over ten years. At the first attempt there was excellent preparation by a stipendiary minister and all seemed to be going well. Then the minister left, and a number of key lay people moved. As a result, when they came to the 'choosing day' there were not many serious candidates to choose from. The diocesan officers running the day concluded that, in the circumstances, it would be right to 'choose' leaders of committees but not to 'choose' potential ordinands. This was seen by some of the congregation as a 'failure' and the whole process ground to a halt for a few years, though some of the committees did begin to start work. Six years later, the last vestiges of a stipendiary minister finally vanished over the horizon and another choosing day was held. This time, two ordinands were identified and were priested in 1998. Because of the history there is considerable scepticism among many of the congregation about whether it will work, but the chosen ones, lay and ordained, are extremely enthusiastic and the diocese, learning from the past, is providing serious back-up and support for the parish in order to ensure that Total Ministry does get off the ground this time around.

The story of the team in Wairoa, in the Diocese of Waiapu, illustrates the extent to which some are prepared to learn on the hoof. In 1992 the stipendiary retired and the bishop persuaded the parish to have a go at appointing a team. There were no rules about how to do this but, with much prayer, an excellent group emerged and they were made responsible for worship and pastoral care. Clearly they still needed a priest and they put forward two candidates. Neither were accepted by the selection panel and the fall-out from that can only be guessed at. Nevertheless, they did not give up but were given the help of a Ministry Enabler in 1994, and this very experienced priest guided them through the next stage. They had a rather more formal choosing day in 1996 and now have one priest and two deacons.

THE STIPENDIARY

As pointed out earlier, Total Ministry only happens when the congregation can no longer afford a stipendiary minister. Sometimes it is a last resort before closure, sometimes far-sighted stipendiaries have been preparing for the day of withdrawal for many years. But there rarely seems to be an overlap between a stipendiary and a priest with local licence, nor is a stipendiary found as a member of a Total Ministry team. Where this does happen, the stipendiary can inevitably feel a bit redundant. Boyd Wilson from Dunedin Diocese describes his feelings with great good humour in *Growing Mutual Ministry*.

> I rather paternally assumed that I would facilitate the training of the ministry group. 'Forget it,' said my wife. 'I for one am really looking forward to being part of a group without the vicar hovering around. And anyway we'll be better off without you.' She was right! (Adams, 1997, p. 18)

THE STIPENDIARY MINISTRY ENABLER

The residual job of the stipendiary is that of 'enabler' and, indeed, in the more 'advanced' dioceses a Ministry Enabler is becoming an essential part of the Total Ministry package. The enabler is distinctly not 'the vicar', even though (s)he is paid for by contributions from a number of Total Ministry parishes.

The last 'vicar' of Chiltern, with the encouragement of the diocese, prepared the parish for Total Ministry. When he left, a former archdeacon who had retired to the area became their enabler. He was big enough and wise enough not to be sucked into being the 'vicar' and, under his guidance, the team grew to maturity and produced two priests of their own. Ten years down the line they are quite capable of running their own show but are very aware that they need diocesan guidance in such matters as producing new members, vision setting, training, ecumenical relations and so on. The diocese, for their part, are getting their act together and are providing an enabler for four Total Ministry parishes in the northern area.

At a personal level, the transition from being a 'vicar' to becoming an enabler is not, of course, an easy one. Tom was part-time minister to three rural congregations and prepared them for Total Ministry over a period of five years. After a traumatic six months when it was unclear whether the money could be found to fund the experiment, he has now been reincarnated as enabler to these congregations and as 'encourager enabler' to a number of other potential Total Ministry parishes. It is a relief not to be an 'inadequate vicar' any more, or at least it would be if his old congregations would let him go! Potentially the job of enabler, both in stimulating new parishes and in maintaining existing teams, is a very exciting one, but it is very much a new invention and, if they are to be effective, enablers need a diocesan support structure which isn't yet in place.

From Dream to Journey is the story of Jan Clark whose husband was vicar of a rural group of parishes in Southland. The parishes decided to begin Total Ministry and Jan was called as a potential priest. She explains how difficult it was to be caught between diocese and parish in the selection process and how hard it was for them to trust each other. However, it all came right in the end and, in 1993, she was ordained and other ministers were licensed.

Her husband remained as priest enabler to the parish for two years and she felt this was particularly valuable. 'Someone who allows a sense of safety while maintaining the challenge to continue the journey is vital at this stage.' Jan has now moved on and, therefore, had to surrender her local licence. However, she has herself been asked to be a priest enabler to another parish and, of course, her past experience is tremendously valuable. In the very conservative rural parishes of the area she discovered how important it was to listen to the stories of the past.

> The saints of the past were renamed and stories of great community gatherings were relived. It seemed to be impossible to start thinking about the present or cast an eye into the future without first knowing just where we had come from. . . . I am aware of the wisdom of the community I work with. My task is often just to help them hold their story so that they can see and name those things which mark the quality of their life together. (Adams, 1997, p. 14)

WORSHIP LEADERS

If Anglican parishes are to 'go it alone' without a stipendiary, they need to have some way of providing worship and of celebrating the eucharist. For the Kiwis this isn't an insuperable problem, given their liking for 'pink elastic'.

The use of extended communion is relatively common, though at least two diocesan authorities are now trying to enforce rules about 'who' 'where' and 'when'. In any case it becomes less of an issue when priests with local licence are ordained.

Those who administer the sacrament, either by extended communion or when a priest is present, will often be 'worship leaders'. All Total Ministry parishes have a worship subcommittee and a number of the members are nominated as 'worship leaders'. They are given practical training for this ministry by the diocesan enabler and they soon seem to gain confidence and do the job very competently.

At Weston, even when there is a priest present, Bob, a young farmer, welcomes the congregation and leads the first part of the service with great panache, introducing readers and soloists in a human and interesting way. He is one of four members of the congregation who are licensed as worship leaders. At Danfield, Geoff, complete with all-enveloping beard, open-neck shirt, guitar and overhead projector, leads the service with great confidence and assurance. At the monthly family service, there are forty or so in the congregation, only a handful of whom are over the age of fifty. Usually there is no priest present but the sermon is preached by a reader (in formal blue suit). During the sermon, the fifteen or so young people go off to a 'Sunday School' in the porch and later came back to show the congregation their work. On average, a dozen lay people contribute to the service, which is always followed by excellent refreshments. At Wanata, in a remote area of the North Island, the Total Ministry congregation has eight worship leaders and, two by two, they take it in turn to lead the service. In a Brethren church in Byford, a different family takes the service each week.

READERS

The other resource are readers, who are generally available even in remote rural areas. The training for readers is very practical and, frankly, minimal. Paul is a retired farmer who was encouraged to train as a reader by his stipendiary minister. He and a friend went to twelve sessions run by the minister where the emphasis was on how to prepare and deliver a sermon. He was then licensed, and finds that he is needed to preach perhaps once every six weeks. He was given two books to read during the course but his training did not involve serious theological study (though he had previously attended four residential events on the lines of Spring Harvest which included Bible study and teaching). Clearly he has not had the chance to come to grips with modern biblical scholarship. He is now being encouraged to enrol on an Education for Ministry course which would certainly begin to meet an obvious need. Indeed EFM and distance learning, which are co-ordinated at provincial level, are playing a major part in a determined drive to offer members of Total Ministry congregations the chance to explore the Christian faith at greater depth.

In the suburban Total Ministry parish of New Brighton, Canterbury, there has developed a 'Sermons or other possibilities of breaking open the Word of God group!' They meet once a month and co-ordinate themes for services, and discuss how these can best be communicated.

PRIESTS WITH LOCAL LICENCE

In these ways and with these resources, Total Ministry parishes ensure that there is no lack of services in their churches. But, like our New Testament ancestors, they do need someone to preside at the eucharist. In such a flexible situation it is hardly surprising that different dioceses use different guidelines for local priesthood. At least one diocese does not have local priests at all while another licenses local priests as NSMs. What seems to be becoming the norm, however, is that the vocation to local priesthood is recognized and such priests are called 'priests with local licence'. They will be members of an established Total Ministry parish and will be 'chosen' by the congregation as well as being tested by the bishop and his advisers.

The process of identifying local priests is simple and straightforward. A diocesan enabler comes to the parish and runs a 'choosing day', as outlined above, with the expectation that two (or more) people will be nominated for ordination. The congregation usually choose people from the pool of readers and worship leaders whose ministry they have already experienced. In Merridon, the congregation nominated William, a reader whose family had lived in the area for generations, and Andrew, a small farmer who is a relative newcomer. Bob, one of the local priests at Chiltern, is a member of a large local family and, because he drives the ambulance, he knows everyone. He is a kind sincere person, the salt of the earth. Their other priest was a farmer's wife who has just moved to another diocese; the 'replacement' is also a farmer's wife with young children, a wise and articulate person who is very conscious of the awesome thing she has taken on.

The list of those who have been nominated by the congregation goes to the bishop who, after consultation, approaches certain individuals and asks them whether they are prepared to consider ordination. If they agree, they are interviewed at length by two clergy whom he nominates (there is no central ABM in the New Zealand church) and, if everyone agrees, they proceed to a twelve-week course organized in their parish by the diocesan enabler. They go to a pre-ordination retreat, are made deacon at the Cathedral, and are subsequently priested in their local church.

How very different from the way we do things in the old

country! And it is easy enough to fault such a fast-track system. Leaving aside the obvious issues about standards, it is certainly surprising that the first time William and Bill met others who were going to be ordained with them was on their ordination retreat. It is even more surprising that the stipendiaries being trained for ministry at St John's College, Christchurch, do not meet priests with local licence during their training. In the light of this, it is perhaps most surprising of all that priests with local licence rarely feel looked down on by stipendiaries or regarded as second-class priests by the congregation.

It would seem that the reason local priesthood obviously works in New Zealand is the result of a combination of factors. The first is the relatively small numbers of stipendiaries. One diocese has thirty, another seventy. Increasingly, their church is being run by lay people, readers, NSMs and priests with local licence. There is, therefore, less likelihood of local priests being present at a church gathering where they feel isolated.

The second reason that local priesthood works is that the 'job specification' does not carry with it the leadership expectations we are used to in England. As we have seen, Total Ministry begins with the recognition of the gifts of all the members of the congregation, and authority for ministry in the parish remains with the bishop, the churchwardens and the vestry – a responsibility which is delegated to a number of functional subcommittees. Within such a structure, priests with local licence are simply members of the worship subcommittee – they are not responsible for the total ministry of the parish. The fact that they are usually ordained in pairs helps to defuse any attempts to put a lone individual on a pedestal.

A casual English observer might be tempted to describe them as 'mass priests', but that is certainly not what it feels like to sit with them at a church meeting. For one thing, they are not allowed to celebrate the eucharist outside their own parish, so they can hardly become mass priests in the traditional sense. But, more importantly, they are clearly respected and looked up to locally, and are generally recognized as the 'right' people to celebrate the mysteries in that place. In the best sense, they are treated as the local 'elders'. This is a role which is, at the same time, doable and also extremely fulfilling. It is a vocation to 'presidency' rather than to 'being a vicar' and, since it is a very different vocation from that of the stipendiary, it does not mean constantly longing to jump the fence into the other field. As Bill puts it, 'To be a priest with local licence is exciting, frightening, but a great privilege.'

A visitor to the team at Kateora would find it difficult to 'spot the dog-collar'. Alan, one of the five priests at Naronga, is adamant that he had no pastoral aptitude or responsibility and that his particular gift is to reflect on the future and be a 'vision' person for the parish. Bill, at Chiltern, is regarded with the greatest respect, one of his gifts being that he is the living repository of local history, but he is neither chairman of the team, nor convener, nor administrator; nor does he wield a special authority because he is ordained. He is simply a highly respected member of the team. In contrast, an experienced stipendiary parish priest retired to Wanata assuming that he would be 'used' by the parish. He was very politely told that, when he had lived and worshipped with the congregation for two or three years, they would consider asking the bishop to give him a local licence. Who there is the second-class priest!

The 1994 handbook from Canterbury has the following job description:

> The Priest with Local Licence is not the pastor, the teacher or the administrator. They gather the church to make eucharist and to offer worship. They are the sacramental people who help the community celebrate, mourn or lament. They are 'broken healers' who help others find healing for their brokenness. Priests with Local Licence call the rest of us to hear God's call, to respond to that call, and offer our life in service to God. Along with the Ministry Enabler they renew our vision. Such people symbolise and make coherent the 'priesthood of all believer's' in that particular congregation.

DOES IT WORK?

While grudgingly admitting that this does all seem uneerily New Testament, it may seem to English readers to be extraordinarily haphazard and fraught with danger. To which our Kiwi brothers and sisters would counter, 'but it works'. And the most telling justification for 'lots of pink elastic' is that it does seem to bring home the bacon. When asked, 'Is it worth it? Does it work?', virtually everyone in Total Ministry parishes would reply, 'Well, we certainly wouldn't want to go back to the old model.' Doris, a lay person who has moved from a large traditional parish to Naronga says, 'It's very different, it's much friendlier, and I've really come to like it.' Meetings and services in Total Ministry parishes are friendly, cheerful, informal family affairs which run on muffins and cups of coffee, and a visitor gets the feeling that a lot of people have a major investment in the enterprise. Total Ministry parishes are probably not so appealing if you want to creep in at the back and escape being noticed, nor if you want a traditional service, traditional preaching and traditional pastoral care. As Doris says, it is very different – a matter of new wine and new wineskins. But in many places which were moribund a great deal is now happening.

Horton, a group of very remote rural congregations on the coast, not only survive now but have developed a pattern for celebrating major festivals which draws in crowds of a hundred and more, much to the amazement of the stipendiary from a large agricultural township who gives them an occasional hand. Oneto was scheduled for closure when a local farmer suddenly realized what was about to happen. He got together a group of local people who formed a local team, and they now run not only a successful small church but also a Christian bookshop which serves the whole area. A network of ten deep-rural congregations on the West Coast of South Island has responded to the ministry of a young enthusiastic enabler appointed by the bishop and are now moving into Total Ministry; four years ago they were moving towards closure.

It is not just that such congregations are surviving and keeping their beloved church open either. Kateora have regular 'outreach' suppers to which they invite those on the 'edge' of the church roll and those who have been contacted via their social welfare programme. They have a monthly family service and, for the weeks in between, have devised a form of postal Sunday school for children scattered over a very wide area. Chiltern have a weekly tea club for children when they arrive back on the school bus.

WORSHIP IN TOTAL MINISTRY PARISHES

All the services now aim to be 'child friendly' and every church has a specific monthly family service. The parishes have a regular training programme, including EFM and ALPHA, and since all the training offered to subcommittee members is open to the whole congregation, the general level of competence is surprisingly high.

A recent visitor writes:

> I attended five acts of worship, and though I never had a sense of mystery and awe, I was often touched by the humanity of presentation. Nor was I ever bored! There seemed to be a number of people in each group I attended who were confident enough to lead prayer without prior warning. None of the services was the property of a lone individual – rather they got close to being the shared offering of a large percentage of the congregation.

PASTORAL CARE

Every Total Ministry parish has a pastoral subcommittee, though this often operates at a fairly rudimentary level. At Merridon it is run down and, frankly, disorganized. One member, Milly, writes that the last meeting was two months before and she has no idea when the next one is going to be. 'Pastoral care' there means care for members of the congregation rather than care for everyone in the locality, and though the intention is to visit everyone on the church roll, in practice this is little more than a pious hope. Those who are actually cared for are those who are regular attenders or who have come into contact with the church because of some 'crisis'. Much the same seems to be true in Naronga and Kateora, though in the former there is a paid administrator who has introduced a more structured approach to visiting. Perhaps two things stand out. First, at the very least, basic pastoral care in Total Ministry parishes is now provided for the regular congregation. Second, this is seen as the responsibility of a lay-led team and only very rarely are priests with local licence involved in leading the subcommittee. Nowhere is pastoral care 'expected' of them.

THE SOCIAL GOSPEL AND TOTAL MINISTRY PARISHES

Perhaps the most unexpected discovery is the extent to which Total Ministry parishes are involved in 'social' activity. The New Zealand economy has gone through a very difficult five years and unemployment is running at over 10 per cent. One response is for those who are in work to contribute canned food, clothes and so on to 'centres for the unemployed'. Virtually all Total Ministry parishes organize such collections in their area, without seeing this as being anything out of the ordinary. Another result of the economic downturn is that, wherever possible, social provision is being privatized, and, of course, a particularly vulnerable group is the elderly. The congregation at Naronga and Tunstock have taken up government grants and become involved in the provision of shared-equity retirement homes. A visitor is immediately struck by the fact that each unit is individually designed, and the human concern and level of involvement of the (Christian) Trustees is impressive. The Presbyterian congregation at Tunstock run an 'Op Shop' (Charity Shop), and the Naronga congregation are working at Spearhead, a depressed Maori area, to establish a mother-and-toddler group and a Sunday school. R.E. is no longer a curriculum subject in New Zealand state schools but members of local Christian congregations are welcome to take (unofficial) classes. The congregation at Naronga, Wanata and Chiltern have accepted the challenge and team members go into their local schools regularly.

Finally, one of the results of not having to find a full stipend for a resident minister is that Total Ministry parishes are suddenly richer than they have ever been in living memory. At Naronga, the sheltered housing scheme has really been made possible because the congregation can now afford to pay a part-time administrator. All the church buildings have been upgraded: Naronga, for instance, has been beautifully reordered (no Advisory Group there!) and the church halls, which most New Zealand churches have, even in rural areas, have usually been brought up to an excellent standard, thus providing a facility increasingly used for secular events by the local community.

ECUMENICAL RELATIONS

Rather sadly, Total Ministry has not generally improved ecumenical relations and at least two shared-ministry arrangements have collapsed under the strain. The problems seem to be twofold. First, our different denominations have very different assumptions about what 'Church' means. The differences can normally be swept under the carpet but they are brought out into the open and highlighted when a congregation is challenged to fulfil their baptism promise and to share in ministry. Second, the role of the minister changes when a parish adopts Total Ministry principles. Increasingly the Total Ministry congregation find it difficult to relate to a traditional-role minister and vice versa.

On the other hand, this is not always the case. The Presbyterian churches at Merridon and Kateora have both grasped the principles of Total Ministry though this has not yet been formalized. Jim is told that, though they do like to see him, the newly trained worship group can get on quite well without him for two Sundays a month! Barbara took a three month sabbatical and, instead of importing a selection of retired ministers from Canterbury, the congregation decided to ask Barbara to give them training so that they could 'do it themselves'. Now Barbara has returned, they have insisted that she spends a full Sunday with each congregation rather than busting a gut to cover three churches on the same day.

PROBLEMS

In all of these ways, Total Ministry parishes show that the model can work in practice. It would be foolish to pretend that there is not a flip-side to the coin. There are inevitable problems and gaps. Training of clergy and readers is probably inadequate and the integration of local authorized ministers into the diocesan structure is rudimentary.

Another very basic point is that the starting point of Total Ministry is a gifting exercise for the whole congregation and the creation of a team is secondary to the harnessing of gifts. Teams, therefore, are usually a slightly haphazard assembly of the chairs of independent subcommittees rather than 'leadership teams'. They often lack cohesion, with no one being quite sure who is supposed to convene meetings or 'drive' the team. The responsibility for leadership of the local church remains in the hands of the churchwardens and the vestry, and this is not always very satisfactory.

Good teamworking does not, of course, just happen and, with the structural uncertainty outlined above, personality clashes can and do happen. At Kateora 'four people left the team two years ago and, since then, things have gone much more smoothly' (not so smoothly as to prevent a heated argument about a historical detail when an English visitor was present!). At Wanata, a reader, a charismatic organist and a newly arrived NSM are quite evidently trying to dominate the team, and are only held in check by a very holy, very wise and very firm Franciscan tertiary! The bishop is sometimes called in personally by churchwardens to 'sort out a difficult person' but, after all, that's what New Testament bishops were for too!

IN CONCLUSION

Total Ministry in New Zealand is thriving and they have much experience and many insights which can help us in the UK to see the wood for the trees. Above all, their experience gives us assurance that we are not in this alone and that it seems to be 'of the Spirit'. As Bill said of ordination, 'It's exciting, it's frightening, but it's a privilege.' Obviously there are dangers and probably there will be a few disasters. But it does seem to hit the nail on the head; it does free the people of God to *be* the people of God.

8

Conclusion

Historians of twentieth-century Britain may well identify 1997, rather than the Millennium, as the pivotal moment for our society. Those of us who were there will tell our great-grandchildren of the election night of May 1st and of Sunday morning the 31st August when we heard that Diana, Princess of Wales, had been killed in a car crash.

We will try to describe the scenes of jubilation on the one hand, and grief on the other, and attempt to explain why we found them so liberating and astonishing. For together these events revealed a new England, a new society which rejected old authority and which had finally turned its back on the culture of Empire. Of course the change has not happened overnight; it has been in gestation since the sixties and it has many facets. But the two which most impinge on local ministry are perhaps the revival of regionalism and the rejection of 'old authority'.

'No one knows what form 'Englishness' will take in the future, if indeed there will ever be a national culture again. But one thing is already clear – that if Britannia is to be ruled, the centre must once again devolve power to the local tribes. Scotland, Wales, Cornwall, Bradford, Moreton-in-the-Marsh, Upper as opposed to Lower Slaughter – government has to begin with base communities if there is to be a consensus for government. 'Subsidiarity' can now be seen as the necessary prerequisite for social cohesion. It is perhaps helpful to see local ministry as part of this development.

The rejection of 'old authority' has naturally included the churches. And to all but the most conservative it has become apparent that the structures of the institutional church which we have inherited are no longer appropriate if we are to preach the gospel in a pluralist society. By contrast, 'base communities' who together share the 'burden of ministry' and of whom one may be ordained – collaborative all-member ministry – not only offer us a structure which resonates with the early church; they also offer a real hope that in this way the gospel may be 'gossiped' in small groups and so listened to again.

Local ministry affirms the base community. This may be a local congregation, or a benefice, or a school, or a factory, or even a golf club – our definition of 'local' needs to be flexible. But we have come to recognize that base communities are the Church, and that the rest of the structure exists to support them, not vice versa. In fact, just what Canon Tiller told us a generation ago.

Local ministry helps the members of the base community to recognize that they have within their number all the gifts they need to do God's will in their place, if they will but listen to his call. They can and should be able to 'do it themselves', including finding someone to be their local priest.

Local ministry is highly suspicious of academic bits of paper, and boards and committees with their earnest addiction to forms and reports and 'standards'. After all, local people know that at grass-roots level it is the gifts of the Spirit, love, joy and peace, which transfigure individuals and communities and places, and that God ministers through the most unexpected people, irrespective of academic background.

And yet those who run local ministry schemes also recognize that we live in a sophisticated world where people are encouraged to ask questions and to think for themselves; a world where detailed information on any subject, including religion, is available at the press of a button. If priests and lay ministers are to serve our society they must be equipped to think theologically about their experiences. It is sad to see the passing of the day of the gifted amateur but we have to accept, if a little grudgingly, that local priests and teams deserve high-quality professional training from those with educational expertise if they are to achieve their potential for the transfiguration of their local place. Indeed, one of the most important achievements of *Stranger in the Wings* was to show the potential of interactive education for helping people to think theologically whatever their academic background.

As we have seen, what has driven local ministry has been a

combination of stark necessity and theological insight. The stark necessity is seen both in the rural areas and in the inner cities. In parts of the USA and Australasia, many rural churches either had to 'do it themselves' or close their doors. In rural England, the hope of the report *Faith in the Countryside* was that the influx of professional people to villages, combined with a burgeoning tourist interest in church buildings, would secure the survival, and in some places the revival, of rural Christianity. But as *Ministry in the Countryside* predicted, the hare has moved too fast for the hounds. It is now common for rural stipendiaries to be responsible for six or more settlements, at which point life without local ministry becomes virtually impossible. As the Bishop of Lincoln said in the debate on *Stranger in the Wings*, 'if it were not for local ministry, areas of Lincolnshire would have by now been abandoned to paganism'. Similarly, in many inner-city parishes the only sure way of averting closure is if the congregation can be brought to have enough confidence in themselves to minister to themselves and to those around them.

At the heart of the local ministry vision is the theological insight that God is calling his people to recognize that mission and ministry are to be done, not just by the ordained but by all the baptized. In particular, ministry needs to be collaborative (St Paul's metaphor of the body) and leadership needs to be shared, clergy and laity together, with shifting chairmanship, consensus decision making and all the things that go with good teamworking. Local ministry seeks to shift the Church from a hierarchical to a collaborative culture, and this needs to go right the way through from parish to diocese, from lay person to priest to bishop.

In this scenario a priest with local licence makes perfect theological sense. The vocation to *stabilitas*, to enmeshment with the local place, allows the priest to be an authentic liturgical representative of the local team and, through them, of the local congregation. Though there are obvious difficulties, their local enmeshment can also give authenticity to the local priest as 'icon of the church' in their locality. Their role as representatives of the catholicity of the Church and as those who ensure that the base community is theologically 'centred' is shared, both with the stipendiary and with the other members of the team who have themselves shared in the ministerial training. All this resonates with what we can glean about the New Testament church.

The one thing local priests should not be is 'clerics', and what most concerns those dioceses which see local ministry as an agent for cultural change is the ordaining of local priests who are not part of a lay-clergy team. For, in their view, the Church does not need more people in dog-collars, it needs more congregations who are responding to their baptismal vocation. Singleton local priests are no more likely to deliver 'Total Ministry' than the singleton stipendiary priests of the past.

The Church needs to affirm the vocation to this collaborative local ministry – to *stabilitas* – as authentic and first class, and must at all costs resist the temptation to turn 'local' priests into 'mass' priests. OLMs are NOT clerics on the cheap; they are, on the contrary, breakers of the clerical mould, for they come complete with their collaborative team around them. The OLM is inevitably a representative of the Church to society but (s)he also represents the priesthood of the base community to the wider Church. OLM is not about providing more priestly hands; it is about recognizing the vocation of local congregations to be God's people in their place, and it is a high and glorious calling.

Stipendiary clergy clearly need a new role model for this brave new world. We have suggested that they will need to take on a quasi-episcopal role, to be 'bishops-in-little' in a large benefice or 'facilitators' in the New Zealand context. We have recorded the tales of a number of stipendiaries who are beginning to see just how fulfilling this new way of working can be. But their remains a dearth of experienced practitioners to provide role models and this is something which only time and experience can provide.

Business management consultants tell us that, while all change is difficult, cultural change is like a surgical operation without anaesthetic. That is why it is such a bumpy ride for those of us who are called to live in 'interesting times'. But the alternative to cultural change for our Church is arterial sclerosis. We need 'less red tape and more pink elastic'.

cococo

Bibliography

Acora (1990) *Faith in the Countryside.* Arthur Rank Centre, NAC, Stoneleigh Park, Warwickshire: Acora Publishing.

Acupa (1986) *Faith in the City.* London: Church House Publishing.

Advisory Board for Ministry (1991) *Local NSM.* Policy Paper No. 1. London: Church House Publishing.

——(1992) *Development of Models of Ministry and Training in Recent Diocesan Proposals for LNSM.* Policy Paper No. 4. London: Church House Publishing.

——(1993) *Criteria for Selection for Ministry in the Church of England Policy.* Paper No. 3A. London: Church House Publishing.

——(1993) *Order in Diversity.* Policy Paper No. 5. London: Church House Publishing.

——(1995) *A Review of Selection Procedures in the Church of England.* Policy Paper No. 6. London: Church House Publishing.

——(1997) *Issues in Theological Education and Training.* Policy Paper No. 15. London: Church House Publishing.

——(1998) *Stranger in the Wings.* Policy Paper No. 8. London: Church House Publishing.

Advisory Council for Church's Ministry (1968) *A Supporting Ministry* (Wesley Report). London: CIO.

——(1987) ACCM Occasional Paper No. 22. London: CIO.

——ACCM Occasional Paper No. 24. London: CIO.

Allen, Roland (see Paton).

Anglican Liturgical Consultation (see Holeton).

ARCIC 1 (1982) *The Final Report.* London: CTS/SPCK.

Arthur Rank Centre, NAC, Stoneleigh Park, Warwickshire CV8 2LZ, publish *Country Way*, a journal which includes many examples of collaborative ministry in action, and also distribute essential reading workbooks for those establishing teams in small congregations (see Francis, Littler and Martineau).

Baker, J. (1992) *Salisbury Diocese: Ministerial Resource and Deployment.* Green Paper. Salisbury: Diocesan Office.

Barrett, C.K. (1985) *Church, Ministry and Sacraments.* Exeter: Paternoster.

Beaminster Parish (1982) *Team Handbook.* Beaminster: Parish Office.

Bishop's Conference of England and Wales. (1995) *The Sign We Give: Report from the Working Party on Collaborative Ministry.* Chelmsford: Matthew James Publishing

Blythe, R. (1986) *Divine Landscapes.* London: Viking.

Board of Education (1985) *All Are Called: Towards a Theology of the Laity.* London: CIO.

Board of Mission (1995) *A Time for Sharing.* Occasional Paper No.6. London: Church House Publishing.

——(1997) *Hidden Treasure* (video). Stoneleigh: Arthur Rank Centre.

Boff, L. (1986) *Ecclesiogenesis: The Base Communities Reinvent the Church.* Maryknoll, NY: Orbis Books.

Borgeson, J. and Wilson, L. (eds) (1990) *Reshaping Ministry: Essays in Memory of Wesley Frensdorff.* Arvada, CO: Jethro. Available from Diocese of Northern Michigan.

Bowden, A. (1994) *Ministry in the Countryside.* London: Mowbray.

Bracegirdle, C. (1996) *Changing Patterns of Ministry in the Diocese of Manchester: The Impact of LNSM.* Unpublished paper submitted for clergy course at St George's House, Windsor.

Bracegirdle, P.H. (1999) *Local Ministry in the Diocese of Gloucester 1994–1999: A Review and Evaluation.* Gloucester: Diocesan Office.

Bradbury, N. (1993)'The minister as midwife', *Theology*, Vol. XCVI, No. 774 (November), pp. 444–7. London: SPCK.

Brown, L.M., Davidson, W. and Brown, A. (1997) *Vision Fulfilling.* Harrisburg, PA: Morehouse.

Brueggemann, W. (1994) *A Social Reading of the Old Testament.* Minneapolis: Fortress Press.

Central Board of Finance of the Church of England (1967) *Partners in Ministry.* London: CIO.

Cope, S. (1987) *The Role of the Laity in the Rural Church.* BTh thesis, University of Southampton.

Coventry, Diocese of (1991) *Guidelines for the Ministry.* Coventry: Diocesan Office.

Davies, D.J., Waktins, C. and Winter, M. (1991) *Church and Religion in Rural England.* Edinburgh: T & T Clark.

Diocesan Submissions to ABM and the Ministry Division for LNSM Schemes. Various submissions held at Church House, Westminster.

Donaldson, C. (1992) *The New Springtime of the Church*. Norwich: Canterbury.

Edward King Institute for Ministry Development (1998) *Report on Local Ministry*. Available from Local Ministry Office, 4 College Green, Gloucester. (The Institute also publishes the journal *Ministry*.)

Ely, Diocese of (1988) *Ministry: A Report to the Bishop from the Ministry Advisory Group*. Ely: Diocesan Office.

Evreux, Diocese of (1990) *La Pastorale Rurale d'accompagnement* (*Eglise en marche*, no. 12). Evreux: Diocese d'Evreux.

Francis, L.J. (1985) *Rural Anglicanism*. London: Collins.

Francis, L.J., Littler, K. and Martineau, J. (2000) *Rural Ministry*. Stoneleigh Park, Warwickshire: Acora Publishing.

General Synod (1974) *Deployment of the Clergy* (The Sheffield Report). Report of the House of Bishops' Working Group, London: GS 205.

——(1985) *All Are Called: Towards a Theology of the Laity*. London: CIO.

——(1985) *Team and Group Ministries: A Report by the Ministry Co-ordinating Group*. London: GS 660.

——(1991) *Team and Group Ministries: Report of the Working Party*. London: GS 993.

——(1992) *Team and Group Ministries Measure*. London: GS 994.

——(1997) *Eucharistic Presidency*. London: Church House Publishing.

Gill, R. (1992) *Beyond Decline*. London: SCM.

——(1993) *The Myth of the Empty Pew*. London: SPCK.

Gloucester, Diocese of (see also Bracegirdle, P.H.) *Local Ministry: An Introduction for Parishes and PCCs*; *A Guide to Choosing and Training New Members*; *A Guide to Remandating for Teams*; *So Your Vicar's Leaving?* (and other relevant booklets). Local Ministry Office, 4 College Green, Gloucester.

Graham, A. (1995) *Priesthood Here and Now*. One of a series of leaflets on priesthood produced by ABM. London: Church House Publishing.

Greenwood, R. (1994) *Transforming Priesthood*. London: SPCK.

——(1996) *Practising Community*. London: SPCK.

——(2000) *The Ministry Team Handbook*. London: SPCK.

Hammersley, J. (1989) *Working Together in Teams and Groups*. Parish & People, The Old Mill, Spetisbury, Blandford Forum, Dorset.

Hereford, Diocese of (1986). *The People, the Land and the Church*. Hereford Diocesan Board of Finance.

Holeton, D.R. (1996) *Renewing the Anglican Eucharist: Findings of the Fifth International Anglican Liturgical Consultation.* London: Grove Booklets.

Howatch, S. (1997) *A Question of Integrity.* London: Little Brown & Co.

Ineson, H. (1995) *LNSM Training: What are we Doing?* Unpublished paper, available from the Local Ministry Office, 4 College Green, Gloucester.

Kent Agricultural Chaplaincy (1980) *Local Ordained Ministry.* Pluckley: Revd J. Sage.

Lathe, A. (ed.) (1986) *The Group: The Story of Eight Country Churches.* Hempnall Group Council, Norfolk.

Legg, R. (1989) *Lay Pastorate.* East Wittering: Angel Press.

Leslie, D. (1998) *Transformative Education and Ministry.* Expanded version of Appendix 5 of *Stranger in the Wings,* available from Liverpool: Diocesan Office.

Lewis, C. (1982) 'The practice of the absence of the priest', *New Fire,* Winter.

Lima Text (1982) *Baptism, Eucharist and Ministry.* WCC.

——(1990) *Baptism, Eucharist and Ministry: 1982 to 1990.* WCC.

Lincoln, Diocese of (1990a) *Exploring Local Ministry.* Lincoln: Diocesan Office.

——(1990b) *Five Course Books in Local Ministry.* Lincoln: Diocesan Office.

——(1990c) *Local Ministry Scheme* (submission to ABM). Lincoln: Diocesan Office.

——(1991) *New Times, New Ways* (Report by Bishop to Synod). Lincoln: Diocesan Office.

Louden, S.H. (1998) *The Greying of the Clergy.* DPhil thesis submitted to the University of Wales.

Macquarrie, J. (1972) *The Faith of the People of God.* London: SCM.

Manchester, Diocese of (1985) *Report of Study Group on Ordained Ministry* (The Dalby Report). Manchester: Diocesan Office.

Martineau, J. (1995) *Turning the Sod. A Workbook on the Multi-Parish Benefice.* Stoneleigh Park, Warwickshire: Acora Publishing.

Mason, K. (1992) *Priesthood and Society.* Norwich: Canterbury.

Mayor, S.H. (n.d.) *Being an Elder in the United Reformed Church.* London: Church Life Department of the URC.

Neale, G. (1995) *Lincoln Local Ministry Scheme: The Praxis.* MA dissertation presented to University of Hull.

Nott, P. (1989) *Moving Forward.* Norwich: Diocesan House.

——(1991) *Moving Forward II*. Norwich: Diocesan House.

Paton, D.M. (ed.) (1968) *Reform of the Ministry: A Study of the Work of Roland Allen*. London: Lutterworth.

Paul, L. (1964) *The Deployment and Payment of the Clergy* (Paul Report). London: CIO.

Pym, B. (1953) *Jane and Prudence*. London: Jonathan Cape.

Rahner, K. (1974) *The Shape of the Church to Come*. London: SPCK.

Ripon, Diocese of (1985) *Two Years On: Local Ministry in 1985*. Ripon: Diocesan House.

——(1989) *Review of the Local Ministry Scheme*. Ripon: Diocesan House.

Roberts, E. (1972) *Partners and Ministers*. London: Falcon Books.

Royle, S. (1992) *A Theological Basis for LNSM*. Salisbury: Canon S. Royle.

Russell, A. (ed.) (1975) *Groups and Teams in the Countryside*. London: SPCK.

——(1980) *The Clerical Profession*. London: SPCK.

——(1986) *The Country Parish*. London: SPCK.

——(1993) *The Country Parson*. London: SPCK.

Rutter, C. (1989) *Local Ordained Ministry*. Salisbury: Diocesan Office.

Schillebeeckx, E. (1981) *Ministry*. London: SPCK.

Skilton, C. (1999) *Ministry Leadership Teams*. London: Grove.

Stetcher, R. (1997) 'A Challenge to the Church', *The Tablet* 20/27 December, pp. 1688–9.

——(1993) *Tiller Ten Years On* Bramcote, Nottingham: Grove.

Tiller, J. (1983) *A Strategy for the Church's Ministry* (Tiller Report). London: CIO.

Tiller, J. and Birchall, M. (1987) *The Gospel Community and its Leadership*. Basingstoke: Marshall Pickering.

Truro, Diocese of (1992) *Local Non-stipendiary Ministry in the Diocese of Truro* (Report by Bishop of Truro's Working Party). Truro: Diocesan Office.

Turner, H.J.M. (1987) 'Ordination and vocation', *Sobornost*, **9** (1). London: Fellowship of St Alban and St Sergius.

West, M. (1994) *Second Class Priests with Second Class Training?: A study of LNSM*. PhD thesis submitted to the University of East Anglia.

——(1998) *OLM: Expediency or Paradigm Shift?* Carmarthen: Trinity College Symposium.

West, M., Noble, G. and Todd, A. (1999) *Living Theology*. London: Darton, Longman and Todd.

Wilson, C.R. and Davenport, L. (1982) *Against All Odds*. Frenchtown, NJ: Jethro Publications.

Winchester, Diocese of (1984) *Lay Pastor's Training Course*. Winchester: Diocesan Office.

——(1990) *A Church for the World* (Report of the Ordained Ministry Review Group). Winchester: Diocesan Office.

Winter, M. and Short, C. (1993) 'Believing and belonging: religion in rural England', *British Journal of Sociology*, September.

World Council of Churches (see Lima Text).

Zabriskie, S.C. (1995) *Total Ministry*. New York: The Alban Institute.

Books, Articles and Reports from America and Australasia

Adams, S. (1997) *Growing Mutual Ministry in New Zealand*. Available from Waiapu Diocesan Office, Napier.

Bennett, Bill (1997) *The Role of the Local Priest in Total Ministry*. Napier: Waiapu Diocesan Office.

Borgeson, J. and Wilson, L. (eds) (1990) *Reshaping Ministry: Essays in Memory of Wesley Frensdorff*. Arvada, CO: Jethro. Available from Diocese of Northern Michigan.

Boyd, D. (1994a) *Licensed Local Ministries in the Diocese of Christchurch*.

——(1994b) *Total Ministry*. Christchurch: Diocesan Office.

Brown, M.B., Davidson, W. and Brown, A. (1997) *Vision Fulfilling: The Story of the Rural and Small Community Work of the Episcopal Church during the Twentieth Century*. Harrisburg, PA: Morehouse.

Cant, Garth (see next entry).

Canterbury Rural Ministry Unit, PO Box 8471, Christchurch, New Zealand, with its Director Garth Cant, is the best source for the reports of the Trans-Tasman Conferences, which contain a number of stories from Total Ministry parishes in Australasia. The Unit also distributes *Rural Network News*.

Dudley, C. (1978) *Making the Small Church Effective*. Nashville, TN: Abingdon.

Dunedin, Diocese of *Total Ministry Curriculum*. Dunedin: Diocesan Office.

Frensdorff, W (see Borgeson and Wilson).

Le Cren, D. (1996) *A Journey into Total Ministry: The Cheviot Story* (see under Canterbury Rural Ministry Unit).

Mathieson, M. (1979) *Delectable Mountains: The Story of the Washing-*

ton County Mission Program. Cincinnati: Forward Movement Publications.

Mavor, J. (1997) *Calling Us by Name*. Melbourne: JBCE Books.

Michigan, Diocese of (1996) *A Plan for Mutual Ministry Development* (and various other relevant documents). Available from the Diocesan Office of the Diocese of Northern Michigan.

Perth, Diocese of (1994) *Becoming Ministering Communities*. Perth: Diocesan Office.

Quinn, B. (1980) *The Small Rural Parish*. Washington DC: Glenmary Research Center.

Ray, D. (1982) *Small Churches are the Right Size*. New York: Pilgrim.

Wallace, R.A. (1991) *They Call Her Pastor: A New Role for Catholic Women*. Albany, NY: State University of New York Press.

Zabriskie, S.C. (1995) *Total Ministry*. New York: The Alban Institute.